Ginger, Lily & Sweet Fire

A Romance with Food

by H. Lamar Thomas

LUMMOX Press

© 2010 H. Lamar Thomas

All Rights Reserved. No portion of this book may be reproduced without express written permission of the editors, except for purposes of review.

ISBN 978-1-929878- 28-4

First edition

Lummox Press
PO Box 5301
San Pedro, CA 90733
www.lummoxpress.com

Printed in the United States of America

Photography by Bryan Redding, H. Lamar Thomas and McGinnis Leathers (pgs. 33 & 143)

Acknowledgments

Chef Lamar's Iron Grill, East West Bistro, St. Orres, Windchimes, Nikolai's Roof, The Abbey and Mansion, all of Mendocino County, California, Atlanta and Athens Georgia; Southern Distinction, Atlanta Cuisine, Atlanta Food & Beer; the Appalachian and Nantahala Mountains.

Family: My Mother, belle of the Cofer/England Clan, Dorothy Mary England-Thomas-Timberlake-Whitelaw, Gary & Debbie Thomas, Lynn & Billy Buckhalt, Eric & Lori B, Celeste & Jason Jackson, Cindy & Chris Parker, Robert Thomas and any and all relations going back down the Cofer/Thomas family tree to the Finns of 1750s Tucker, Georgia USA (Yes, our family is that old here).

Friends, Mentors, Chefs/Authors, Bands, Business and Loves:
Don & Sanni Chambers (beloved), Jordan Thomas, Larry Hicks, Dan Hart (as dear as a brother, in memoriam), Richard Mehlinger, Elizabeth(s) Hart and Kilgore, George Gore, BJ Bracewell, Mike & Susuan Timlin, Jarad Blanton, Peter Keane, Gabriel & Fernando Quintinilla, Joe Chandler, Mark Condon, Sharon Anderson King, Melanie Paulk, Jan Hickel, Gina, Valerie Fan, Renee, Silke, Chris & Mary Aubry, Deanna & Brian, Bryan Redding, Bill W., Aaron W., Victoria Lee, Mary Alise, Binky, Kathy, Heaven, Diana F Five Star Day, Kim Chee, Jasper J, Gary F, Jaamy Zarnegar., Melissa Clegg, Janine, Tom & Melanie Maicon, and on and on and on....

Louis Osteen(set the food fever), Alice Waters, Norman Van Aken, Ken Hom, James Fraioli, Jacque Pepin, Jean-George Vongretchen, Susser Lee, Morimoto, David Chang, Harold McGee, Sam Choy, Julia Childe, Heinz Schwartz & Hans Bertram (in memoriam), Anthony Bourdain, Fuschia Dunlop, Rosso/Lukens Silver Palate Cookbooks, Silver Spoon Cookbook, the ACF, Edna Lewis, 1000

Recipe Chinese Cookbook, Virginia Willis, Steven Raichlen, Rebecca Lange, Selby Wright, Andrea Griffin, Rolling Pin, UGA, Alton Brown, David Larkworthy (5 Seasons), Luna Bakery, Boo & Rebecca Backyard Harvest, Farm 255, Last Resort, The National, Alice Mills (THE Red Mule Grits), Herve This, Richard Blaise, Ricardo Ullio, Linton Hopkins, Bacchanalia, Jittery Joe's Coffee (Charley Mustard), Veggie Patch, Honolulu Fish (Lael), Inland Seafood (Rani), Clean Fish, Dan Miller Yesterdays Catch, Carolina Trout, Seafood Choices Alliance, Monterey Bay Aquarium, Sea Web, Market Fresh Produce, Karen Fooks Food, Royal Produce, Buckhead Beef (Blake), Greg S&D Coffee, Southern Foodways Alliance, Atlanta Foods Saxon, IGF Craig, Jose Castro Desserts/Catering, Tammy Cheesecakes, Cecilia & Juan Cakes, Sea Shepards, America's Test Kitchens, Will Harris Ranch, Colorado Lamb, Cowgirl Creamery and Sweet Grass Dairy, Slow Food, Georgia Organics, Drs Young, Mitchell, Hulsey, Pylant, Max Sidner; Food Arts, Saveur, Guns And Gardening, Food And Wine, Cooks, Southern Living, Jackson Street Books, Avid Books, Janet & Jim Geddis….

    Drive By Truckers, Patterson Hood, Don Chambers+Goat, Drivin N Cryin/Kevn Kenny, REM, PJ Harvey, Patti Smith, Pylon, Nick Cave, Jack White, Bobby Sleppy Nuci's Space, The Firing Range (Jeff, Ivan, Tim), Ray Foreman/Clark Street Review, Nimrod Literary Journal, Wisconsin Review, Richard & Sujayta Winfield, David Halpern, James Biddle, Don & Jane Newt, Mike Stock, RD Armstrong Lummox Press and Art Director Chris Yeseta, 688, 40 Watt, Apple Computers, Dr Pepper and Coca Cola, Lord Byron, St John Perse, Walt Whitman, Cormac McCarthy, Foucault, Bukowski, Rimbaud, Carruth, Rilke, Thomas Wolfe, Bachelard, Heidegger, Spinoza, Mark Strand, Song Of Songs, Buddha, Jesus, Love, Peace and collard greens, libraries and kitchens of America, China, Southeast Asia and everyone who ever inspired me in food and literature this and all that follows is for you.

Ginger, Lily & Sweet Fire

A Romance with Food

Welcome to the place of all origins and births, to the romances of life, language and love, yes, to the house of Food, welcome to the pure democracy of New World Cuisine…It is a house that is open to all people. I entered long ago in my travels across America and into China. I learned to fuse together flavor ideas from disparate cultures, preserving the national origin of the food without losing what was uniquely American about it in my hands. I am not unique. I am a part of the celebration of all cultures through their foods. From the time of my apprenticeship over twenty years ago it has been my one driving force to bring these cuisines to the American table. There is an element of rebellion to my work in that it is always changing and open to the new. I have always sought to remove the cult of personality from cuisine and to give that cuisine to the ordinary cook and diner. Eating is not a luxury, it is a necessity. Yet, in the most ordinary of events we can find the extraordinary of experience. Show me the produce section of your local market and I will show you a part of the language of the world. For me, as I hope it is for you, this is a world of inclusion. It is the very source of the Romantic pursuit of making the Ideal into the Real by way of familiarization. Love? Yes, you can find love in the strangest places, even in the kitchen. And in this kitchen all languages are spoken, all cultures are celebrated.

Introduction

GINGER, LILY and SWEET FIRE
(A Romance with Food)

THERE IS ROMANCE IN THESE PAGES. The flavors that I will teach you to mingle and unlock in this book are, to my mind, the very essence of romance. In GINGER, LILY AND SWEET FIRE, spice, flora, and heat come together to bring home the magic of four great areas of contemporary world cuisine: Thai, Mediterranean, island, and New American. Once known as fusion, this exquisite blending today goes by the more particular title of New World Cuisine. The flavors of ginger, lily and sweet fire are the links that hold this diverse, expansive cuisine together as a cohesive whole.

The old spaghetti store has been replaced by Northern Italian grottoes featuring handmade ravioli with squid ink pasta and fresh house cured Buffalo mozzarella. The venerable local Chinese restaurant has been met with a flood of Thai, Singapore, Hong Kong, Korean, and Sichuan restaurants presenting whole striped bass seared in lemon grass and ginger, pad Thai (a Thailand national pasta), and soft shell crabs with pineapple sage and galanga broth. Where is the General Cho's Chicken? It's still there, but the chicken is grain fed and raised in a "stress" free environment. Island cuisine is not just coconut cream pie, or pork with mango, no, Island cuisine is as varied as the worlds from which it was born, such as North Africa, France, Portugal, and Spain. Jamaican jerk dishes are as rich in complexity and flavor as any sauce from the heart of Escoffier country. And what of our own land, America? Steak and potatoes, fried chicken and boiled corn, roast beef with vegetables, they are still here, but we have expanded upon the traditions of our cultural regions. The steak now has an oyster and bourbon sauce, the chicken is fried in walnut oil, and the potatoes are purple, mixed with yucca and seasoned with roasted garlic and Irish sea salt.

Designed for the home cook, this book is an exercise in culinary internationalism that to my eye and palate has no equal on the cookbook shelf today. Describing it in terms of cookware, it is the American grill meets the hand-hammered wok, the brick oven, the clay pot and hibachi. Examples of this cuisine are adding chrysanthemum and tiger lily flowers to a classic brown sauce; making a barbecue sauce with black currants, shrimp paste and sweet soy sauce instead of ketchup and vinegar; blending Italian Mascarpone cheese with lime and Sambal Oelek; egg rolls made with shiitake mushrooms and crunchy bean sprouts with a miso dressing; breading fish with crushed Japanese wasabi fried green peas; enriching Thai coconut soup with zucchini, yellow squash and heavy cream; adding nori and arugula to a spinach cream sauce, and the list continues every day. So, as you can see by the examples and in

Introduction

the following chapters you will learn the origins as well as the evolution of the great cuisines of the world.

Over the last decade, the exotic tastes of these regions have traveled to America and been embraced by diners everywhere from New York to Los Angeles. I have been fortunate to be at the center of this movement, from my base at the East West Bistro. Having studied with chefs such as Louis Osteen, Hans Bertram, and Heinz Schwab, and having worked with Japanese, Thai, Chinese, Korean, Lebanese, Israeli, Turkish, Moroccan, Jamaican, Peruvian, Colombian, Hungarian, German, Swiss, French, and, yes, American-born chefs, I have acquired the international perspective necessary to making this exciting taste innovation work on its own terms. From each nation I have taken a little bit of language, culture, flavor, and technique and here show you how to mix it together in a way that will set your sense of romance afire. And even better, I was able to spend a little time in Shanghai with various chefs in that melting pot of China where I learned the mysteries of salt and oil flavors.

For a suburban Georgian like myself, experiencing the pleasures of this cuisine was like traveling the world from my hometown. As I became expert in the World Cuisine, I learned to fuse or blend together flavor ideas from disparate cultures, preserving the national origin of the flavor without losing what was uniquely American about the fusion. A movement was born. I am a part of this birth. From the time of my apprenticeship over twenty years ago it has been my one driving force to bring these cuisines to the American table. There is an element of rebellion to my work. I have always sought to remove the cult of personality from cuisine and to give that cuisine to the ordinary cook and diner. Eating is not a luxury, it is a necessity. Show me the produce section of your local market and I will give you the best of possible choices of world discovering menus. How am I unique in all of this? I show you how to make the ordinary into the extraordinary, and you do not need a "no limit" charge account to do it. This is a cuisine of inclusion.

My work with the great organizations Sea Web and Seafood Choices Alliance afforded me the honor of inclusion in the cookbook "Ocean Friendly Cuisine, ed. James Fraioli with forward by Jean michel Cousteau" along with Jacque Pepin, Emeril Lagasse, and several other talented chefs; and the cookbook "Wild Alaska: 100 Recipes From American's Top 25 Chefs, edited by James Fraioli". Of the many things a chef must be (in addition to Renaissance man), we must hold ourselves responsible for the survival and eco-friendly harvesting of our foods. Whenever you shop ask country of origin and nature of harvest for your seafood, meats and produce. Make a difference.

My life has been one of a devotion to poetry, food and philosophy. I believe that

Introduction

nothing in the world is accomplished without passion. My passion for knowledge, for taste, and for the Arts has been my driving force throughout my culinary career. I am one of the lucky ones. I apprenticed in the classical French traditions, cut my teeth on Nouvelle Cuisine, grew with the advent of the freedoms expressed with Northern California cuisine, and became a man with the opening of the world markets, and experiments of my predecessors. All these things came together in my work as both Executive Chef and as food columnist for Georgia Life, Southern Distinctions Magazine, Lummox Journal and Atlanta Cuisine. It is the duty of a chef to represent their culinary history and future in such a way that the diner and cook are able to join in on this quest. I give you this map of cuisine here, in *GINGER, LILY, AND SWEET FIRE*.

I have worked from Atlanta to Mackinac Island, San Francisco to Mendocino, and the Outer Banks back to Athens, Georgia. Everywhere I went the people wanted to know the cuisine of where I had been. I gave it to them with the option that they do so in return for me. Curiosity for curiosity. I learned about the foods many of us want to cook at home. I learned that we want to create these dishes in our own home kitchens. We want to be surprised and enticed by what we have in restaurants. We all want to learn new things. We want to learn what the other parts of the world are like. What better way, without travel, than to bring these cultures home into our kitchens where we may touch, smell, prepare and eat the great bounties of the world.

The cuisine will touch your heart, and also your mind. There is a poetry to dining. Poetry, like love, shows up in the strangest, and the most ordinary of places. Look into your kitchen, look into a garden, it is all there. The greater percentages of our romantic experiences are seamlessly connected to dining experiences. By the time you have prepared the book's four season sequences of seven three-course menus, you will have finished a course in culinary cultural geography, and learned a bit about romance as well.

Be sure to take a special someone along for the journey. Shopping for these recipes, preparing them together, and dining on the myriad exotic flavors will be a romantic experience you won't soon forget. A little spice. A little sweetness. A little fire.

You'll enjoy them all, and experience a bit of romantic poetry, in a mixing bowl that has no equal in the world. All you need is a spirit of adventure, a love of the world, and a desire to cook like you never have before.

Remember, love shows up in the most remarkable of places, even the kitchen. The world must be made romantic.

A DEDICATION

*To the love and the beauty in a life
devoted to making the ideal real
through poetry, food, and philosophy,
to making the real ideal
through a love of conversation,
dining, and the arts.
And most of all
to the woman of ginger scented skin,
who is forever rolling
and evolving, who embraces
the spiritual, and the sensual.
She who is many and is still one.*

Contents

CHAPTER ONE ~
GINGER, LILY and SWEET FIRE ... 20

THE FIRST MENU ... 24
Chicken coconut soup
Green cabbage, cucumber and red onion with spiced rice vinegar
Baked tilapia with cashews, yellow and red peppers
Sides of jasmine rice and broccoli with sesame
Chilled slices of mango and pear with chocolate cream

THE SECOND MENU ... 33
Steamed mussels with lemon grass and tomato
Dijon and sesame crusted chicken breast
Bananas and coconut cream

THE THIRD MENU ... 42
Baked aromatic chicken with spinach
Sambal shrimp and Thai noodles
Chilled tangerine with red grape syrup

THE FOURTH MENU ... 48
Coconut shrimp with blackberry-horseradish sauce
Vegetable fried rice with tofu and roasted shallots
Pumpkin custard

THE FIFTH MENU ... 56
Sweet and sour vegetable soup
Panang curry with ziti pasta, chicken or vegetable
Banana smoothie with raspberries

Contents

THE SIXTH MENU ... 61
Pan-fried Japanese eggplant
Pompano steamed in banana leaf (haw moke) served over vegetables
Mango rice pudding

THE SEVENTH MENU ... 67
Chicken and sundried tomato egg roll
Baked trout or tilapia with lemon grass, ginger and pear
Traditional sticky rice with stir-fried vegetables
Sliced apples and gouda

Contents

CHAPTER TWO ~
MEDITERRANEAN HILLSIDES and BEACHES ... 72

THE FIRST MENU ... 76
Romaine lettuce, granny smith apples, dried dates, serrano peppers, sunflower seeds and scallions with parmesan oil and vinegar dressing
Penne pasta with an artichoke heart and wild mushroom marinara
Ricotta cheesecake

THE SECOND MENU ... 85
Bruschetta with basil, romas and feta
Seared shrimp and poblano peppers with lemon
Parmesan risotto, garnished with tomato coulis
Cantaloupe with minted cream

THE THIRD MENU ... 93
Spinach soup with red bell cream
Oven broiled amberjack with fried capers, pistachios, and white cheddar cheese
Sides of roasted garlic spaghetti, sweet zucchini and onions
Fresh berries and brown sugar

THE FOURTH MENU ... 100
Frittata with shrimp, potato and onion
Pan seared beef filet with apple-almond harissa
Tiramisu

Contents

THE FIFTH MENU ... 108
Field lettuces with toasted pine nuts, crisped pancetta, peppers and basil dressing
Roasted eggplant with garbanzo beans, wild rice, Parmesan and tomato sauce
Espresso crème brulee

THE SIXTH MENU ... 115
Steamed artichoke with basil-lime butter
Foccacia pizza with sage, olives, tomato, and chicken with roasted garlic spread, goat cheese and mozzarella
Raspberry sorbet

THE SEVENTH MENU ... 122
Crimini mushroom and bean soup
Lamb leg steak with avocado, pecans and red wine
Sides of green beans and citrus orzo
Plum tart

**SALT AND SEE WHAT TASTES CAN BE:
AN ESSAY ... 128**

Contents

CHAPTER THREE ~
ISLAND and OASIS ... 136

THE FIRST MENU ... 138
Shrimp, calamari, and plantains sautéed and glazed with peppers, ginger beer, mint and coconut cream
Baby back pork ribs with mango BBQ
Chilled passion fruit with cashew crisps

THE SECOND MENU ... 146
Scallops with jalapeno and pears
Tomato and basil cous cous with vegetables and chicken
White chocolate meringues poached in orange water

THE THIRD MENU ... 152
Chicken breast poached in tamarind and soy with molasses and rum glaze over mixed greens
Sautéed lobster medallions with a sambal oelek
Whipped mascarpone
Mango Napoleon

THE FOURTH MENU ... 159
Mixed peppercorn, allspice and coriander crusted tuna with wasabi fruit coulis
Jerk chicken with plantains black beans and pineapple-cucumber cole slaw
Warm dates stuffed with almonds, served with tamarind "lemonade"...

Contents

THE FIFTH MENU ... 165
Crab cakes mixed with cheddar and mesquite seasoning, curry aioli
Grilled mahi-mahi with carambola
Banana and papaya eggrolls

THE SIXTH MENU ... 170
Grilled cilantro flatbread with amfisi olives and Tomato
Macadamia and coconut crusted wreckfish with lime sauce
Pink guava mousse

THE SEVENTH MENU ... 178
Steamed asparagus with prosciutto and apple aioli
Molasses, cayenne and ginger beer roasted duckling
Gingerbread with apricot

Contents

CHAPTER FOUR ~
FLOWERING of AMERICA ... 186

THE FIRST MENU ... 190
Spinach and rose petal salad, drunken raisins, almonds, rice vinegar, cardamom, and Sichuan pepper
Grilled salmon stuffed with poblano peppers, Asian pear and thyme
Kiwi white cocolate mousse with crème de cassis

THE SECOND MENU ... 196
Portobella mushroom pizza, stuffed with mango, jalapeno, red and yellow bells, cilantro, feta
Basmati rice with rosemary roasted vegetables
Pistachio biscotti with an iced latte

THE THIRD MENU ... 201
Boston lettuce with mandarin orange, red hots, red onion, and wasabi dressing
Sautéed Wahoo with pomegranate and toasted cashew velouté
Port wine cheese, graham crackers, golden delicious apples and fresh figs

THE FOURTH MENU ... 208
Corn chowder
Grilled beef filet stuffed: smoked gouda, onion, spinach
Strawberry chocolate shortcake, maybe golden or red raspberries, olali berries, huckleberries

Contents

THE FIFTH MENU ... 215
Shiitake egg rolls with miso vinaigrette and wasabi
Sichuan and black pepper grilled turkey steak with rose hips and zinfandel sauce
Bread pudding with sweet rosemary syrup and cherry cream

THE SIXTH MENU ... 223
Shredded duckling and vegetables baked in rice paper
Grilled tuna with a golden pepper and poblano honey coulis
Praline tulip with espresso cream

THE SEVENTH MENU ... 229
Pan-fried tofu with tortilla and tomatillo salsa
Sautéed lamb loin medallions with pear mint veloute and saffron cream
Chocolate decadence

GLOSSARY ... 237

INDEX ... 249

CHAPTER ONE

GINGER, LILY and SWEET FIRE

*She was there alone by the counter
watching the herbs and fruits
like a perfect still life with wonder,
and it was here, downtown by the pines
in a neighborhood of open fires
that I saw her, and I saw my reflection,
so I rose and stood beside her
and together we began,
with the ginger and the lily,
we began our lives together.*

*F*USION THAI! All the menus in this chapter are variations on Thai dishes, hence the title "Ginger, Lily and Sweet Fire." Don't worry, all you are looking for is bright, complex taste that blends and combines, hence opening up the heart and the eyes.

These are dishes that are quick to cook but take a little time in the cut and chop department. It takes two to tango, why not the same in the kitchen?

The first step for all recipes and menus is getting things together. Let me make a suggestion, not only for this particular recipe, but also for all recipes: read the whole menu, think about the ingredients and the cooking process, **make lists of what you need**. The menus in this book are arranged so that all the contrasts of flavors combine into a well-balanced experience. If some of the essential ingredients are unavailable then don't try to cook the dish. Once you understand, through trial and error, what flavors you like, then go ahead and mix and match recipes throughout the book. After you learn the cooking methods and the way flavors interact by putting different foods together this will all become both challenging and fun.

Remember, while one-person chops, the other organizes the stove and begins side dishes. Some things can be prepared ahead and reheated, like the soups and some desserts. Most of the time such suggestions will be given with the recipe, but where this is neglected, please feel free to improvise. Influence your partner, goad, plead, agree, and most of all, work together and make the unfamiliar familiar.

Don't make the cooking painful. This stuff is quite enjoyable once you get the knack for the art and science of it all. Practice and experiment. Preparing and dining upon the foods you have created is such a beautiful and sensuous moment in life, savor and share it, it is romantic, and that's what the table is all about: to share.

Put on your apron. Let's begin.

Chapter One • GINGER, LILY and SWEET FIRE

• KEY INGREDIENTS LIST >>

SAMBAL OELEK: A very hot concoction of Thai bird chilies and vinegar. You can make your own by seeding and chopping dried peppers, soaking them in water and cooking in vinegar for about 10 minutes. For one cup it takes 30 red chilies.

Sriracha (Red Rooster Vietnamese chili sauce) is often used as a substitute, but it has sugars and is quite different in flavor. Sriracha is great tasting, but it is not pure Thai.

PALM SUGAR: used everywhere we would normally use white granulated, molasses, light brown, or turbinado sugars. Palm sugar is very sweet. Pureed in a Vita Prep or high powered blender with coffee or black tea it becomes foamy with the appearance of being a dairy additive when in fact it's just delicious date palm sugar.

YELLOW ROCK SUGAR: No slow cooked pork or choi dish is quite right without this hard sugar. I have used it in collard greens along with Three Crabs Fish sauce and the difference was over the top.

NAMYA: A mixture of shrimp paste, curry paste, coconut milk and lemon grass. It is often referred to as noodle sauce. Spicy.

NAMPLA: this is fish sauce, made from shrimp, calamari, cuttlefish, or anchovy. The raw smell is a bit off putting, but once it is in a cooked dish the flavor is unmistakably what we know as a Thai taste in a dish. The better the fish sauce the better the dish, so always go for highest quality.

SWEET BEAN PASTES: A variety of pastes using Chinese black beans (soy beans), yellow beans and red beans cured with ginger, garlic, salt and sugar. It's good for marinades and sauce; also used in dim sum dishes as the filling for sweet lily buns.

CHILI BEAN PASTE: Same as above but without the sugar, and with the addition of chili peppers.

CURRY PASTE: Any blend of spices and oils that gives a distinct flavor of aromatic peppers. This is not your packaged dry curry powder. Most curries have the small red chili known as the bird or Thai, ginger, paprika, turmeric, cumin, fenugreek, and garlic. Curry pot dishes will sometimes have curry leaves in them, but the curry leaf is not "curry" itself. It is called curry leaf because of a similarity in flavor to the thousands of curries that exist in the world.

OYSTER SAUCE: Practically a condiment. It is made from a reduction of oysters and sugars into a thick, dark liquid. The taste really doesn't come across as oysters; it's really reminiscent of sea salt and black beans. It makes a great addition to stir fries and stews. Worcestershire sauce isn't everything.

SWEET SOY SAUCE: Marketed as Indonesian, Thai or Philippine. It is thick soy with the addition of molasses and brown sugar. If you can't find it, make it: mix 1 cup of soy sauce with 1/4 cup each of molasses and brown sugar. Goes well with egg rolls, sushi, tuna, salmon, and sometimes even as a sprinkle on salads. Once you get used to using it you'll wonder why it's not more popular, my bet is that it will be soon. I make my own but you can find it in true international markets.

SOY SAUCE: There are a lot of brands out there. It's a mixture of soybean juice, wheat, water and salt. Look for the ones that are soy, salt and water only; they are known as Tamari soy sauce. Soy sauces have a heavy taste that's used in the place of salt for a lot of dishes. Thin soy is good for lighter dishes, and soys like mushroom soy, dark soy, and tamari are good for heavier combinations that use an unsalted stock. Experiment, try them all and you will be very surprised.

MUSHROOM SOY SAUCE: My favorite. Soy sauce cured with mushrooms. There are no mushrooms in it. It has more of an earthy taste than generic soy.

GOLDEN MOUNTAIN/MAGGI: This is a blend of soy and tamarind sauce which has a distinctive flavor that acts as an enhancer of sorts, and it is prevalent in Thai and South East Asian over to Hong Kong and Singapore cuisines.

CHILI OIL: Peanut oil with an infusion of peppers. You can make your own by simmering your favorite peppers: serrano, jalapeno, poblano, chili, etc. in peanut oil. Pour into Mason jar, or whatever jars you might have and store in a dark haunted place for a week or so. Strain. It should be hot. Flavored oils are the way to go. You can flavor any oil the way you want so that when you're cooking all you've got to do is add the oil. Hints: basil, rosemary, tiger lily, orange, Sichuan peppercorn, lemon, garlic, gingers. Simmering is not necessary for these, just bottle and rest.

PRICKLY ASH OIL: Stinging hot, like Sichuan peppers it hits slowly and then numbs your tongue.

WASABI OIL: This is a favorite of mine for its aromatic ability to control the taste buds without even putting it on the food. Put a dash in a spoon, inhale and then eat a bite of sushi, inhale again. Feel the magic!

SESAME OIL: Thick, nutty, brown oil made from extracts of sesame seeds. Use sparingly and as a last addition to cooking as it is very strong, and burns easily. I like to sear salmon and tuna with this, but it takes a lot of care and practice. Not recommended for the beginner.

PEANUT OIL: The absolute best oil for Asian cooking. It is medium bodied, has a mild flavor, does not burn at high temperatures, and comes from a good family. If you just can't use peanut oil, then use soy oil or corn oil for your stir-fry dishes. Avoid corn oil, I don't trust it. There's too much processing going on with this oil, and there is recent research that shows it's not as healthy as it was originally shown to be.

LEMON GRASS AND GALANGAL: Lemon grass, along with galangal, Thai basil, bird chili peppers, fish sauce, and tamarind are essentials to Thai cuisine. Lemon grass looks like long stalks of river grass. We use the lower white to green portion of the peeled stalk for seasoning. It imparts a light lemon-grass flavor, hence the name, 'lemon grass'. Galangal or baby ginger is a somewhat earthier flavored ginger than the regular ginger we often use. Galangal larger, has a slick brown skin, and is not as sharp as common ginger. It is most commonly known by its use in chicken coconut soup, but is used throughout Thai and Southeast Asian cuisines in stir fries, curry pots, and soups.

Chapter One • GINGER, LILY *and* SWEET FIRE

• *THE FIRST MENU* •

CHICKEN COCONUT SOUP

GREEN CABBAGE, CUCUMBER AND RED ONION WITH SPICED RICE VINEGAR

BAKED TILAPIA WITH CASHEWS, YELLOW AND RED PEPPERS WITH RASPBERRY JUICE AND MINT SERVED WITH JASMINE RICE, AND BROCCOLI WITH SESAME

CHILLED SLICES OF MANGO AND PEAR WITH CHOCOLATE CREAM

CHICKEN COCONUT SOUP

This is a variation on the classic Thai coconut soup that I adjusted to match my Southern love of things creamy and of things squash. It is creamy with a slight fire and, if you choose, rich with additional vegetables. Lemon grass and sambal oelek are essential to the fragrance and spice of this popular dish. Welcome to Thai cuisine.

Try to plan and prepare ahead. As an example, all the vegetables in this menu can be chopped and cut ahead of time and kept in separate containers in the refrigerator. You can make the soup a day or two in advance. Just reheat it on low and bring to a boil, turn it down to simmer for ten minutes, stir the whole time, and there you have a soup in 15 minutes.

5 oz	peanut oil
1 clove	garlic
6 0z	chicken breast, diced
10	button mushrooms, sliced thin
½ teaspoon	dried lemon grass.
1 tablespoon	ginger shaved with a cheese grater
¼ teaspoon	dried red pepper or 1 dried chili pepper
10 ounces	coconut milk
6 ounces	heavy cream
1 cup	chicken stock
2	fresh limes, juiced

1 tablespoon	cilantro, chopped
2 stalks	scallions, sliced thin
¼ to ¾ teaspoon	sambal oelek depends on how hot you want the soup. Be careful. Taste!

Gently cook the chicken and garlic on low heat in the peanut oil. As the chicken begins to turn white add the mushrooms, stir and add the spices and peppers. Add the liquids and bring the soup to a simmer. Add cilantro, scallions and sambal oelek. Let the soup simmer for at least fifteen minutes so that all the flavors arrive to their fullest taste.

Now the fun part. If you feel adventurous and like your soup slightly thick, do this: mix 1 tablespoon of flour with 2 tablespoons of cold butter, mash it around either with your fingers or with a spoon until the flour is mixed completely with the butter. This is a beurre manié. When the soup is simmering, with bubbles rising to the top of the pan, stir in the flour mix. The soup will slowly and lightly thicken as you stir. At this point you have a fairly traditional chicken coconut soup.

To bring to an even more authentic flavor add galangal root to the soup. This is also known as baby ginger, laos or ka. The powdered form works but the taste is so faint and dry that it really isn't worth the trouble, so do your best to find the dried or fresh form. The taste of dried galangal is sort of like ginger but with an aroma similar to a root cellar or basement. Don't think musty, think rich soil. The fresh tends more towards a lemon background. It's the same with wines: you taste the soil as much as you taste the grape. Galangal is also in the coveted list of aphrodisiacs.

If you like your soup heartier and with a bit bolder flavor, add diced vegetables such as zucchini, onions, carrots and yellow squash. If you want to make it vegetarian just eliminate the chicken and use vegetable bouillon. Shrimp can also be substituted for the chicken, which would

---

If you are lucky enough to have fresh lemon grass, use the bottom two inches of the stalk, peel away the outer skin, thin slice the inner layers. The lemon grass stalk will be pale green and white. If you want to use the whole stalk for more intense flavor pound the bottom half with the hilt end of your Chinese cleaver, or with a meat hammer. Place the whole stalk in the soup broth.

Chapter One • GINGER, LILY and SWEET FIRE

influence you towards adding clam juice or a shrimp base.

A soup for two people only requires about 3 tablespoons of each vegetable, which of course means that you have vegetables left over for other meals.

GREEN CABBAGE, CUCUMBER AND RED ONION

The second course is a bit of a snack, and this is optional, it all depends on how much time you have and how hungry you are. The nice thing about cabbage as a break in a spicy meal is that it cools and refreshes between courses. A lot of Thai meals include the salad throughout the meal, so that you can munch the greens to settle the seasonings more comfortably on the tongue. Keep that in mind when you are preparing other semi-traditional meals that involve lots of hot spices. Also, just to add to the vocabulary of your palate, cabbage is sometimes highly spiced as an accompaniment to mild entrees.

green cabbage	hand tear four large leaves into about twelve pieces
cucumber	one, peeled, seeded and sliced thin. To peel, use a vegetable peeler and peel four lines down the cucumber, cut it in half, and with the handle part of the peeler scoop out the seeds by pulling the utensil towards you. Slice the cucumber very thin.
red onion	one medium. these guys are tricky. If it isn't very firm get ready for tears and strong taste. Peel and slice thin across the middle of the onion. This gives you a sweeter taste. If you cut it from end to end you will get more of a strong onion flavor.

Use Marukan **spiced rice vinegar**, or Japanese Mirin. Both are readily available in upscale grocery stores. If you can't find either, here's what you do:

12 ounce	bottle of rice vinegar (pour out 2 ounces and set aside).
1 tablespoon	sugar
¼ teaspoon	ginger

¼ teaspoon	white pepper, or ground Sichuan pepper
¼ teaspoon	ground coriander
¼ teaspoon	ground cardamom

Shake and let it set overnight for best results, if you don't have the time it's okay to shake and serve, the flavor just won't be as deep.

Be bold in setting up the plate. Spread the cabbage out over the plate, then sprinkle the cucumber and onion slices over the cabbage. Now shake the bottle, hold your finger over the mouth of the bottle and open just a little and sprinkle the vinegar over it all. Coarsely chopped cilantro makes a nice touch here. But, if you can't find good fresh cilantro then use parsley. The plate should look busy. An edible flower or flowering herbs goes quite nicely in this arrangement *(see Edible Flowers in* **GLOSSARY***)*.

If it's too bland for you and you want to make it more of a salad, add diced tomato, black olives and feta cheese. Hey, you've gone Italian, but why not, food is there to enjoy.

Third course, the entree:
BAKED TILAPIA WITH CASHEWS, RED AND YELLOW PEPPERS WITH RASPBERRY JUICE AND MINT

2 six ounce	tilapia fillets. Buy the boneless, portioned fillets— it will save you time and heartache.
10 thin slices	red bell pepper
10 thin slices	yellow bell pepper
¼ cup	cashew halves, more or less
3 tablespoons	peanut oil, oil for fish
2 tablespoons	butter for sauté, you can substitute any of the flavored oils or olive oil, but note that it will change the texture of the sauce.
1 tablespoon	butter for sauce, no substitute.
1 cup	raspberry juice. Cran-raspberry is equally good.
2 sprigs	mint. You should have 12 to 15 leaves.
¼ teaspoon	coarse salt
1/6 teaspoon	ground black pepper

Rub a tablespoon of peanut or vegetable oil on the tilapia, then

Chapter One • GINGER, LILY *and* SWEET FIRE

Baked Tilapia with cashews, red and yellow peppers with raspberry juice and mint

lightly salt and pepper the fish. Place on a sheet pan and put into a 375° oven. Bake for fifteen to twenty minutes. Fifteen for moist, twenty for well done.

THE SAUCE

In the meantime, or ahead of time, prepare the sauce.

Heat the butter in a saucepan on medium high heat until it begins to froth and sizzle. Turn down to medium and add the peppers, stir them around until they begin to shine and are just crisp, add the cashews and continue to cook till the cashews start to turn a dark tan. Add the raspberry juice and turn the heat to high and bring to a boil, let it boil until the sauce reduces by one half, turn it down and simmer until there is about two or three tablespoons of sauce in the pan.

Sprinkle a pinch of salt and pepper over the sauce and stir it in. Turn the heat off and stir in one tablespoon of whole cold butter until it is fully incorporated into the sauce. Add the mint leaves. Set aside in a warm place until the fish has finished cooking. This sauce takes about 10 minutes. It will be a little thin, with a rich,

---

An easy way around the pinch and touch of small measurements with salt and pepper is to mix them together in a bowl. As an example, use 2 tablespoons of coarse salt to 1 tablespoon of ground pepper, dip your thumb and the next two fingers into the mix just the tips, lift out your clenched fingertips, this is a pinch. Get the picture? Pinch the mix. Once you get it down you will make your cooking life really very easy. This is the way it's generally done in restaurants, and the reason is the obvious one of ease. Also, when you see pictures of chefs scattering seasonings all over a sauce pot with hand high in the air, the reason for this wild display is to evenly distribute the spices onto the cooking food. And yeah, we can be messy at times.

well-blended flavor of nuts and fresh fruits.

ALTERNATE METHOD:
Salt and pepper and lightly flour the tilapia. Heat an ovenproof skillet. Add one ounce of corn oil. Place the tilapia skin side up in the skillet and sear the fish on high heat. Turn it over after about 30 to 45 seconds. After you turn it over add the peppers and sauté for a minute, and then add the cashews. Cook till tan, add juice and mint and place in oven. Cook for 15 minutes. Remove from oven, place fish on plate. Stir cold butter into skillet and pour over fish. This gives you a crisp fish with a much richer sauce. The sauce will have more of the flavor of the fish and will be richer in taste but less clear in color. This is the preferred method for flavor, but if you are trying to stay away from flour, or don't want to bother with any pan cooking, the first baking method is still a good way to go.

SIDES:

½ cup	jasmine rice, rinsed
1½ cups	water
1 tablespoon	sugar
1 teaspoon	salt & pepper
1	dried lily flower

Bring the water and spices to a boil, add the rice, bring back to a boil, cover and turn down to simmer and cook for twenty minutes. Take off the lid and fluff the rice with a fork. It will be kind of sticky; not the dry separated kind of white rice. Cover and set aside until ready to eat.

BROCCOLI WITH SESAME

2 heads	broccoli cut into flowerets
1 tablespoon	sesame oil
1 quart	water
1½ tablespoons	salt & pepper

Boil water with salt and pepper. Set a strainer or steamer basket in the water. The water will be just below the steamer. Add the broccoli and cover. Cook for three minutes for crisp bright green broccoli, longer if you want it soft. Remove the broccoli and set on plate, and sprinkle with sesame oil.

Chapter One • GINGER, LILY *and* SWEET FIRE

> **A SIMPLE GARNISH TIP AS ALTERNATE TO "WEDGES"**
> **To cut a lemon or lime wedge:** cut it in half from stem end to end, then make two more cuts on each half following the same procedure from stem end to end. Lemons are easiest; limes need a very sharp or serrated edge knife. If cutting limes, cut from the flesh not the skin. Cut the fruit so that you have six wedges. Now, hold the wedge with the skin side on the table. Place your sharp knife at the stem end in the middle of the pith (the white between the skin and flesh) and gently push the knife back and forth to the front of the wedge until you are just a fraction of an inch from the end. Stop. Don't cut it off; you want it to kind of flap there. Cut a line on each side of the flap of skin from the connected end to the other end. Don't cut a complete "V," leave the base open "\/". Fold the centerpiece of skin under. It will look like an impressionistic bunny or like the OK sign you make with your fingers.

ONCE THE FISH IS COOKED:

Place fish at bottom edge of plate, spoon sauce over fish and place rice at top left, broccoli at top right. Garnish? You bet. In the center of the plate set your lemon and lime "bunnies" and place a sprig of mint between them. That's it.

CHILLED SLICES OF MANGO AND PEAR WITH CHOCOLATE CREAM

1	mango, barely ripe. It should be semi-soft and firm skinned.
1	pear, Anjou or Bartlett are the easiest to find and are the best eating pears. If Asian pears are available then use them.
3 oz	chocolate, sweet
4 oz	heavy cream
1 slice	crystallized ginger. Buy it in the specialty food section of the grocery store or at a local Asian market.

Using the large slots on a cheese grater, grate the chocolate onto a chilled plate. Whip the cream to soft peaks with a hand whisk in a chilled metal bowl. It only takes about a minute. Since this is such a small amount you don't need to use an electric mixer, plus you have more control in getting the cream to the desired texture.

Fold in the chocolate. Cover and refrigerate.

There are two ways of peeling the mango. If it is firm, then peel before you slice. If it is soft, then peel after you slice. If you peel it before you slice when it is soft then you risk losing the juices to the cutting board, and you don't want that. You should have 12 ½-inch thick slices.

Wash the pear. Cut it in half and remove the core with your paring knife. Cut 12 ¼-inch slices.

Chop the ginger into tiny pieces. The crystallized ginger will be tricky to mince because it will stick to your knife. Rub the blade with a little vegetable oil. The oil will help you with a smoother cut, and don't worry; it won't flavor the ginger.

Arrange the mango and pear slices in alternating layers in the shape of a fan in the center of a dessert plate. Spoon the chocolate flecked whipped cream at the base of the fan. Sprinkle the minced ginger over the fruit. Mint's a great garnish, and if you have some left over from the entree, place a small sprig of mint in the cream with the leaves falling over towards the front of the plate.

If your taste for fruit is more domestic, or the seasons prohibit availability then you can use cantaloupe and apple instead. If you are feeling really exotic, papaya and Asian pear are out of this world.

Chapter One • **GINGER, LILY** *and* **SWEET FIRE**

*In a place out of reach
on the world's blue edge
there were hot stones and coals,
the hearth and light,
and it was here the two were formed,
golden fish upon the stones,
flickering shadows and voices
warm in the night,
warm to the welcome, yes hello
in a season of tides,
in a night of stars and a simple feast.*

• THE SECOND MENU •

STEAMED MUSSELS WITH LEMON GRASS AND TOMATO

DIJON AND SESAME CRUSTED CHICKEN BREAST WITH VEGETABLES, FETTUCINE, APRICOT AND SOY SAUCE

BANANAS AND COCONUT CREAM

Please don't be afraid of buying mussels. Just plan this meal when the grocer gets them in. Make sure they are all closed tightly. Don't use any that are open, which means they are dead and you really can't eat them. Place the mussels in cold water with a handful of cornmeal. This will plump them, and they will pass any impurities possibly gathered in the shipping and storing process. You can keep them in the water for at least an hour and as long as overnight. Lift them out of the water under cold running water; throw away any that have opened. Now you are ready.

If you cannot find fresh black mussels then use New Zealand green lipped. They are big, meaty and full of healthy amino acids; and on top of that they are delicious. They are bigger and meatier but the flavor is not as acute. This kind of mussel is a picture of neon drama. They have bright green and black rippled shells, and pale yellow flesh, it fairly jumps up off of the plate.

You will need a pot of boiling water, a cone-shaped strainer, and a large high-sided skillet for this dish.

MUSSELS WITH LEMON GRASS AND TOMATO

20	black mussels
¼ cup	pure olive oil (virgin isn't necessary for this)
2 tablespoons	chopped garlic
2 stalks	green onion, diced up to the deep green part. Use the green for garnish.
1 stalk	lemon grass, peeled and chopped (use the first two inches from the root. If you can't get fresh, try to obtain the dried stalk and then grind it in your mill. Powdered works, but use extra. Like any powdered herb the taste is a shadow of what you're looking for… Powdered = 2 tablespoons)

Chapter One • GINGER, LILY and SWEET FIRE

2 tablespoons	fresh ginger. Peeled and minced.
2 whole	tomatoes, seeded and chopped
2 tablespoons	basil, chopped
1 cup	tomato sauce
1 teaspoon	salt and pepper mix

Wash the mussels in very cold water and place them into the strainer, lower the strainer into the boiling water and let them cook until they all are opened. Lift the strainer out and set it aside in the sink to drain.

Heat the oil in the skillet on high heat. Add the garlic and onion, then lift the pan off of the stove and turn the heat to medium high. Stir, add ginger, tomato and tomato sauce, heat until it begins to bubble and add the mussels. Be careful at this stage, the sauce may pop if you're too rough in stirring the mussels and sauce. Stir the mussels so that they take in all the sauce. Add the basil, salt and pepper, and lemon grass. Stir. Let them cook in the sauce for a couple of minutes so that all the flavors blend and incorporate into the mussels. The taste will be deep and flowery, with a hint of citrus.

A splash of lemon juice, red wine or both adds a nice touch to this dish. The lemon or wine will brighten the flavor. As with all recipes, when you've got it down and can replicate the dish, then experiment and build on what you like. Use lime, orange, guava puree, peach juice, pear juice, currant juice, etc.

OK, let's talk about herbs. It's a known conceit of chefs and gardeners to use fresh herbs as much as possible and we expect everybody else to do the same, and that's not fair. Granted, we cannot replace the flavor and beauty of fresh, herbs, but we can at least approximate in a pinch. We all have a cabinet full of dried herbs, or at least a few essentials such as oregano, thyme, basil and bay, and now we hope that lemon grass and cilantro are there as well. Here's what you do to get the best out of the dried stuff: Wash and dry your hands. Place the herbs in your palm, now clasp your hands together with your thumbs opposing, and rub the herbs into a powder. Open your hands and smell. Pretty neat, huh?

The oil from your hands, plus the flavor release from mashing the herbs does the trick. That's as close as you are going to get to fresh from dried. It's a primitive version of the mortar and pestle, and that's not a bad thing, it works. When you try this method do it directly over the dish as you prepare it so that you get the most out of your effort.

The **coffee mill**. This thing is great for quick grinds and the powdering of peppercorns, dried lemon grass, coriander seeds, kosher salt, chilies, et al. Use and wipe out with a dry cloth or paper towel.

The **mortar and pestle** (marble or wood). Use this and use this often. It is as old as food. Some prefer the wooden variety for its earthy feel and texture. I like the clink and clean sound and feel of marble. They are most useful for blending herbs and seeds, for curries and compound spice mixtures. Just put your coriander or cardamom seeds in and mash them around with the pestle. Inhale, yep, that's what dinner smells like. It's nice to use when two are cooking together, which is what this book is all about, because you can blend herbs and talk and move around in the kitchen without getting in the way if you are the one doing the grunt work, uh, being the assistant.

Chapter One • GINGER, LILY and SWEET FIRE

Slowly, ice melting around the shells,
sleek, black ships waiting,
smell of the sands and tides
rising from the refrigerated air...
and she turns from the mounds
of chopped tomato and vidalia
to the stalks of lemon grass
and deep green fresh basil.
"Come here, peel away the skin
from the base like this,"
and the room filled with the fragrances
of crushed tangerine and lemon leaves
from the single bulb of lemon grass.
And if I didn't know better I would swear
I was standing in the groves
of the Indian River,
but I wasn't, it was we in the kitchen
with the greens of Mandalay,
with mussels from the heart of Hudson Bay.

The Second Menu

The next dish is a stir-fry and I recommend that you use a wok. Otherwise use a very large, high sided skillet. You need even heat for optimum cooking.

The wok: Use a carbon steel, stainless steel or copper-bottomed wok. Carbon steel is the best because of its ability to evenly transfer heat. Season by rubbing with corn oil and rock salt and heating it on medium heat for about thirty minutes. Maintain by cleaning with warm water only, no soap. If it rusts then clean with an abrasive cleaner and soft sponge. After you have cleaned it re-season the pan. There are non-stick woks on the market now that are pretty good; you don't have to worry about acidic reactions staining the pan. The choice is yours, authenticity or modernity that actually works.

Sesame and dijon crusted strips of Chicken Breast sautéed with mixed vegetables, apricot and soy over fettucine

The hottest part is the bottom. The sides are where you push the parts of a dish that require less rapid cooking, or when a sauce is reducing and you don't want the particular ingredient to overcook. An average wok will hold about a gallon and a half of liquid. They require very high heat for the best results. Even heat is essential; this helps you to cook an entire dish in one place with speed and control over the process.

Always oil the wok before cooking in it. Don't use virgin olive oil, as it will catch fire. The oil with the highest resistance to burning is corn oil. Use corn, peanut, vegetable or a blend of olive and corn, or a blend of olive and corn or peanut oil. If you are using butter then add it late in the stir-fry. Once you are used to using a wok you will find it difficult to just use a regular sauté pan. The wok, like the iron skillet is essential to a well-rounded kitchen. The iron skillet holds heat longer. The wok returns to high heat faster. You blacken Cajun dishes in an iron skillet, you sauté in a wok.

Chapter One • GINGER, LILY and SWEET FIRE

As the book progresses and your skill increases you will more fully understand how the wok works. Experience and, trial and error teach more than any volume of literature can.

SESAME AND DIJON CRUSTED STRIPS OF CHICKEN BREAST SAUTÉED WITH MIXED VEGETABLES, APRICOT AND SOY OVER FETTUCINE

½ cup	all purpose flour
3 tablespoons	butter
1 tablespoon	sesame oil
10 ounces	chicken breast sliced thin into 20 strips
2 tablespoons	brown mustard
2 tablespoons	honey
1 cup	sesame seeds

Dust chicken in flour. Coat chicken in honey mustard mix. Roll chicken in sesame seeds so that it is completely covered. Set aside on a plate.

VEGETABLES

5 medium stalks	asparagus sliced long and thin
2 medium	carrot peeled and very thin sliced
1 medium	yellow squash cut in 4ths and sliced thin
1 large	yellow onion cut in 4ths and sliced thin

SAUCE

3 tablespoons	apricot preserves
1 teaspoon	prepared horseradish
¼ cup	soy sauce
1 tablespoon	brown sugar
1/3 cup	apple juice (optional)

PASTA

8 ounces	fettuccine (will yield 12 oz cooked)

Cook the pasta, rinse in cold water and set aside until ready to mix with entree.

In a large skillet or wok, sauté the chicken and onion in butter. Stir with care, you don't want to burn or dislodge the sesame seeds. Add sesame oil. Add the vegetables, turn up the heat and cook until the asparagus is shiny and just crisp. This is the very definition of *stir-fry*.

Add the juice and horseradish and cook until it begins to boil. Add apricot, soy and sugar. Stir. Reduce heat to simmer. Taste. Adjust if necessary.

With the pasta still in a colander wash it under very hot water and then shake off all the water and drain.

Turn heat on sauce up to high. As it begins to boil add the pasta, and stir so that it is all mixed together and hot. Remove from heat and divide between two plates. Eat.

BANANAS AND COCONUT CREAM

You are going to make more than you can eat in one sitting for this dish. Why? Because you will freeze the leftovers and make milkshakes with it for a later menu. *YUM!*

4 cups	coconut milk. Shake the can before you open it so that the milk and cream mix.
2/3 cup	sugar
¼ cup	honey
1 teaspoon	salt
2 pounds	bananas, firm. If red bananas are available use them and cook longer, they are great for cooking.

Place everything except the bananas in a medium saucepan and bring to a low boil, simmer and stir occasionally with a whisk for about ten minutes. There should be no lumps and it will be slightly thick, just enough to coat a spoon with a thin film. Don't let it rise to a hard boil, this will separate the milk and scorch the pan!

> **If you have access to fresh pastas, then by all means be experimental and buy them. Just remember that cooking fresh pasta is quite different from the cooking methods for dried. Just drop it in boiling water for about a minute or two, stir it around and immediately mix it with the sauce. A flavored pasta such as tomato, lemon or orange would go well with this dish. Otherwise, stick to the recipe until you feel more comfortable with branching out which we will do in later chapters.**

Chapter One • **GINGER, LILY** *and* **SWEET FIRE**

> Is it to your liking? Does it need anything? This is the part where you have the chance to design the dish to your personal tastes. If you are happy with it then by all means continue, if not, then think about what you have added and what you might like more or less of. If more, then add, if less, then add more liquid to cut the flavor. Maybe you like ginger or garlic, basil or cilantro. This is your moment and no one else's. Both of you taste it, that's what this book is all about, cooking together for your own happiness and pleasure.

Peel and cut the bananas in two-inch long slanted slices. This is called cutting "on the diagonal." It looks like an oblong circle. Add to the mixture and stir with a spoon until it returns to a low boil. Simmer two to three minutes.

Remove from heat and pour into small bowls. You may eat this warm or at room temperature.

If this seems too unusual and you want to do something to make it a little more familiar, then pour it over thick slices of pound cake. It's good either way. Freeze the leftovers. There's a recipe for that later in the book.

So it's like this, OK?
You cook, I'll chop,
I'll do anything,
Anything to be here
Where we are close,
*We are **doing**,*
We are in our lives together.
Together. . . through the steam
And color of our finished table
It is just you and I
In a moment shared,
In a moment here.

Chapter One • GINGER, LILY and SWEET FIRE

• *THE THIRD MENU* •

BAKED AROMATIC CHICKEN WITH SPINACH WITH INDONESIAN SWEET SOY SAUCE DRESSING

SAMBAL SHRIMP AND THAI NOODLES WITH A SIDE OF CABBAGE, CARROTS AND BROCCOLI

CHILLED TANGERINE WITH RED GRAPE SYRUP

This menu is a burst of flavors from the highly aromatic to the spicy hot, winding down with a cool, sweet ice of tangerines and grapes. It's all pretty easily assembled and requires a minimum of preparation. In fact, most of it can be set up ahead of time. If you are cooking in the summer, or anywhere where it's hot and humid then this is the menu for you, you'll sweat and cool down, and best of all, you'll have a nice meal. The entree is a stir-fry, so get out your wok, cook fast, and turn down the AC.

BAKED AROMATIC CHICKEN WITH SPINACH WITH INDONESIAN SWEET SOY DRESSING

THE CHICKEN

8 ounces	chicken breast, 1 breast, skinless/boneless
1½ tablespoons	Chinese 5 spice mixture
1	granny smith apple
1/8 cup	rice vinegar
1/8 cup	soy sauce
1 tablespoon	brown sugar

Rinse the chicken breast under cold water and cut off any fat, also trim the flesh off any bone. Thin slice the apple and lay four pieces on the breast. Rub the brown sugar into the breast. Sprinkle the 5 spice powder on the chicken and apple. Place in small baking dish with the liquid. Cover with lid or aluminum foil. Bake for 20 minutes at 350 degrees. Remove from oven. Let cool a little at room temperature. Cut into small cubes.

While it's cooking, work on the spinach salad.

The Third Menu

Chinese five spice powder is a blend of clove, anise seed, star anise, ginger and cinnamon. It will sometimes have fennel. It's good for marinades and for spicing up a dish when the imagination's running low. I tend to use it primarily for hot and cold combinations because I like the way it wakes up a dish and brings together opposites. Once you become comfortable with using it you can make your own blend, that way it's easier to adjust the flavors to your particular needs and tastes. Remember, that's the great thing about learning your way around the shadows in your kitchen, making things the way you like them. Putting together your own spice blends is one of those exquisite tasks that takes away the mystery, but in that same taking binds you into a whole new mystery, that which is found in the creating the AHA! of a blend that marks it as your very own. Curries and masalas operate on the same principles of what combines, and we will be soon cooking those in other places. Use that mortar and pestle.

SALAD

25 leaves	spinach. It equals 8 ounces stemmed and washed
¼ cup	raisins, soaked in white wine overnight
2 tablespoon	sunflower seeds
2 whole	roma tomatoes, diced. If yellow tomatoes are available, use them. Whenever a variety such as pear tomato, yellow or tiger striped is available, use it. You'll be surprised.

Arrange on plate by placing spinach leaves first and then sprinkling other ingredients over spinach. Refrigerate.

DRESSING

1 cup	dark soy sauce
1 tablespoon	molasses
2 tablespoons	brown sugar
¼ cup	rice vinegar
2 tablespoons	cornstarch
2	lime juice and lime zest. For the zest, grate the skin on a cheese grater using only the green part, not the white, which is bitter. Strain the juice through a sieve

Mix all dressing ingredients together in a stainless steel bowl. Now

Chapter One • **GINGER, LILY** *and* **SWEET FIRE**

go to the stove and turn it on low heat. Hold the bowl with a towel or potholder. Stir the mixture with a wire whisk over the heat until it begins to thicken. Once it has thickened remove from heat. Keep warm.

Remove salad from cooler, scatter diced chicken over spinach, and drizzle dressing over the whole thing. It should be hot and cold. Warm chicken, hot dressing, cold salad.

STEAMED AND CHILLED CABBAGE, BROCCOLI AND CARROTS

5 large leaves	green cabbage
1 bunch	broccoli or four small heads stems trimmed
2	carrots peeled and sliced thin on diagona

Steam the vegetables until they are tender inside. Check with knife point. If it goes in easily with gentle force, you're OK. Don't add anything else unless you really want to. The pure taste of the vegetable will complement the sharp flavors of the entree. Chill.

By the way, I hope you have a bamboo steamer, if not, use one of those cute little folding steamer inserts you can buy in cooking sections of food and department stores, or specialty stores.

SAMBAL SHRIMP AND THAI NOODLES

¼ cup	peanut oil
16 medium	shrimp peeled and deveined. The technical term for medium is 26/30. You can go smaller if you like, and we usually are constrained by what is available in the grocery store anyway so buy what's best looking in amounts you can eat.
1 tablespoon	sambal oelek
1 clove	garlic very thin sliced or shaved on grater.
4 stalks	scallion, chopped
1 teaspoon	paprika
¼ cup	soy sauce
1/3 cup	Chinese cooking wine or sherry
6 ounces	Thai wide rice noodles or rice sticks

Soak these in very hot water until they are soft. Keep in water until you are ready to use, then drain.

In your wok or skillet heat the oil. HOT. It must be very, very hot. This is a stir-fry. As the oil begins to smoke, carefully slide the shrimp down the sides of the wok, stir, add the sambal and cook until the shrimp turns white to pink. Push the shrimp up the sides of the wok and add the other spices. Then stir shrimp in with the spices. Smoky, huh? Add the wine. Drain the noodles, then add to the shrimp and stir so that they kind of fry. You may need to add more oil, do so in small increments by the spoonful. Watch out so that the noodles don't stick to the pan. They'll do that if they aren't completely drained, or if the pan isn't hot enough. Add the soy sauce. Turn the heat down to medium. Use that wok; push everything around the sides of the bottom part where there is the most heat. Now, if it looks at all dry just add a little water. Pour in thin streams, and please don't splash. You're done. Cooking time is about five minutes. Yeah, it's fast.

Sambal Shrimp and Thai Noodles

Evenly divide between two plates. Place vegetables in center of table. You might want some bread with this dish, if so go for sourdough style. It will be spicy hot.

I sometimes like to put a couple of dashes of chili oil in with the peanut just to give it that extra heat. Also, peanuts or cashews are a nice garnish on top of the pasta. Like all the other dishes, experiment after you try out the initial recipe. You might like it hotter than what I've presented.

Chapter One • GINGER, LILY and SWEET FIRE

> If you grow or have access to organic roses sprinkle them on and around the bowl. Just think about the heights you take this little dessert to with a touch of imagination. By the way, almonds, peaches, apricots, apples and pears are all members of the rose family. It has something to do with the number of seeds, shape of seed, and with the number five.

You are now going to make a simple syrup. This is a syrup that occurs throughout the cuisines of the world. It's useful and you'll be glad to know this little sweetener.

Except for the crushed ice you can do it all in advance. If you can't do the crushed ice, that's OK, vanilla or white chocolate ice cream takes this dish to another heaven altogether.

CHILLED TANGERINE WITH RED GRAPE SYRUP

1 cup	sugar
2 cup	water
1 cup	white grape juice
3	tangerines, segmented. Use canned mandarin oranges if fresh is unavailable.
1 tray	crushed ice. Crush in a blender.

Mix sugar and water in saucepan and bring to a boil. Stir so that you dissolve all the sugar. Turn to medium low temperature. Cook and stir until it is thin enough to coat a spoon and it drips off the spoon in a smooth stream. That's simple syrup.

Now add the grape juice and continue to cook for five minutes. Watch that you don't burn it or boil it too hard. Keep the temperature down and stir. When it returns to a syrupy texture, remove from heat and chill.

Place the crushed ice or ice cream in bowls. Fan the tangerine segments around the ice. Drizzle about a third of a cup of syrup over each bowl. Save the rest for something else. Enjoy.

There's obviously a lot of opportunity for variations on this dish. In the syrup you can use orange blossom water, mint, jasmine, clove, rose water, different juices and so on.

The Third Menu

*Green chilies and garlic burning
in the blue gas flame on the stove in May;
breathe, breathe, it's so thick and rich
in here today, and you know, I rushed home.
I rushed home from work today...with green shrimp,
papaya and sweet pepper, tangerines and clove...
and there you were as tired as I,
and for you this is yours. Sit back and breathe,
let this be your air, your silence, your laugh,
whatever,
tonight it's all on me.*

Chapter One • GINGER, LILY *and* SWEET FIRE

• *THE FOURTH MENU* •

COCONUT SHRIMP WITH BLACKBERRY-HORSERADISH SAUCE

VEGETABLE FRIED RICE WITH TOFU AND ROASTED SHALLOTS

PUMPKIN CUSTARD

You have the chance to shine here with exotic dishes that are as simple as fried shrimp, rice and custard.

The one possible problem with dessert could arise from an improperly calibrated oven. If you have never checked your oven temperature with an oven thermometer, now is the time to do it. The majority of failures with custards occur from ovens that are not the temperature that they say they are. Oven thermometers are usually located on the hanging racks at the top of the shelves in the grocery store. In fact, there's lots of neat stuff up there. The best place to look is in the section where they keep all the baking paraphernalia.

There are so many different rices on the market now that I sometimes have trouble deciding just what kind or flavor I want to cook. If you are going for traditional then use standard long grain white rice. After that the easiest option is Uncle Ben's Wild and Long Mix (I swear), and then on to the good stuff: brown rice, Louisiana wild rice, pecan rice, jasmine rice, nishki rice, and basmati rice, and if you are shopping a farmer's market that targets the whole world then you are going to find even more rice variations. Go for it. Buy a little of each and find out for yourself which you prefer. They are all unique in flavor. My favorites for side dishes are jasmine and basmati. Jasmine for its flowery aroma and soft grain, basmati for its popcorn-like scent and "looseness." The best overall for this particular fried rice is the Long and Wild mix from Uncle Ben's. I'm not afraid to admit using it, and you shouldn't be either. It's easy, follow the directions, don't add too much water, and there you have it. The shelves are full of rice mixes like the Long and Wild, but the Uncle Ben's has been the most consistent for me in putting together a quick fried rice.

The Fourth Menu

COCONUT SHRIMP WITH BLACKBERRY-HORSERADISH SAUCE

12 large	shrimp (the technical name for large is 16/20). Peel and devein leaving the tail intact (to devein just cut the back side of the shrimp where you see the dark line. Slice down to the vein so that it opens up like a butterfly. Then wash under very cold water).
1	egg beaten with 3 tablespoons water. This is called an egg wash.
4 tablespoons	flour, for dusting the shrimp.
1 cup	coconut, shredded, unsweetened.
2/3 cup	peanut oil

Dust the shrimp in the flour; put them in the egg wash. Wash your hands. Now, with your left hand lift the shrimp out of the egg wash and with your right hand roll them in the coconut. Put them on the floured plate. Refrigerate until ready to use. They fry best when very cold.

Frying: On high heat, heat the oil in a wok, or high sided medium saucepan. Flick a dash of flour into the oil, if it sizzles and pops then you're ready. If it burns turn down the heat. If it just sits there and spins then wait about 30 seconds and try again.

Hold the shrimp by the tail and lay them into the oil. If you are afraid of burning yourself (a healthy fear) then use a pair of tongs. When they are all in the oil and the oil

Coconut Shrimp with blackberry - horseradish sauce

Ginger, Lily & Sweet Fire • 49

Chapter One • **GINGER, LILY** *and* **SWEET FIRE**

is sizzling, turn the heat down to medium. If you keep it on high the whole time you risk burning the coconut.

Let them cook 45 seconds on each side, turn again and watch the color of the coconut; it will be a golden tan. When it reaches golden, lift them out with your tongs and place on a paper towel to drain any extra oil.

SAUCE

½ cup	blackberries, high quality preserves. When fresh is available, use them.
1 teaspoon	ginger, minced
2 tablespoons	honey
1 lime	lime juice
1 tablespoon	horseradish (prepared horseradish) it's in the dairy section.
2 teaspoons	lemon yogurt
2 round slices	lemon, for garnish
2 round slices	lime, for garnish.

Put everything except, the yogurt, lemon and lime wheels into your food processor or blender and puree. That's it. You can make this at any time and refrigerate, or simply blend and serve.

THE PLATE

Sauce: Spread the sauce evenly over the plate. Put a teaspoon of yogurt in the center of each plate. With a fork or knife pull from the yogurt to the outside of the plate so that you get thin white lines running through the sauce. Place six shrimp around each plate with the tails to the outside of the plate.

An intersecting lemon and lime wheel adds a dramatic touch to this dish. Do this by thin slicing a lime and a lemon across the equator of the fruit, and then cut it to the center. Open up the lemon slice and turn the sides in opposite directions, then do the same with the lime and place it on top of the lemon in the center of the plate.

VEGETABLE FRIED RICE WITH TOFU AND ROASTED SHALLOTS

8	shallots, peeled. If you can't find shallots, use pearl onions.
8 ounces	tofu, very firm, cut in ½ inch cubes.
1/3 cup	balsamic vinegar
1/3 cup	water, mix with vinegar

RICE

2 cups	The standard measurement is twice the water to amount of rice used. Jasmine and basmati require a little more so instead of two cups use 2 1/3 cups water. let cool at room temperature, loosely cover and refrigerate.

VEGETABLES

Group A: put these together to the side.

1	red bell pepper, diced in 1/4 inch squares
1	onion, diced
2 stalks	celery, diced

Group B: put these two to the side.

2 heads	broccoli cut in flowerets
1	yellow squash, diced

Group C: put these two together to the side.

12 to 18	snow peas. Remove the stems and cut in half. If you can't get snow peas then use green beans, asparagus beans or sugar snap peas.
6	mushrooms, cut in wedges, four to the mushroom. I suggest crimini, snow crab (harisium), portobella, or shiitake.
3	eggs, beaten, set aside in bowl

SEASONING

1/3 cup	peanut oil
1 tablespoon	garlic, minced
3	chili peppers, dried
1 tablespoon	ginger, minced
1 teaspoon	salt and pepper mix

Chapter One • **GINGER, LILY** *and* **SWEET FIRE**

2 tablespoons	soy sauce
6 leaves	basil (½ teaspoon if dried)
2 stalks	scallions, sliced thin for garnish

Pour the vinegar and water over the shallots and tofu in a small pie pan, cover with aluminum foil and bake for thirty minutes on 350°. Remove from oven, do not remove lid. Set it aside until ready to use with rice. Just before using pour off the vinegar and save that for a dressing.

You will cook the rice ahead of time and refrigerate it. This is done so that the gluten adheres to the grains and doesn't stick to the pan. Cold rice stir-fries better than warm or hot rice for this very reason. If you cook it when it is hot it will stick to the pan. This makes serving time a lot easier too because there is less to do at the last minute.

I have friends who cook their rice in the microwave, they say it works, and I have to agree that the taste and texture really is excellent. On rice I'm sort of a traditionalist, when I'm preparing rice there are three other methods, in a covered pot on the stove, in the oven, or best of all in a commercial rice cooker where it's perfect every time.

There are as many ways to season as there are people in the world, yet for this particular dish all we are going to do is salt the water. All the taste is in the extras.

While the shallots and tofu are roasting you can chop the vegetables for the rice, and prepare the custard base.

That's a lot of ingredients, huh?

YOU CAN ARRANGE IT ALL ON A LARGE PLATE; JUST KEEP THEM IN THE SEPARATE GROUPS BECAUSE YOU WILL SAUTÉ THEM IN STAGES ACCORDING TO LENGTH OF TIME NEEDED FOR EACH GROUP TO COOK.

You really need a wok; I hope you have a wok by now. If not then use the largest skillet you have in the house. The even high heat is absolutely necessary for this to work right. Stir-fry: Wok or high-sided skillet. Very high heat, very little oil, quick cook time, stir and toss the whole the time, splash of liquid at the end.

Heat the wok. Add the oil. Add the chilies and cook until they begin to darken. Add the vegetables in group A. Add the egg and scramble. While it is scrambling add the ginger and garlic.

Stir in the vegetables in group B. Make sure the pan is very hot, and that it has enough oil to cook the rice. Add the rice and stir, stir, stir. Check to see that it is hot. When the rice is very hot add all the rest of the seasonings and stir some more. This all takes about five minutes.

Now, uncover your shallots and tofu, add the shallots and tofu to the vegetable rice and stir some more. Whew! Cook for two more minutes. That's it. Divide between two large plates and sprinkle the scallions over the top of the rice. This is a good time to test out those chopsticks.

A cold pilsner or iced mint tea goes well with this.

By the way, please don't eat the red chili peppers. You'll just sit there and cry and choke and otherwise embarrass yourself.

DESSERT

People tend to shy away from making cooked custards at home, and yet when they go out to eat, this is a favorite dessert. It isn't hard to make, in fact it's easy. I think we tend to be afraid of the whole process, like there's some mystery. Well, there isn't a mystery, just chemistry. Just follow the directions, use good baking dishes and make sure that oven is calibrated.

PUMPKIN CUSTARD

2 tablespoons	butter
4 tablespoons	granulated sugar
4 tablespoons	pumpkin puree
4	eggs, large
2	egg yolk
1 tablespoon	sugar
2 tablespoons	heavy cream
¼ teaspoon	vanilla extract

Preheat oven to 350°.

In two 6 ounce baking ramekins (high sided bowls) rub butter around the insides. Pour granulated sugar into the bowls and spin it around so that it is coated, pour out the remaining sugar and use in the recipe.

Whisk the eggs together in a mixing bowl. Then beat in the puree

Chapter One • **GINGER, LILY** *and* **SWEET FIRE**

Pumpkin custard

and the rest of the ingredients. Pour into bowls leaving it a half inch from the top. Place the bowls in a roasting pan. Pour water in the pan so that it is halfway up the sides of the bowls. Cover with aluminum foil. Bake for 30 minutes. Leave the door closed. Do not peek. After the cooking time has elapsed, remove from oven. Check it with a toothpick or knife point by sticking it in the center of the custard. If it comes out clean then you are done. If it looks grainy then it's overcooked, if it is wet then it isn't done.

Let it cool down a little, about 15 minutes. Now you can eat it two different ways. Gently tap the edges of the dish, shake it a little, lay a plate on top of the bowl, turn the plate and bowl over together, shake it again, and lift the bowl off of the plate. If all goes well and according to plan then the custard should release from the bowl and rest nicely on the plate. Or eat it from the cup. Crisp, thin cookies would go well with this dessert. Any flower petals?

DIALOGUE

Waiting for letters, spare change and jewels.
They're all hidden in a stack of magazines
in a bowl to the side of the kitchen door,
you know, where we threw last nights
unwanted correspondence, the wadded up recipe
for cinnamon gravlax with oregano custard...
"Well, it's mentioned in the back pages of
New York, and there's a chef in Boston who did it
for the stars." I'm sorry it didn't work,
but the words all sounded so very good.
"The words, the words all sounded so very good."
Well now I'm glad we know not all things combine,
at least it's worth a try, hey, we worked.
"Thank goodness we had other things to eat,
bananas and peanut butter, wheat bread and chips,
and yeah, we work."
I promise next time, "next time to read
the whole recipe?" How was I to know to buy
the salmon in April, in the rain,
at the moment before dusk with a blue coat on?
"Pass the salsa, will 'ya?"
I think tomorrow night we'll do something more
familiar. "Like a simple pasta?"
Yeah, a simple pasta...

Chapter One • GINGER, LILY *and* SWEET FIRE

• *THE FIFTH MENU* •

SWEET AND SOUR VEGETABLE SOUP

PANANG CURRY WITH ZITI PASTA, CHICKEN OR VEGETABLE

BANANA SMOOTHIE WITH RASPBERRIES

The vegetable soup can be made ahead and reheated. The curry paste can be made at any time within a month or two of using it. The pasta you've got to cook to order. The banana smoothie uses the leftover bananas and cream from an earlier recipe. This is an easy one.

The one odd ingredient you will need for the soup is fermented black beans. They can be found in any Asian grocery. They look like raisins. The black bean in this form is very traditional in Chinese cooking. It is sharp and earthy tasting. It doesn't take much of these to season a dish, and if you use too much it will make the food a little too salty. My favorites are the ones that have been seasoned with ginger and orange peel. Read the label or ask the grocer for help.

SWEET AND SOUR SOUP

1 quart	water
10 beans	fermented black beans
2 thin slices	fresh ginger
10 julienne slices	lemon grass, white only from stem part. No fresh? Use 1 teaspoon dried. Neither? Zest of 1 lime and 1 lemon.
1/3 cup	rice vinegar
1/3 cup	soy sauce
4	dried chili peppers
3 tablespoons	fresh cilantro, or 1 tablespoon if using dried.
10	Sichuan peppercorns, crushed coarse
2 tablespoons	sugar

The Fifth Menu

Put everything in a pot on the stove set to simmer. Let it simmer while you chop the vegetables, about 10 minutes. This will incorporate all the flavors into a nice stock. Then add:

½	onion, minced (very fine dice)
1 stalk	celery minced
1 head	broccoli, tiny flowerets = 1/3 cup
two leaves	bok choy, thin shredded. No bok choy? Then use whatever cabbage you can find.
10 leaves	spinach thin shredded.
1/3 cup	yellow squash, diced
5 medium	Mushrooms thin sliced.*

Be bold, don't just use button, try crimini, wood ear, shiitake, (see GLOSSARY) etc. There are so many great mushrooms available now, so reach out and explore the differences.

Put everything into the pot and simmer for 15 minutes. Stir every few minutes. Taste. After the soup has simmered for 15 minutes turn it up to boil for a couple of minutes before you serve it, this soup should be very hot, temperature-wise. Adjust flavor or go ahead and eat.

That should be it...unless...

Vegetable soups really are stock pots, so you can use whatever vegetables you like in them, extra suggestions would be jicama, Japanese eggplant, corn, turnips, potato, leeks, and on and on. The defining characteristic of this soup is not what's in it. For this one it's the underlying flavor, sweet and sour.

I have used chili bean paste for this and it adds a unique taste of earth and fire. You can make your own or you can buy it.

PANANG CURRY WITH ZITI PASTA, CHICKEN OR VEGETARIAN

THE CURRY PASTE:

1 teaspoon	sambal oelek
2 teaspoons	lemon grass
1 teaspoon	ground caraway
1½ teaspoon	garlic
3 stalks	cilantro with stem
¼ cup	lime juice

Chapter One • GINGER, LILY *and* SWEET FIRE

1 cup	tomato paste
½ tablespoon	salt and pepper
1/3 cup	vegetable oil

Put everything into a food processor and blend until smooth. There will be green flecks from the cilantro. Taste, it should be tomato with a sharp after-bite of "heat". If it is too acid from the tomato paste, add more salt and pepper. Maybe it's not hot enough, add more sambal. If it's not herby enough, then add more cilantro and blend again. The ground caraway gives that low, back of the tongue smoothness to the curry. If you don't taste that, then add more caraway.

So, you really should be able to taste all the ingredients both separately and as a whole, that is, you will be able to identify the flavors as being what they are within the context of the whole of the panang paste. Remember, this is the base for the dish, so it is going to be intense. Caveat emptor: it is not complete until mixed with the cream, vegetables and pasta.

PASTA

10 oz	Ziti, penne or bow tie. Cook and set aside.

THE ENTREE

3 tablespoons	peanut oil
8 ounces	chicken breast, diced
4 stalks	green onion chopped
1	carrot, peeled and minced
10	snow peas, cut in half on diagonal
4	asparagus, medium, sliced thin on the diagonal
2 tablespoons	curry paste
1	avocado, sliced thin into about 10 wedges
½ cup	coconut milk
½ cup	heavy cream
¼ cup	peanuts or cashews, chopped

The Fifth Menu

> Why the suggestions on balancing the flavors? Because we don't all taste in the same manner, from the personal likes to the basic physical ability to taste: the herbs may be old, the spice a poor blend, the tomato paste a lesser grade, or quite simply, the measurements may have been inaccurate and you need to correct the seasoning. There is nothing wrong with correcting to your tastes. Often it is forced upon us that we should in many cases acquire a taste for something, and a lot of the time this is true, who has eaten asparagus as a child and hated it, only to return as an adult and loved the thing?

Heat a large skillet on high, add peanut oil. When it begins to sizzle add the diced chicken and turn heat to medium. Stir it around a lot so that it doesn't stick. Remember the chicken is not floured so you don't have that extra protection from the pan. Go fast!

In this sequence add the vegetables: carrots, cook till crisped, asparagus till the skin blisters a little. Add the curry paste and let it simmer until it looks kind of thick and scary.

Add the snow peas and avocado and immediately pour in the coconut milk and cream. Stir and turn heat down to low.

Add the cooked pasta and mix it all together so that the sauce gets inside the tunnels in the pasta.

The sauce should be thick but not gloppy, and it certainly should not be runny and thin. It will have a slight pink-orange (peach) color and the taste will be smooth and creamy, then hot. The nuts calm down the fight that sometimes occurs between creams and peppers.

Divide between two plates and top with chopped nuts and green onion. You may like bread with this, and a crusty French bread would match with this spicy dish.

If making the curry paste for this dish whets your appetite for making more curries of your own, then look through any of the recent Thai and Indian cookbooks that are heavy on curries. Once you get the knack it's hard to go wrong with these, they store well and are great additions to most any stew or sauté.

Chapter One • GINGER, LILY *and* SWEET FIRE

DESSERT
BANANA SMOOTHIE WITH RASPBERRIES

Are the bananas and coconut cream still in your freezer from the earlier recipe? No? Can't blame you. If not, here are the base ingredients.

4 cups	coconut milk, shake the can before you open it so that the milk and cream mix.
2/3 cup	sugar
¼ cup	honey
1 teaspoon	salt
2 pounds,	bananas, firm. If red bananas are available use them and cook longer, they are great for cooking.
1 pint	raspberries, no fresh? Whole frozen only
	plain yogurt (optional: 1 cup vanilla or white chocolate ice cream)

If you do have the leftovers in the freezer, take them out and puree with the yogurt. Pour into ice cold parfait or pilsner glasses, fold in raspberries and top with a sprig of mint. Eat with a spoon or just slurp, either way it's a great way to end a meal that's no fuss and just childish enough to be fun.

It isn't necessary to cook the bananas if you already have them in the freezer from the earlier recipe. Just put everything together, except the raspberries, using ice cream instead of yogurt and blend.

Sprightly options would be to add a favorite clear soda, orange juice, rose water, tamarind juice, pineapple juice, and so on. If it's hot and humid, August and boring, you might want to freeze the raspberries (or buy frozen) and chop them into the puree. It gives the whole thing a sharp chill and crunch that's incredibly rewarding in the dog days. Actually, it's rewarding anytime.

• THE SIXTH MENU •

GREEN PAPAYA AND GREEN BEAN SALAD

POMPANO STEAMED IN BANANA LEAF (HAW MOKE) SERVED OVER VEGETABLES

COCONUT RICE PUDDING

This is a set of food that you are going to love and swear a lifetime's fidelity to, though difficult, it is a love well earned. It is a showoff meal with a combination of flavors from the strong to the sublime, and finally heavy sweet.

You have to plan ahead for this one because the papaya isn't always available. Most difficult of all, you have to find a market that has fresh or frozen banana leaves. The fish does not have to be pompano; it's just a suggestion because it's one of my favorites. This is a problem for the home cook. Cookbooks frequently suggest things that simply are not available to the home cook. We don't do it to shame you, it's just that all the odd stuff is easier to get if you are in the business where constant communication with purveyors sets up the line of supply and demand.

I've passed over a lot of otherwise great recipes on the principle of avoiding overt obscurity. Don't be afraid to ask your grocers to get what you want, often they will accommodate you. Also, if there is an international farmer's markets within sane driving distance then go there and shop to your heart and wallets content. Take a cookbook or a list of goods that you want to try. Buy things you've never heard of that look interesting. Talk to the employees, talk to other shoppers. It's truly the culinary land of Oz.

If a recipe calls for pompano and that isn't available use snapper, wreckfish, halibut, or even pomfrit, opah or farmed trout. If it's salmon the recipe wants then use tuna, striped bass, amberjack, arctic char, or Pacific marlin. If you can't find fresh fish that you are comfortable with then buy a high quality quick frozen fish. If you have to use frozen and you are grilling or baking, use it from the frozen state, **do not thaw**. If you thaw under running water the juices escape in the water and the fish ends up with a bland frozen taste. If you cook it still frozen then the juices remain in the dish. Just don't buy frozen trout; it isn't worth the time of day.

Chapter One • GINGER, LILY *and* SWEET FIRE

> **Fish sauce is very THAI, when alone it smells like a wet dog, but when cooked or combined it adds a distinct flavor that is reminiscent of the anchovy in Italian cuisine. Along with lemon grass and galanga this is one of those ingredients that identifies a dish as Thai.**

GREEN PAPAYA AND GREEN BEAN SALAD

You will need a papaya that is still firm and not quite ripe. If you can't find that then use a firm mango. What is important is the crunchiness.

1	serrano chili, thin sliced
1 teaspoon	garlic, chopped
1	shallot, chopped
1	papaya, shredded on a grater
10	green beans cut in 2 inch sections
1 teaspoon	sugar
¼ teaspoon	salt. You can substitute soy sauce if you like.
1 tablespoon	fish sauce
½	lime, peeled and quartered
5	cherry tomatoes, quartered
¼ cup	peanut oil
3 tablespoons	rice vinegar
4 ounces	salad greens

In a bowl, mash the peppers, garlic and shallot together till they are coarse, not mushy. Add the papaya and firmly press and mix.

Bruise the green beans by lightly hitting them with the back of a pan or meat hammer. Add to mix. Add the rest of the ingredients, squeeze in the lime juice and add the peeled wedges, firmly press and mix with a heavy spoon. Stir in the oil and vinegar. Now stir in the tomatoes, keeping them whole. It will be slightly wet and pulpy.

Arrange the greens on two plates and divide the mix over the lettuces. What you will have is a sweet, sour, hot, salty salad that is unique and a burst of flavor.

For the haw moke you will need a steamer, preferably a bamboo steamer that comes with your wok set. They are not expensive and are superior to any other kind of steaming utensils.

POMPANO STEAMED IN BANANA LEAF OVER VEGETABLES

The first time I had this dish was at the Thai Cafe on California Street in San Francisco in 1980. I literally shed a tear of happiness over this dish. I had never had anything better before in my life. There are several variations of this dish. It is kin to a fish mousse in French cuisine, but, then again it's not.

4	dried chilies
1 stalk	lemon grass
6 large leaves	basil, use holy or purple basil if it is available, for a slight cinnamon or anise taste
1 tablespoon	garlic, chopped = 2 cloves
1	shallot, chopped
½ teaspoon	turmeric
1 tablespoon	soy sauce
10	Sichuan peppercorns crushed
4 tablespoons	coconut cream: get this by scooping the cream off the top when you open the can.
½ teaspoon	sugar
8 ounces	pompano, cut in thin 1 inch pieces
1	banana leaf. Buy more if you're nervous and it's the first time
2	limes, zested on grater, use the zest.
10 medium leaves	spinach

Cut and discard the seeds from the chilies. Chop and soak the chilies in hot water.

Use the bottom three inches of the lemon grass, peel away the tough outer skin and slice crosswise as thin as you can.

In your mortar, or food processor, make a paste from the drained chilies, garlic, shallot, lemon grass, turmeric, soy and peppercorns. Remove to mixing bowl.

Add coconut cream, sugar, and the fish. Stir so that it is well mixed and pasty. Set aside.

Cut the banana leaves into 8 X 11 inch rectangles. Cut two more rectangles at 3 X 5 inches. Cut six long thin, string-like strips of banana leaf for tying the packets. Set the large leaves on a cutting board, shiny side down. Place small leaves inside large leaves. Divide and stack spinach on each, then stack basil leaves on top of spinach.

Go back to the fish mix (it is a curry). Stir in the lime zest. Divide the mix between the banana leaves. Fold the edges of the leaves over so that each overlaps in the center.

You will have a tube shape. Now, fold the ends over to close it. Turn each over. Lay the strings down, three per pack on the cutting board. Set the packets on top of the strings. Tie it up. Not too thick, you don't want to squeeze out the mix.

Fill the bottom of the wok with water, set the steamer of top of the water. Bring to furious, propulsive boil. Place packets in steamer rack. Cover. Cook ten minutes. No more, no less. At the end of that time, lift the steamer off of the pan and set it aside. With a spatula, and be careful, lift the packets off of the steamer and place on vegetables.

VEGETABLES

10 leaves	bok choy sliced thin, napa cabbage if bok choy is unavailable.
1	zucchini, very thin sliced, lengthways
1	yellow onion, thin sliced crossways
2 stalks	celery, thin sliced long ways
12	snow peas
½ cup	mung bean sprouts
2 tablespoons	peanut oil
1 tablespoon	ginger, grated
1 tablespoon	soy sauce

Sauté the vegetables in the peanut oil and ginger. When they are tender, add soy sauce. Pour on plate and set banana leaf package on top.

This is a good place for day lily flowers, chive flowers, or even nasturtiums. Sprinkle the petals over the plate. Cut the leaf open when you are ready to eat. Don't eat the banana leaf, it's there for flavor and packaging only. I hope you enjoy this dish as much as I have. It's a classic of Thai cuisine.

An alternative dish in banana leaf is to just use a fillet of halibut or pompano and top with panang curry and raw shrimp, wrap in aluminum foil and bake. Bake at 400° for thirty minutes. To steam, wrap in Romaine lettuce leaves, or if available use lotus leaves. Steam for twenty minutes.

COCONUT RICE PUDDING WITH FRESH FRUIT

1 cup	sushi rice
1 cup	water
1 cup	coconut milk
½ teaspoon	salt
1/3 cup	fruit juice of the fruit you choose to eat. You can use any canned or bottled juice.
1/3 cup	honey
½ teaspoon	clove, ground
1/3 cup	shredded coconut
enough for 2	plums, mango, nectarine, strawberries, kiwi, banana, peaches, whichever is at its peak ripeness and is your favorite.

Combine everything except the fruit and cook till the liquid is absorbed, about 20 minutes on low heat. Leave covered until ready to eat.

Set the warm rice in mounds on a small plate. Slice and arrange the fruit around the rice, letting the juice drip onto the rice.

Chapter One • **GINGER, LILY *and* SWEET FIRE**

*Early evening opening into a Van Gogh sky
of fog brightened stars and shadowed trees,
wicker chairs creaking as we lean back and yawn,
sharing a sweet spring water and Anjou pears.
Coltrane's Meditation flows and rises
from the stereo, rises with the chirps and whistles
of thrashers and buntings in the bamboo garden.
It's so peaceful here, after dinner,
relaxed and easy, where this is the wish:
the working world slips away and it's just us,
here on the front porch, feeling the night
wrap around us, silky and moist, alive.*

• THE SEVENTH MENU •

CHICKEN AND SUNDRIED TOMATO EGGROLL

BAKED TROUT WITH LEMON GRASS, GINGER AND PEAR, TRADITIONAL STICKY RICE WITH VEGETABLES

SLICED APPLES AND GOUDA

The only hard part about this menu is the egg roll. Make more than you need for one sitting. After you fry them you can freeze the leftover egg rolls and use them another time. Just reheat in the microwave, re-fry, or warm in the oven. Cooking it again in oil gives the best flavor and does retain the integrity of the dish. Egg roll skins can be bought at any Asian grocery, and I have found them in standard grocery stores lately. Sundried tomatoes can be found in the specialty sections of the produce department. If you can, buy the dry ones and soak them in hot water yourself, otherwise just use the ones packed in brine or oil, be sure to rinse them off.

This recipe is a variation of one by Ken Hom from his excellent book *East-West Cooking*. He is an inspiration and definitely one of the best writer-chefs on the New Hong Kong blends of cooking. Highly recommended reading and cooking.

CHICKEN AND SUNDRIED TOMATO EGG ROLLS

4	eggroll skins
2 tablespoons	zucchini, fine diced
2 tablespoon	yellow squash, fine diced

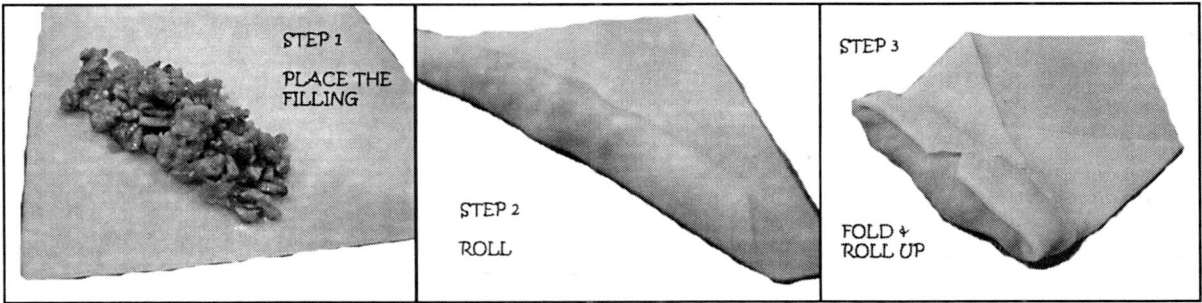

Chapter One • **GINGER, LILY *and* SWEET FIRE**

1 ounce	bean thread noodles soaked in hot water and then chopped when softened
2 tablespoons	red bell pepper, fine diced
2 tablespoons	scallion, fine diced
6 halves	sundried tomato, thin sliced
3 ounces	chicken breast, very thin sliced
3 tablespoons	rice vinegar
1 tablespoon	sesame seeds
1 tablespoon	cilantro, chopped
1 tablespoon	basil, chopped
3 tablespoons	mushroom soy sauce
1	egg, beaten with 1 tablespoon water
1/3 cup	cornmeal
1 cup	peanut oil

Mix everything except the egg roll skins, cornmeal, and egg together in a mixing bowl. Sprinkle the cornmeal on a cutting board. Lay the skins on the cornmeal. Portion the mix into the skins; this will be about 3 tablespoons per egg roll. Roll the skin over the top of the mix. Brush the egg wash over the skin. Fold in the ends over the edge about a fourth of an inch. Roll the egg roll like a cigarette. Keep the edges closed. Make sure you have it covered in cornmeal, and that it is tightly closed.

Heat the oil in a wok, or small high-sided pan. Temperature should be at 350°. Gently set the egg rolls into the oil and fry, turning them over every 2 minutes, six minutes. Remove and drain on a paper towel. Cut one open to check that the chicken is cooked. It should be. Cut them on the diagonal and serve on the following sauces.

Baked Trout with lemon grass, ginger and pear

SAUCES

SWEET SOY, WASABI AND APRICOT HORSERADISH

3 tablespoons	sweet soy sauce
1 teaspoon	wasabi: you can buy this powdered and mix it to your taste, or as a paste.

APRICOT PRESERVES WITH HORSERADISH AND LIME JUICE:

1/3 cup	apricot preserves
1 teaspoon	prepared horseradish
1 teaspoon	lime juice. 3 tablespoons per serving

Blend all ingredients together until smooth.

Spread the sauces, except the wasabi, separately on the plate so that it looks swirly. Put dabs of wasabi on the edges of the plate, set egg roll slices around the plate.

A nice garnish for this would be green onion stems sliced long down the stem so that it curves. Place three to five strands over the plate. Also, diced sweet peppers and Bermuda onion are nice additions to the rim of the plate.

BAKED TROUT WITH LEMON GRASS, GINGER AND PEAR WITH TRADITIONAL STICKY RICE AND VEGETABLES

RICE

1 cup	nishki rice
2 cups	water
1 tablespoon	salt
1 ounce	rice vinegar
1 tablespoon	granulated sugar

Bring the water, salt, vinegar and sugar to a boil. Add the rice. Bring to a boil. Turn heat down to simmer. Cover and cook for twenty minutes. Remove from stove and leave covered for an additional twenty minutes. Or just keep covered until it's time to eat.

You want the rice kind of plain so that it doesn't disturb the taste of the fish. There is a lot of flavor going on with the trout, so the rice needs to act as a "chaser."

Chapter One • **GINGER, LILY** and **SWEET FIRE**

TROUT

2 6 to 8 ounce	trout
1/3 stalk	lemon grass, mince the white part
4 ounces	ginger, very thin sliced
4 tablespoons	mushroom soy sauce
3 tablespoons	rice vinegar
1	Anjou pear, thin sliced
1	jalapeno, seeded and thin sliced
12 seeds	cardamom crushed
6	scallions: whole
1	carrots: thin sliced
10	green beans: cut long
1	onion, thin sliced
8	oyster mushrooms, thin sliced
2 tablespoons	peanut oil

Rub the trout with the peanut oil. Place in roasting pan. Gently rub all the herbs and spices in and on the trout. Layer it with the pear and vegetables. Pour on the soy and vinegar. Cover with aluminum foil or banana leaf if you still have any around. Bake at 375° for 15 minutes.

Place rice on plate. Set trout on rice. Spoon liquid and vegetables over the fish. You may want to garnish with lemon and lime wedges.

DESSERT

SLICED APPLES AND GOUDA

This really isn't Thai at all, but this is fusion cuisine, and we are looking for what combines, so let's rebel a bit.

2	apples, use whatever appeals to you in the market.
4 ounces	gouda, cut in tiny wedges rose petals or honeysuckle flowers sprinkled over plate.

For this, the larger the plate the better. If you like crackers with your fruit and cheese, the Bremner wafer or lavash is a great addition. Russian style black bread or a thick wheat is good as well.

The Seventh Menu

> **If at the end of any of the meals you are just too full to have a dessert, try eating just a few slices of ripe mango sprinkled with fresh lime juice. You'll feel better for it.**

Well, that's the end of our chapter on Thai fusion cuisine. I hope you have learned and experimented with a few new dishes. If you like what we've done then buy other books on more authentic Thai cooking and charge full steam into the tropics.

The next chapter, Mediterranean Hillsides and Beaches explores a different style of cooking, but don't put away the wok and herbs. We are bringing together the cuisines of the world, so with a just a wave of the flourish wand you can transform otherwise traditional cooking into a uniquely personal meal.

Ginger, lily and sweet fire,
the click of marble and stainless steel.
Summer rain on a tin roof steaming.
Outside it rages, crisp, clean and stormy,
so let's just go slow, simmer and roast,
cook on low heat, let the hours pass.
Savor and cradle the day in our arms,
or better yet, let the day hold us.

CHAPTER TWO

MEDITERRANEAN HILLSIDES and BEACHES

Small waves, ripples,
a green basin shines,
the soft sun colored stock
clinks clam and oyster shells,
calamari swarm like drunken clouds,
and the kitchen becomes a haven
of lost spices and aromatics.
Dizzy with the fumes of roasting garlic,
the steaming fronds of saffron and bay,
it pulls me in, and I cross the hearth.
And yeah… I remembered the rosemary bread,
you stir, I've got the china
Barolo, and raspberry sorbet.

THIS CHAPTER IS AN EXPLORATION of the cuisine that invites us into the coastlines, green valleys and arid hills of southern Spain, Italy, and North Africa. It seems like a broad stroke, and it is, but our purpose here is to touch upon, assimilate, and connect with how the foods of these lands come together in the American kitchen. Were not going on a sauce boat up the Tiber, just a skiff.

There are more than tomatoes, olives, oregano and semolina to the cuisine of these lands, and yet it is through these four things that we visualize the Mediterranean table. We will use these ingredients in many places, but not all. Get ready for custards, shellfish, lamb, sharp cheeses, risotto, and the fruits of an abundant garden.

Italian food is fun; it is not somber and contemplative. When arranging a meal, do so with a light heart and an empty stomach. Let yourself go, use a heavy hand with the spices, don't be afraid of buying the boldest wine on the shelf, find a good fresh pasta, and, oh yeah, buy some yeast, because were going to make bread in this chapter.

By now you should have the idea that this is not a manual of overtly traditional recipes. The Romans and Ottomans who settled the Mediterranean were not only great warriors, they were great assimilators. There is always the give and take. What we are doing is building upon the foundations of classic dishes and expanding upon them with contemporary tastes. This is a book of romances: cultural, culinary, and personal, and for each to succeed there must not only be a passion, there must be an ability to expand beyond the center of that passion. Food represents so much more than the plate upon the table. How often do we remember events by the food or drink around that event? How many relationships contain elements of a previous relationship? What culture is able to close itself off from its past and still progress? If you love the freedom and spontaneity of a life that gathers in the world and reaches outwards from the source of that life, then

Chapter Two • MEDITERRANEAN HILLSIDES *and* BEACHES

open up the cabinets, turn on the stove, and empty out the cooler, this is about the pleasure of the sensual and the changing, about romance and the foods that best influence the heart and the soul. Have fun with it, that's the best I can ask.

Before we get started I want to brief you on olive oils. Olives are one of the greatest fruits of the earth, the juice of the olives, olive oil, are perhaps surpassed only by wine as one of the supreme gifts of the marriage of earth and invention. We know the health benefits, from low in fat to that of widening the gap between good HDL and bad LDL cholesterol, but what about the benefits of use and flavor. . .beyond question there is no better. Corn oil lowers both HDL and LDL equally and does not widen the cholesterol gap, it lowers each by the same ratio. Corn oil and peanut oil have their place in different kinds of cooking that require different flavors, but the health factor has to be put aside when using these oils. No, olive oil reigns supreme.

When you taste virgin olive oils you will experience one of the following flavors: nutty, grassy, artichoke, fennel, green apple, peppery, sundried tomato. It will be smooth, pungent, slightly bitter, and like the California or Greek, fruity. Oils from different regions have different flavors. Colors range from wheat to green. If the flavor is rusty, metallic, musty and greasy then it isn't any good. You can choose blends, or single olive oils like the Calamata, which is very strong, but the easiest key to identifying the oil you want is by country and region. California production is still on the rise, and I have had some excellent oils from both the Napa Valley and Sonoma.

Unfortunately you can't readily find them at your local grocer, and you'll have to go to the specialty shops, but the find is worth the search. The most popular oils in the stores do list place of origin, so read the label. This is a very general list, and as I keep emphasizing, taste and you will learn: Tuscany: peppery, Riviera: delicate, Umbria: earthy, Southern Italian: strong, olive, French flowery, North African:

mild, Greek: fruity to strong olive (it's a guessing game with Greek oil), Spanish: fruity and aromatic, Napa Valley: fruity to nutty (depends on the vineyard, fortunately the label tells you), Sonoma: olive to nutty. If you want to spend the money buy the ones listed as stone ground, cold press, first pour, and if you can't find that then buy the extra virgin which is all that except it may not be stone pressed. There are so many now available that it's no big deal to buy little bottles of all the oils and try them out for yourself. It's even more fun to do blind tastings in the same manner as wine tastings. You will be surprised at what you discover. Well, those are the Cliff Note guides for extra virgin olive oils.

Do not buy oil in the can unless you plan to use it all up within a month or so. Store in a cool, dark place and avoid extreme temperature fluctuations. Always keep the bottle sealed shut.

When you use plain olive oil for cooking you can always add a little extra virgin at the end just to enrich the dish without risking the oil catching on fire. This is important, as noted at the beginning of the chapter, extra virgin olive oil will flame at a lower temperature than lesser grade oil. Cook, beware.

The first menu is information heavy, we will cover the areas of oils, pasta cooking and pastas, an extension of the basic marinara, and best of all, how to make a ricotta cheesecake. These are the staples. When you have learned how to make, or build, these basics of Italian cooking you will find yourself freed from a lot of previous apprehensions about going beyond the all purpose jar of tomato and freezer cured desserts. I swear, well, I at least hope.

Chapter Two • MEDITERRANEAN HILLSIDES *and* BEACHES

• *THE FIRST MENU* •

ROMAINE LETTUCE, GRANNY SMITH APPLES,
DRIED DATES, SERRANO PEPPERS, SUNFLOWER SEEDS
AND SCALLIONS WITH PARMESAN
OIL AND VINEGAR DRESSING

PENNE PASTA WITH AN ARTICHOKE HEART
AND WILD MUSHROOM MARINARA

RICOTTA CHEESECAKE

AT THE GROCERY STORE:
These are the things you need to look for at the store:

Tight, deep to light green bodied romaine with no brown spots or wilted tips. Shake off the water at the produce shelf; this stuff (extra weight) does you no good once you put it in the plastic bag.

The apple needs to be tart and crisp, which is why I suggest the Granny Smith. It must be free of blemishes, tight-skinned, firm and have a slight sour/tart apple smell. The color should be light green.

The serrano pepper must be small, firm and shiny. If you shake it and hear or feel the seeds rattle, then put it back and make another choice. The serrano is a very hot and spicy pepper, so if you are at all sensitive to this degree of heat then go for a large jalapeno or even a poblano pepper, and if those are too hot then use banana peppers. Because it will be very finely minced the heat of the pepper combines with the other fruits throughout the salad and will not be as intense as you may at first imagine. Be daring. Serranos and jalapenos are my favorite peppers because of the variation in flavor from pepper to pepper. They are all hot, but they also have a variety of citrus flavors that become evident once you acquire a taste and ability to learn how to combine them with other fruits, vegetables, and meats.

Do not buy grated parmesan or anything resembling processed parmesan. Buy it in the little wedge of either Italian or Argentine origin. It's easy to shred or grate on a typical cheese grater. The taste is milky and sharp, the price is easy, and the reward of fresh taste far exceeds the convenience of

The First Menu

You will need a couple of heavy pots that hold at least 4 to 8 quarts liquid. A 2-gallon two-handled pot is the best for cooking pasta, and you can get by with a 4 quart pan for the sauce. You'll need one large slotted colander for draining the pasta. For the cheesecake, a 9 inch spring form cheesecake pan. A spring form pan has a removable bottom and a spring latch on the side to tighten and release the bottom. It is designed this way so that you can easily remove the cake without damaging the integrity of the dessert. More on that later during the recipe.

There are no odd ingredients to this menu, so don't worry about scratching through the back shelves of specialty shops and grocery stores to stock up for the meal.

shaking a treated powder out of a green tube.

The olive oil should be extra virgin. It will have a yellow to green color and a heavy olive scent, and it's thicker than the other grades of olive oil. The grades of olive oil tell you the level at which they were processed. Extra virgin is first press, virgin second, pure is third, and just plain olive oil occurs somewhere along the watering down stage. Pure and diluted olive oils are for cooking. Extra virgin and virgin is for seasoning dressings and final additions to cooked foods. The reason for this is because the first grades burn at a low temperature and the flavor of hot olives overpowers the rest of the food. The easy formula is virgin cold, pure hot. I'll go into more detail on olive oils in the fourth menu.

Balsamic vinegar has been a favorite of restaurants for a very long time. It has been slowly rising into vogue in the consumer market since the middle 1980s. Everybody say hurrah! for California cuisine and the likes of Alice Waters and Jeremiah Tower, for it was through them that the use of gourmet vinegars became a child of the popular market. Balsamic is an aged red wine vinegar with a thick, deep color and flavor that is more akin to a table wine than a vinegar. As a note, it is also good for your digestion.

When you mention the words dates or figs to some folks they seem to screw up their faces in disgust. I've never understood why, but if you or your partner is opposed to dates use any dried fruit of your choice. I use dried dates in this recipe for the chewy texture and the intense sweetness. The combination is superb.

Why the lengthy instructions on shopping? To make sure you buy the best.

Chapter Two • MEDITERRANEAN HILLSIDES and BEACHES

> The pasta must match the sauce for the optimum experience. A hearty, bold pasta for a hearty, bold sauce, hence the penne for the marinara. Think of it this way: small pasta small sauce, big pasta big sauce. (See GLOSSARY)

FIRST COURSE

ROMAINE LETTUCE, GRANNY SMITH APPLES, DRIED DATES, SERRANO PEPPERS, SUNFLOWER SEEDS AND SCALLIONS, WITH PARMESAN OIL AND VINEGAR DRESSING.

THE SALAD

8 outer leaves	romaine, and the heart. rinsed and the heart and torn by hand.
1	granny smith apple, diced. Put in bowl.
2 tablespoons	chopped dates.
1	serrano chili, cut in half, remove seeds, mince (wash hands, knife and cutting surface, and do not touch your eyes or anything else, believe me, you don't want the burn.)
2 tablespoons	sunflower seed.
3 stalks	scallion sliced very thin.

THE DRESSING

½ cup	virgin olive oil
¼ cup	balsamic vinegar
½ teaspoon	garlic, minced
½ teaspoon	brown sugar
A pinch	black pepper (a pinch equals the tip of a regular teaspoon)
¼ cup	parmesan, grated fine.

In a blender set to medium speed, slowly pour in two thirds of the oil so that it emulsifies (thickens). Add all the balsamic vinegar, slowly. Add garlic, brown sugar and black pepper. Now add the rest of the oil. Turn blender off. Add parmesan and pulse the blender two or three times to mix the cheese in but not to puree it.

Put all salad ingredients together in large mixing bowl. Pour dressing over salad, toss it around and serve.

PENNE PASTA WITH AN ARTICHOKE HEART AND WILD MUSHROOM MARINARA

THE SAUCE

½ cup	pure olive oil
½	onion medium yellow onion, diced.
2 stalks	celery, diced.
2 tablespoons	garlic, chopped.
6 each	shiitake, crimini, and portobella, mushrooms, sliced
4	bay leaves
½ teaspoon	basil
½ teaspoon	oregano
1/3 teaspoon	cinnamon (yes, cinnamon)
1/3 cup	balsamic vinegar
12	roma tomatoes, chopped.
10 ounces	tomato sauce
6	artichoke hearts, cut in half (1 small can)
1 tablespoon	salt and pepper (remember the mix? 1 to 1/3)
1 small bunch	parsley, fresh, chopped; it will equal about 2 tablespoons (when you look at it in the store the leaf part will cover the palm of your hand)

You can make the sauce early and reheat when you need it.

THE PASTA

6 ounces	Dry penne, boil in 2 quarts water for ten minutes or until the texture is the way you like it for your tastes

In a 2-quart heavy-bottomed soup pot, heat the olive oil on medium. Add the celery and onion and cook until they begin to soften. Add the mushrooms and cook about a minute. Add all the herbs. Turn on high and stir for about two to three minutes and then add the vinegar, and turn to medium low. Add the tomatoes and tomato sauce, simmer for 15 minutes. Add

Penne Pasta with an artichoke heart and wild mushroom marinara

Chapter Two • MEDITERRANEAN HILLSIDES *and* BEACHES

> If you must have meat then use a thick slab salt bacon or pancetta. Pancetta (belly) is an Italian style bacon that is not smoked, except in the northern regions. It has a sweet-salty taste and is similar to prosciutto except that it is not as salty or raw. If you are using it in a recipe always dice it, and to make use of the fat for the sauce, cook from the beginning with onions and peppers. I know, it's not the healthiest sounding thing in the world, but what we are concerned with here is the best possible dish. And by the way, the only thing I've ever figured out that's unhealthy about food is sitting around and doing nothing. An active life uses everything you eat. That easy chair is more unhealthy and damaging to the system than all the carbohydrates and fats in the world.

the artichoke hearts and salt and pepper. Simmer uncovered for around thirty minutes. Remember to stir a lot, and don't you dare cover it, all that covering does is water down the flavor and make the sauce watery and bland. When it is done, turn off the heat and stir in the parsley. This brings together all the flavors and adds that last complement of fresh herbs.

After you have cooked and washed the pasta place it in a large mixing bowl and pour in two cups of marinara. Toss it around and serve. Garnish with grated cheese and a sprinkle of chopped parsley. Bread? Toasted garlic French is always nice. Thick slices of sourdough brushed with melted butter, hopped garlic and oregano, and baked for five minutes at 400° is good too. Just a suggestion.

Fresh grated parmesan or its country cousin the sharp Romano on top is a good traditional touch. If you like other cheeses, go for it.

> **Fresh pasta versus dried pasta:** Fresh pasta is made with egg and flour and is soft. Dried pasta is made with water and flour and is, well, dried. Fresh pastas need a butter or cream sauce to enhance the velvety texture of the pasta, and must be mixed with the sauce, never topped with a sauce. Dried pastas are more versatile and can be topped or mixed. You can freeze fresh pasta. It must be used as soon as it is cooked, boiling water for three to five minutes, no longer, and you don't need to rinse it, just mix immediately into the sauce and serve. Once you have learned how to cook fresh pasta, and only experience can do this, you will fall in love with the texture and delicate flavor. I guarantee. For more information go to Marcella Hazans Essentials of Classic Italian Cooking, she covers it all.

The First Menu

I've done this with Monterey jack, cheddar (from Wisconsin to Sharp Italian), fontina, and gouda and have been pleased with each one. Fresh gorgonzola is a knock out if you like heavy blue or green *veined* cheeses. There are so many wonderful cheeses in the world that it's a shame not to try them all.

Try this, buy cheeses you don't know a thing about, have seen but never tried, or that just look interesting. Buy them in small pieces. Nibble. Think about flavors that would go well with them as you eat. Strong cheese needs an equally strong companion, mild cheeses need mild flavors. In this situation it isn't so much the yin and yang of combinations as it is the marrying of intensities.

The golden coin of the Rubaiyat,
it spins and spins throughout
the dawn and day and dusk,
and yet at night it stops and shines,
one light upon the table,
one flower on the mantle...
cluttered, empty plates,
a smoldering candle smokes and sputters,
and I start humming the dance
from Cavelaria Rusticana,
swaying, holding, a little waltz
together in the kitchen at night,
and we shine back into the coin,
giving definition, giving heart
to the great feast of today, and tomorrow.

Chapter Two • MEDITERRANEAN HILLSIDES *and* BEACHES

DESSERT

RICOTTA CHEESECAKE

Stop shaking your head and saying no, no, no. It's easy, but you must follow the directions exactly. There is no sure cure for cracks, we do all we can to prevent them, yet even the best efforts are set astray by uneven temperatures (the major cause) or collapsed egg whites (not whipped enough). There isn't much you can do about large cracks, and small cracks will sometimes heal themselves as the cheesecake cooks or settles. Fruit glazes and sour cream toppings were no doubt created for just these problems, so when the cracks do appear, glaze away. Also, one of the earliest recipes for cheesecake appears between 234-149 BC. in the book *Marcus Gavius Apicius by Cato, De Agricultura*. So, it's been around a long time; it can't be that hard, can it?

You will need: a mixer, a 9 1/2 inch spring form pan, baking paper, a grater, 325° oven, and an oven thermometer to make sure the heat is consistent in your oven. That's it on the special equipment.

CRUST\PAN

1 cup	walnuts
1 tablespoon	brown sugar
2 tablespoons	sugar
¼ teaspoon	cinnamon

Put all the ingredients into a food processor and blend into fine crumbs. Cut a circle out of the baking paper and fit it over the bottom part of the spring form pan. Butter the bottom and the edges. Press the crumbs all around and up the sides of the pan. Put the pan in the refrigerator.

CAKE

3 ounces	cream cheese
1¾ cups	ricotta
¼ cup	yogurt
¾ cup	sugar
3 large	eggs, separate yolks and whites
1 teaspoon	lemon zest from one lemon
2 teaspoons	lemon juice
4 tablespoons	all purpose flour
Pinch of	salt

The First Menu

If you are using a regular mixer use the paddle attachments instead of the whisks. If you are using the food processor use the plastic blades instead of the metal.

Beat the cream cheese until it is smooth and soft, add ricotta and yogurt and continue beating until smooth again. Turn it off and scrape down sides of bowl. Beat and scrape again, and again until it is smooth and velvety. Add sugar and continue, then add egg yolks, lemon zest, and lemon juice. Scrape. On low speed, gradually add flour and salt. If you rush it you ruin it.

Remove and set aside, clean out the bowl so that there is absolutely no residue left in it, rinse with cold water and wipe clean.

Put in regular whisks and beat the egg whites until they are stiff. Begin slowly and increase speed as you go. This thickens and expands the whites more evenly. Now, you may have to turn the machine (pulse) on and off as you go to check the texture. The finished whites will have what are called stiff peaks; the ridges will hold shape when you turn the mixer off. The mix will still be shiny white, not paper white. If it is over mixed they will appear dry and grainy. If this happens throw it away and start again.

Fold your perfect egg whites into the cheesecake mix. Do this either with your clean hand or with a rubber spatula. Fold gently as you do not want to collapse the whites. When it is smooth and well combined pour it into the spring form pan. Place in center rack of preheated 325° oven and bake for 45 to 50 minutes. If you must look at it, wait at least 20 minutes before doing so. Remember, one way that cracks occur is from extreme oven temperature fluctuations.

When it is done the sides will be puffed up and tan, and across the top of the cake it will be a light gold color. Tap the edges and it will shake just a little in the center. If it jiggles it isn't done yet. If you are really stuck on the toothpick in the middle thing, then go ahead and stick it in, just remember that there will be a little moisture left to the

So it cracked. You have two choices: Mix a cup of sour cream with two tablespoons honey, 1/4 teaspoon allspice and a dash of the extract of your choice, blend and smooth over the top of the cake. Or you can take one cup or your favorite jam or preserves, smooth it out a little bit, and then spread it over the top. Fresh berries placed in the sour cream aspire toward the sublime.

Ginger, Lily & Sweet Fire

Chapter Two • MEDITERRANEAN HILLSIDES *and* BEACHES

cake and that it will not come out completely clean. If it is done, then turn off the oven and let it stay there for one hour. After an hour take it out and let it cool at room temperature for at least two hours. Avoid drafts, another crack inducer. After that, dig in, if you are making it in advance, wrap loosely with plastic wrap and refrigerate.

To remove from pan, release the spring latch on the side of the pan, and lift it off. You can either leave the cheesecake on the bottom pan or slide it off onto a cake platter. There are ten to twelve servings to a cake, but if it's for a party cut it small at fourteen slices and garnish with fresh fruit. Blueberries, blackberries, strawberries and raspberries are all charmed accomplices to the boldness of a cheesecake.

A break, a moment,
a few minutes lost,
tomatoes bubbling in red wine and olive oil,
a car door slams,
steel hinges squeak,
foot falls on the mat and across the living room,
crushed bay in my palm,
water glass trembles,
and there she was, a sudden kiss of iris and clove.
Funny how nervous,
the ceremony of unpacking,
turning and smelling, pushing and shaking,
praying the fish fresh,
the basil unblemished,
and the meal as perfect as the moment she walked in.

• THE SECOND MENU •

BRUSCHETTA WITH BASIL, ROMAS AND FETA

SEARED SHRIMP AND POBLANO PEPPERS WITH LEMON

PARMESAN RISOTTO, GARNISHED WITH TOMATO COULIS

CANTALOUPE WITH MINTED CREAM

Everybody seems to have a favorite bread, a favorite baker or brand, and for those with the time there is a favorite recipe. There are three breads I find it difficult to live without: Foccacia, ciabatta, and unleavened flat bread. The present recipe calls for a ciabatta. Foccacia and ciabatta are Italian breads, they require three rises, and take close to three hours to prepare. Flat bread is Near East and Mediterranean. For the sake of authenticity and presentation I'll include a recipe, but if you don't have the time or the feel for baking, don't try. Baking isn't for everyone and I've seen a lot of good cooks reduced to childish frustration over the peculiarities of yeast, and uh, well. . . that scene has at times included me in the center.

Our first course is bruschetta. Bruschetta is grilled bread. It is then topped with something. Hmmm, it sounds like an open-faced sandwich on thick sliced bread, well it is. We give it a nice name, serve it on country French or ciabatta and it becomes more than the lowly open-faced sandwich, it becomes *bruschetta.* This is a dish whose beauty resides in the simplicity of presentation and taste. There are many recipes around that suggest a sort of concasse, or chopped arrangement of ingredients, which is a preparation that makes it more salad sandwich than a set of distinct flavors. It's your choice, and if it's done right, and tastes good, then it's good.

BRUSCHETTA WITH ROMA TOMATOES, BASIL LEAVES AND FETA

USE COUNTRY ITALIAN OR FRENCH BREAD
10   ¾ inch thick slices, cut on an angle so that the slices are about 3 inches long.

Chapter Two • MEDITERRANEAN HILLSIDES *and* BEACHES

ROASTED GARLIC OIL

4 cloves	garlic, baked in 1/4 cup olive oil until tan, at 375° for 20 minutes. After roasting let it cool, then mash with fork until it is a light paste.
10 large	basil leaves
20 slices	roma tomato, about a 1/4 inch thick
5 teaspoons	feta cheese, chopped coarse, not powder and not chunky, make sure the knife is dry or else the cheese will stick to the knife. Buy a high grade feta, some are too moist and won't chop. It will be labeled as dry feta.
2	lemon wedges

Bruschetta with Roma tomatoes, basil leaves and feta

Brush the bread with the garlic oil and bake for 5 minutes at 375°. The toast or bruschetta will be tan. Remove from oven and place a basil leaf on each slice of bread. Then set two slices each of roma tomato on the basil. Sprinkle the chopped feta on top of the tomato. That's it. The lemon is for squeezing the juice on top of the bruschetta right before you eat it, if you like the tart flavors. Try a piece without the lemon first, and then one with just a few drops of the fresh juice. Decide from there.

Variations include sliced olives (your favorites), sautéed mushrooms, a thin slice of prosciutto, capicolla, smoked salmon or any other smoked seafood.

The next dish is a good example of my flavors and cuisine.

SEARED SHRIMP AND POBLANO PEPPERS WITH LEMON PARMESAN RISOTTO, GARNISHED WITH TOMATO COULIS

Why are people afraid of risotto? It takes a little concentration, you must stay with it, and the results are wonderful. This is a good dish to make with someone who has cooked risotto before. Otherwise, follow the directions carefully. Do as I say. Remain calm, do not answer the phone, do not panic, just stand there and stir. You do not have to endlessly stir into the dark of night, just stir a lot. Think of risotto as a Northern Italian food of the gods, an ambrosia, rich and teasing, or more simply as a kind of rice porridge, though not quite so humble as British literature would have us believe, you know, Charles Dickens and all that. This is a good dish for two to make together as one may sear the shrimp and vegetables while the other stirs the risotto. After you have learned this version you will be able to approach other risotto recipes with confidence.

Seared shrimp and poblano peppers with lemon parmesan risotto

The coulis can be made ahead of time. Classically, a coulis refers to the juices obtained from cooked meats from which sauces and gravies are made, and directly poured over a finished dish. Today a coulis is more often used to denote a puree, or the juices of cooked vegetables. For the purpose of the present dish a tomato coulis is used, and this can be made either by pureeing 3 large garden tomatoes, or by cheating and using V-8 juice or its equivalent. What you need, and what is required is the fresh, sharp, fruity taste of the tomato.

As an option:

Roasting provides a mellower, deeper flavor for coulis, or purees and juices. Sweet peppers are unmatched for this process. You can do it with tomatoes, zucchini, onions, mango, hard skinned squashes, etc., but you must use the juices that escape to the pan as well as the pulp. Just place the vegetable on a roasting pan, add a enough water to just coat the bottom of the pan, cover with aluminum foil or a roasting bag, cook at 350 for 45 minutes. Remove and let cool, and then pour it all into a blender and puree. It's best to remove the seeds from the sweet

Chapter Two • MEDITERRANEAN HILLSIDES and BEACHES

peppers after roasting. By the way, live dangerously, buy odd or unusual kinds of tomatoes, peppers and vegetables; you will be surprised at the taste of foods that don't necessarily conform to mass farming techniques. Support difference in produce and you will support a wider diversity not only of product, but also of survival for the small Eco-conscious farmer.

The recipe for the risotto makes 4 servings.

Use only arborio rice, also known as 'piedmont rice'. It is a medium grained, plump Italian rice that works every time. Never rinse this rice as washing it will remove the starches that aide in making it creamy. Fortunately, arborio is now available in most markets. Of course you can use the basic technique of adding liquid and stirring to any rice and still obtain a moist porridge like dish, but with lesser rice you miss out on the outside creamy consistency and inside al dente bite of arborio rice. This is again a yin-yang marriage of types; creamy, deep, and rich contrasting a bright flavor and firm texture. I have had some success with Chinese Pearl rice, and with pearled barley in making substitute recipes for risotto, it's just that it's not really classic risotto.

RISOTTO

2 tablespoons	butter
3 tablespoons	extra virgin olive oil
1	leek, the white only, finely minced. If leeks are unavailable, use 1 small white onion
1	carrot, peeled and minced
1 stalk	celery, minced
½ teaspoon each	dried oregano, basil and thyme
2	bay leaves
½ teaspoon	ground black pepper
1 1/3 cups	arborio rice
3 1/3 cups	chicken stock. Either mix bouillon and water, buy a good quality stock in the store, or make your own
1/3 cup	heavy cream
6 tablespoons	lemon juice, (3 lemons, juiced)
½ cup	parmesan cheese, grated

THE RISOTTO:

Sauté the vegetables on medium heat until they begin to soften, about five minutes. Add the herbs; stir until they begin to cook, two minutes. Add the rice and stir so that it is well coated with the oil and herbs. Slowly pour in half the liquid, stirring the whole time. With the heat on medium, continue to cook and stir until the liquid is almost dissolved. At that point add the rest of the liquid and continue stirring at one minute intervals. The process takes about fifteen to twenty minutes. Add the cream and parmesan followed at the very end with lemon juice. Is it runny? Looks like porridge? Then you are there. Taste for seasoning and consistency. Remember that the rice should have a very slight resistance, and that the liquid should be a little runny. The tastes will at first be lemony and fresh followed by a deep, creamy herb palate that seems both light and heavy at the same time.

SEARED SHRIMP AND PEPPERS:

While the risotto is cooking heat a medium skillet on high heat. Searing involves very high temperatures and very little oil, so be ready to go fast. Splash a drop of water in the pan. If it sizzles and evaporates then you are ready. Add the peppers and onion and toss around in the pan until the skin begins to blister (puff and turn tan), add the oil, stir and then add the shrimp and sauté for two minutes. Total cook time is about five minutes.

SEARED SHRIMP AND PEPPERS:

12 medium	shrimp, peeled and deveined
½	red bell pepper, cut in 8 thin strips
½	poblano pepper, cut in 8 thin strips
½	yellow onion, sliced thin
2 tablespoons	olive oil

THE COULIS:

Wash and cut off the stem ends. (Tomatoes have been found to carry salmonella, a kind of food toxin, and washing and cutting out the

---

Now, there are those who will say that cream is cheating, but we use it here as an additional flavor. If you are on a low cholesterol diet eliminate the cream and butter and increase the water and olive oil content. Also you will be able to refrigerate any leftovers and make rice cakes for a later meal. And for that you just pat the rice out into little cakes and sauté with olive oil until crisp on the outside and hot on the inside.

Chapter Two • MEDITERRANEAN HILLSIDES *and* BEACHES

> The hardest part about buying melons is buying the right melon. Touch: the melon should be heavy and the skin will give slightly when you press it. Smell: it will smell like a melon. No smell no buy. Give it a shake: if you hear or feel movement, or a sloshing sound, then it's over ripe and you don't want it. If you are planning ahead and the price is right, then it's OK to buy a melon that is not quite ripe. Set it on the table for a couple of days and it will ripen there. When ripe put it in the produce bin of your refrigerator. Let your senses be your guide in choosing melons. SEE GLOSSARY.

stems eliminates the possibility) Cut in half and squeeze out the seeds. Place in blender and puree. That's it.

TOMATO COULIS

4	tomatoes, large, very ripe

When all is cooked and ready pour the risotto into large high-sided plates, or bowls. Swirl the coulis in spiral pattern over the top of the risotto. Top with the shrimp and peppers. If you like more cheese, have some grated parmesan on hand. The same goes for lemon, you might enjoy a bit more fresh squeezed juice on the dish.

DESSERT

CANTALOUPE WITH MINTED CREAM

After all the complicated arrangements this is easy and elegant, and you probably had it as a snack as a child.

6 slices	cantaloupe, skin cut off
¼ cup	heavy cream lightly beaten
5 leaves	fresh mint, cut in what is called a chiffonade, very thin.

Fan the melon on a plate with the bottom ends touching and the tops set apart so that it looks like a…fan. Combine mint and cream. Drizzle over melon.

The Second Menu

Alternative servings: buy different melons and fan them out in alternating colors. Use cheese instead of cream. Cream cheese whipped with honey is delicious. Mascarpone is classic Italian. Danish saga is a creamy bleu cheese that ranks among, if not the best for bleu cheese lovers. Sprinkle with a Vermont goat cheese for an old country appeal. Drizzle with a favorite sweet wine or liquor. Blueberries or raspberries are nice additions. So are chopped and toasted nuts. Lightly glaze the plate with peach and berry purees. If it's summer, put a few honeysuckle flowers on the plate.

Want to look professional for that special meal? Puree a pack of frozen blackberries, strain the seeds. Spread the puree in a thin glaze on the plate. Fan the melon in the center of the plate. Around the edges put a series of small circles of slightly thickened sweet cream (seven will do). Take a toothpick and put it in the center of each dollop of cream and pull outward so that the cream leaves a streak in the puree. Do this five times to each dot of cream. Looks good, huh? Remember, you can be as simple or as complicated as you like, just don't ruin the dish with extravagance. Respect the taste of the melon as you would any other food.

Chapter Two • MEDITERRANEAN HILLSIDES *and* BEACHES

Pine nuts and pomegranates,
San Pellegrino with crushed apple and lime,
it's not much, but it's good,
and in the simple pleasures
of exhaustion and repose
she rests with the rhythms
of a plain heartbeat.
All comfort and lace
behind a cobalt glass
of warm spring water
she whispers the Spanish
of Neruda's love poems.
Nestled in her speech
she sips and sings
of flowing hair,
of nets and waves
and long sultry nights
that rise with wonder.
In comfort and lace
she sits and smiles
and opens her palm
to the hand that is mine,
the one that always reaches,
the one that's always hers.

• THE THIRD MENU •

SPINACH SOUP WITH RED BELL COULIS

OVEN BROILED AMBERJACK WITH FRIED CAPERS, PISTACHIOS, AND WHITE CHEDDAR CHEESE WITH BALSAMIC VINEGAR AND PAN JUICES

SIDE OF ROASTED GARLIC SPAGHETTI, SWEET ZUCCHINI AND ONIONS

FRESH BERRIES AND BROWN SUGAR

After gas and electricity the most radical change to have occurred in the kitchen was the invention of the food processor. By the late Eighties it was possible to go out to dinner and have a whole meal composed of things processed, reduced and strained to essences and intensities previously unknown to the palate. We chefs became a bit carried away with the little demon. Today, we are adapting to a better understanding of when and when not to puree and process. But oh, the beauty, you can even make bread dough in them, and the ease of time and labor are such that not having one is almost unmentionable. The following meal involves the processor, a blender and, miracle of miracles, a peasant style entree. Strangely enough, entrees that are seasoned with chopped and intact ingredients are seen as being unique and inventive. It's nice now that we can have a little bit of it all and appreciate the combination of styles.

SPINACH SOUP WITH RED BELL PEPPER COULIS

There's nothing unusual about this soup. It's simple and direct with an intense spinach flavor.

8 ounces	spinach, pureed
1 small	onion yellow, diced very fine .
2 tablespoons	butter
2 cups	half and half
¼ teaspoon	basil
1/5 teaspoon	ground thyme
1	bay leaf

Chapter Two • MEDITERRANEAN HILLSIDES *and* BEACHES

½ teaspoon	garlic
½ teaspoon	salt and pepper
2½ tablespoons	beurre manie (beurre manie is a hand blended mix of cold butter and flour). In a bowl mash together 1½ tablespoons of butter with 1 tablespoon of flour until it is a thick

In a medium sized high-sided pot sauté the onion and butter until the onion is soft and not yet turning color. On medium high heat this will take about three minutes. Add the herbs and cook for two more minutes. Add the half and half and allow the liquid to cook until it almost boils, it will bubble a little, when this happens turn the heat down to low and let it cook for five more minutes. This process is called scald. If the cream rises in the pot and starts to boil over you are close to burning the bottom of the pan, change cooking pots, or else you will scorch the soup. It's a touchy area, this scalding, you have to watch your temperatures, and keep it high enough to simmer but low enough so that it doesn't boil over the pot.

OK, you've scalded the liquid, now turn up the heat and immediately stir in the beurre manie. This will thicken the soup just enough to coat a spoon, not thick, not thin, just a little. Add the spinach. Turn the heat down to medium low. Add the salt and pepper mix. Simmer five minutes.

RED BELL PEPPER COULIS

1 large	red bell pepper, seeded and stemmed
3 tablespoons	apple juice

Put in blender and puree until it won't puree anymore. It will not become completely smooth, so don't worry about that, what you want will look a little grainy.

Pour the soup into two large wide soup bowls. The small deep ones don't serve the purpose. Using a tablespoon, place three circles of the coulis on the soup so that it does not fully sink and that there are red spots on the top. Take the tip of the spoon and from the center of each circle pull the spoon outward into the green soup making three curved lines. It's easy to do that little extra to give your food a more artistic appeal. Don't be restrained, think of Kandinsky, Mondrian and Jackson Pollock.

> *The hardest thing about this entree is finding good fresh fish. Pester and plead with your grocer to please get in usable fresh fish. I've gone to the grocery store too many times wanting fresh fish and have just stood there in near shock over the horrible display of what they are trying to force upon us. Find out their delivery days, talk to the person behind the counter, and ask questions. Pick up the fish, touch it. If it smells fishy then don't buy it. Fresh fish has no odor. Gently press the flesh with your finger, if it moves back into place it's OK. If it holds your fingerprints reprimand the grocer, wash your hands and find a better store. Demand excellence from these guys. Who cares about the lobsters in the tank, that's a lure for the impulse purchase. Unless you live in an area where the market demands fresh seafood, or on the ocean, it is going to be a little rough finding quality seafood. If you can't find what you want, then. . .then do the unmentionable, go to the frozen section and buy what you can find that matches what you need. Look for good color and no ice marks on the fish. If you can't find amberjack, then look for these options: mahi-mahi, tuna, wahoo, cobia, turbot, orange roughy, or wreckfish.*

OVEN BROILED AMBERJACK WITH FRIED CAPERS, PISTACHIOS, AND WHITE CHEDDAR CHEESE WITH BALSAMIC VINEGAR AND PAN JUICES. SIDE OF ROASTED GARLIC SPAGHETTI, SWEET ZUCCHINI AND ONIONS.

There are two things required for the dish that may be unfamiliar to you. They are fried capers and roasted garlic. Here's what you do:

TO FRY CAPERS: Heat 1/3 cup blend of olive and corn oil to 300° in a high sided skillet. Drain 4 tablespoons of capers. Carefully! Add capers to hot oil. Agitate pan or stir with long spoon. Fry three minutes until capers are crisp. They will look shrunken. Pour capers and oil through strainer into a heat proof container so that you can save the oil for use later. That's it. They will taste crunchy and sharp, but not as sharp as capers right out of the jar.

TO ROAST GARLIC: Heat oven to 400°. Peel garlic bulb. There are a lot of methods and gadgets for this; I prefer doing it under warm

Chapter Two • MEDITERRANEAN HILLSIDES and BEACHES

water. The warm water loosens the skin and keeps the clove from sticking to you fingers. Place garlic cloves in one cup of pure olive oil. Roast for twenty minutes. Let cool and blend to coarse consistency. Don't drain the oil, which's where a lot of the flavor is.

Finally, to the entrée:

Oven broiled Amberjack with fried capers, pistachios, and white cheddar cheese

THE ENTREE

2-7 oz	amberjack fillets
1 teaspoon	salt and pepper mix
1 teaspoon	crushed oregano leaves
1 tablespoon	virgin olive oil
2 teaspoon	fried capers
2 tablespoons	shelled fresh pistachio nuts
2 tablespoons	grated Italian sharp white cheddar or feta if you can't find the cheddar.
5 tablespoons	balsamic vinegar
2 tablespoons	heavy cream
1 tablespoon	chopped parsley

Turn oven on to broil. Oil then salt and pepper both sides of the fish. Rub oregano on top side of fish. Place fish skin side up in baking dish. Pour balsamic vinegar into dish. Broil 12 inches from heat source. Turn fish over once. Cook five minutes per side. Remove from oven. Place fish on warming plate. Turn off oven and place fish back in oven. Now, don't get rid of the pan, put it on the stove on med high heat and add the cream to pan and balsamic juices. Stir and heat until it starts to bubble and thicken. Salt and pepper if you think it needs it. When it has cooked and reduced to about 1/3 cup, add the parsley and turn off the heat. Mix capers, pistachios and cheese. Now, don't do anything else until the pasta dish is finished.

You can cook the pasta while the fish cooks. It will save time.

The Third Menu

If you must buy frozen fish then follow this instruction: Do not thaw. Thawing and rinsing under running water removes the natural juices from the fish and makes it taste bland when you cook it. If you are sautéing it, then thaw the fish out by leaving it in your refrigerator overnight. NOT on the countertop, and NOT under running water, YES in the refrigerator. For broiled, baked, poached and steamed dishes cooking from the frozen state really will give you an approximation to fresh. This method does not transfer to other meats, fish only. When you think that it is done, just pierce it in the center with a knife and look for clear juices. In a restaurant demand fresh, we have the means of acquisition, but for the home it is sometimes necessary to go below freezing and that is forgiven. There are a lot of books on fish cookery, find one that covers all the methods. I know I mentioned this is the first chapter; I just want you with me on these methods.

PASTA

8 ounces	spaghetti, angel hair or cappellini noodles
2 tablespoons	roasted garlic including the oil.
1 tablespoon	caper oil that you saved from frying the capers
1	medium zucchini, about 6 inches long cut in julienne strips
1	medium yellow onion, sliced thin (julienne)
1 teaspoon	salt and pepper mix

I like doing this in a wok. If you remember how to use a wok from the first chapter then we are in luck. If not, then use a high-sided sauté pan. Cook the noodles, strain and set aside. Heat pan to high and add caper oil. Add onions and sauté till they begin to soften, about a minute. Turn heat down to medium. Add zucchini and roasted garlic. Stir. Add noodles and salt and pepper. Cook and stir so that it is all mixed together.

Pour pasta on large plate. Set fish on top of pasta. Pour sauce over fish. Sprinkle mix of capers, nuts and cheese over the whole dish. And as the wait-staff says: Enjoy.

DESSERT

FRESH BERRIES AND BROWN SUGAR

Use one cup of whatever fresh berries are available. Such as raspberries, blueberries, strawberries, blackberries, and if it's that time of year where nothings happening use something interesting like an off variety of apple or pear, or even imported mango or papaya. They will all work for this simple and rich dessert.

1 cup	berries
½ cup	light brown sugar
4 tablespoons	heavy cream

Turn oven onto broil. Divide cream on two heatproof serving plates. Set fruit on top of cream. Cover fruit with brown sugar. Place 6 inches under broiler and cook until sugar melts. Watch out, it can burn. It will take less than five minutes and more than one minute, so you have to keep an eye on it. When the sugar has melted, take it out of the oven and let it stand for one minute. If you like vanilla yogurt this is a good time to use it. Place a teaspoon on top of each fruit dish. If not, just eat it as is. The sugar should harden a little when you let it stand and this is supposed to happen so don't despair. Rejoice in the rich, warm flavors of the sweet berries.

Late arrival,
window shakes as the front door slams,
covers pull up against the coming light,
    and a sweet voice flows across the dust...
in your room you feel the dreams of 5 in the afternoon,
hard, cold, and real...and suddenly, warmly,
the images fade and are spiced with the cadence
    of a voice, the timbre of the comfort
        of a woman you know you love...
like a tickle inside your ear:
Hello?   Hello?
How bout an espresso? Let's just stay home.
Uummm, and you wake and you know days off are so fine.

Chapter Two • MEDITERRANEAN HILLSIDES and BEACHES

• THE FOURTH MENU •

FRITTATA WITH SHRIMP, POTATO AND ONION

PAN SEARED BEEF FILET WITH APPLE-ALMOND HARISSA

TIRAMISU

This is a big and hearty meal, so plan to take your time with the dinner. The shopping is easy. The frittata and tiramisu can be made in advance. Frittata, harissa and tiramisu, are each traditional dishes in their regions of origin. Frittata/Tortilla is Italian/Spanish, Harissa is Tunisian, and Tiramisu is Italian. Everybody wants to take credit for a great dish, even Nero wanted to claim the blending of garlic and olive oil as his own. Garlic is originally Asian, at least this is what historical botanists show, and I'm not equipped to argue with their research. This is the great thing about food, none of us own it. Purists tend to get in the way of pleasure and experimentation, so, if you are at all prone to statements that resemble this: It's not that way in . . . then close the book now. Really. Now, about the shopping: it's all in the grocery store; you will not have to search.

You will need a 10 inch ovenproof skillet, mixing bowl, and a whisk. This will take thirty about minutes. If you're good with a knife and a whisk then it will take twenty-five. Ten minutes cooking time for the potatoes and onion, ten minutes for the frittata. Ten minutes for chopping and mixing. The whipped garlic oil takes about thirty seconds in the blender. If you are doing this with your partner, one chops, one whips, then one cooks. The one not cooking can set up the materials for the entree.

FRITTATA WITH SHRIMP, POTATO AND ONION, AND WHIPPED GARLIC-PARSLEY OIL

6	large eggs, beaten
20	small shrimp
5	red potatoes, should equal a pound, diced small = a quarter inch square
1	large vidalia or walla walla onion, diced small
2 tablespoons	butter
2 tablespoons	olive oil blend

½ teaspoon	paprika
1 teaspoon	salt and pepper mix
¾ tablespoon	thyme, fresh if you can get it
2	garlic cloves, crushed and minced

Wash the potatoes. Slice each potato into four rings, then slice again long ways four times, then slice across the potato strips so that you have little squares, hence a small dice. Put the diced potato into cold water and leave it there until time to sauté. Dice the onion into small squares. Mince the garlic. Set aside while you prepare the garlic-parsley oil.

GARLIC-PARSLEY OIL

2	cloves garlic
3 tablespoons	fresh parsley
½ cup	extra virgin olive oil

Place garlic and parsley in blender, blend till smooth. Slowly, in a thin stream pour in the oil while blending on medium-slow speed. It will whip into a semi-thick texture. Stop and set in refrigerator.
BACK TO THE STOVE:
Heat the olive oil blend in a 10-inch iron or ovenproof skillet on medium heat. At this time turn oven on to 350°.
Crack the eggs into a mixing bowl, and add a teaspoon of water. Whisk the eggs to a thick and deep yellow. You don't need to beat them, just whisk them around and incorporate the yolk and white. Add the salt, pepper, paprika and thyme. Beat in. This isn't an omelet so it isn't necessary to beat hard. Set aside.
Drain the diced potato and pat dry so that there is no water on the flesh. Add the potato to the hot skillet, and stir so that it does not stick. Turn heat to high, keep the skillet agitated. As it begins to soften and brown (five minutes) add the onion and garlic and sauté till golden. Melt the butter in with the potato and onion, turn heat back down to medium. Pour in the eggs.
Now, don't do a thing except watch for when the first bubbles begin to appear in the egg. When this happens put it in the oven and bake for ten minutes. After ten minutes check the egg by tapping it on the top to see if there is resistance, it should be bouncy, but firm. If that's not good enough, then do the toothpick test, it should come out dry. Just remember, it is not an omelet.
OK, it's cooked. Take it out of the oven. Let it rest for five

Chapter Two • MEDITERRANEAN HILLSIDES *and* BEACHES

minutes before you cut it. Cut in four equal wedges. Set on plate; brush the top of the frittata with the garlic-parsley oil. A good garnish is black or concord grapes (best season, September through November), otherwise use red flame grapes.

Save whatever leftovers there may be for sandwiches, or breakfast.

PAN SEARED BEEF FILET WITH APPLE-ALMOND HARISSA

Beef is just a choice, you may wish to be more traditional and use lamb or chicken. Wild game is extraordinary with any variety of Tunisian harissa.

A word about *harissa*: Harissa is comparable to the Indonesian sambal oelek mentioned in Chapter One. They are both primarily composed of hot peppers and oil, and a harissa can be built from a sambal oelek. That's what I usually do, and only because it's simpler. When you have time go all the way and make the harissa from scratch. Here's the basic recipe for one cup:

HARISSA

3 ounces	dried red chilies. if you have anchos, add or use only ancho (it's up to your tastes)
1 clove	small garlic, peeled and crushed in your pestle.
1 teaspoon	ground coriander seed
1 teaspoon	ground caraway seed
½ teaspoon	ground allspice
1 medium	red bell pepper, roasted and peeled
1 teaspoon	salt
4 ounces	virgin olive oil (if you can, use Spanish for this)

First roast the red bell pepper in your oven at 450°. It will take about 20 minutes. You want it to turn black, but not burned. Watch closely, and don't worry about opening the oven too frequently. When it has cooked, wrap it in plastic wrap and refrigerate.

When it has cooled, unwrap it and drop it into cold water. Peel the blackened skin off of the pepper. Be careful not to tear it up too much. Some of it will come apart, but that's no big deal as long as you keep most of the flesh intact. Rub the seeds and pith (the white part) out of the pepper with your fingers. Set aside.

Here's the tricky part: sometimes I like the seeds in hot peppers for their extra heat. If you just want the flavor of the flesh of the pepper, break off the stem and shake out the seeds, then soak the peppers in very hot water for at least thirty minutes. Drain and dry the peppers with a paper towel, or if you have one, a cheese cloth. Now, put all the ingredients except the oil into a food processor (or use your mortar and pestle) and grind them into a paste. Slowly pour in the oil until it becomes a thick paste. That's a classic harissa.

You can play with the flavors by adding cardamom, cloves, cinnamon, and cilantro. It's a great condiment and once you learn how to use it you will find hundreds of places to mix it in. When you are cooking with harissa, just heat 4 tablespoons oil and stir in 1 teaspoon of tomato paste, cook it through and then add a tablespoon of harissa, then add the liquids that you want to cook into a sauce. In the present case we'll use apple juice and white wine, but that does not restrict your options, as tomato fillets and tomato juice, or cream, or chicken stock all work.

TABLE CONDIMENT:

¼ cup	harissa
2 tablespoons	water
1 tablespoon	lime juice
1 tablespoon	apple cider vinegar
2 tablespoons	olive oil

Mix it all together in a bowl. From this you can add harissa to salad dressings, brush it on meats, stir into rice or cous cous, or add to a favorite sauce to bring out a distinct North African flavor.

APPLE ALMOND HARISSA

2 tablespoons	olive oil
2 tablespoons	tomato paste
¼ cup	table condiment mix
1 cup	apple juice
1/3 cup	white wine
2 ounces	sliced almonds, toasted
¼	granny smith apple, diced
½ teaspoon	salt and pepper mix

In a small high sided pan heat the olive oil on medium high until it turns clear, add the tomato paste and stir, cook one minute, and then add the harissa mix. Cook and stir with a wooden spoon for two

Chapter Two • MEDITERRANEAN HILLSIDES and BEACHES

ABOUT CUTS OF BEEF:
When you are at the grocers shopping for this meal try to go at a time when the butcher is present in the meat section. Talking to the butcher is fun, be curious, and ask questions about the cut of meat you are buying. In this case you are purchasing 14 ounces of center cut beef tenderloin. This particular cut is called the tornado. You will cut it into four equal portions of 3.5 ounces each. Have the butcher trim off all silver skin (a tough inedible silver colored layer of sinew that is often left on the meat, but better removed). The meat should be a deep red with thin white veins of fat through out the center of the cut. This is called marbling. If the veins are too thick there is too much fat, if there are translucent veins then they are going to be chewy, if there is no marbling then there isn't going to be much flavor to the meat. Remember, fat is flavor, but too much is just unmelted grease. The tenderloin is the tenderest cut of beef. The New York strip off of the strip loin is the most flavorful. In between are the rib eyes and sirloin, then the skirt, flank, shoulder, and roast. Some people love lots of fat on their beef, take Prime Rib for instance, this is a very fatty and rich cut of beef that is flavorful, tender and impressive looking. But there are those of us who don't feel too good after eating prime rib or the rib eye, it's just too rich, so, go for the tenderloin, you wont be let down.

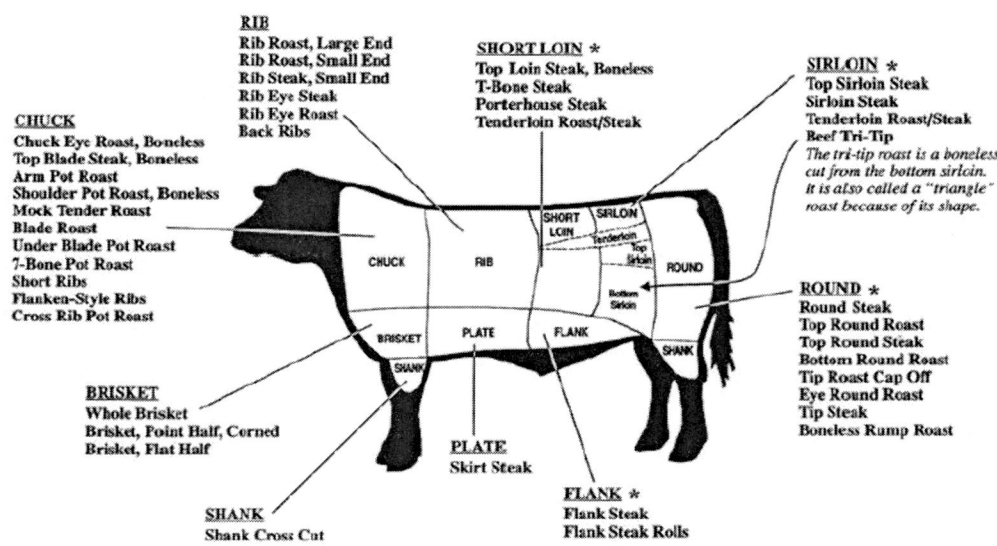

— BEEF CUTS —
Where They Come From

CHUCK
Chuck Eye Roast, Boneless
Top Blade Steak, Boneless
Arm Pot Roast
Shoulder Pot Roast, Boneless
Mock Tender Roast
Blade Roast
Under Blade Pot Roast
7-Bone Pot Roast
Short Ribs
Flanken-Style Ribs
Cross Rib Pot Roast

RIB
Rib Roast, Large End
Rib Roast, Small End
Rib Steak, Small End
Rib Eye Steak
Rib Eye Roast
Back Ribs

SHORT LOIN *
Top Loin Steak, Boneless
T-Bone Steak
Porterhouse Steak
Tenderloin Roast/Steak

SIRLOIN *
Top Sirloin Steak
Sirloin Steak
Tenderloin Roast/Steak
Beef Tri-Tip
The tri-tip roast is a boneless cut from the bottom sirloin. it is also called a "triangle" roast because of its shape.

ROUND *
Round Steak
Top Round Roast
Top Round Steak
Bottom Round Roast
Tip Roast Cap Off
Eye Round Roast
Tip Steak
Boneless Rump Roast

BRISKET
Whole Brisket
Brisket, Point Half, Corned
Brisket, Flat Half

PLATE
Skirt Steak

FLANK *
Flank Steak
Flank Steak Rolls

SHANK
Shank Cross Cut

*Cuts with the least fat

minutes. Add the liquids and stir in with a whisk. Let the sauce come to a boil and then turn the heat to medium low and simmer until it begins to thicken; this will take about ten to fifteen minutes. Add the almonds and apple and season with the salt and pepper mix. Cook another ten minutes on medium low. Set aside.

Searing is a method of cooking that does not use flour and is cooked at a very high temperature. This seals the meat and keeps all the good flavors inside, also the absence of flour prevents any burnt flavors from interfering with the quality of your meal.

PAN SEARED BEEF FILET

4 3 ½ ounce	center cut filets
¼ cup	cooking oil (20% olive 80% corn)

Preheat a large iron skillet and add the oil, turn heat to high. When the oil just begins to smoke, using tongs, place the meat into the skillet starting from the center and then setting the remaining three around the pan. Agitate the pan, call it names, and shake it gently so that the meat does not stick to the surface. You will cook it two minutes per side to reach medium rare. When you turn the meat over and it has cooked two minutes on the second side, pour off the oil, remove the meat, and then add your Apple Almond Harissa (6 oz) to the pan. It will spit and sizzle so stand back. Let this cook and reduce until it has thickened enough to hold onto the back of a spoon. Taste. When it is ready pour over the meat, or into a side dish, gravy dish or sauce boat.

This is the kind of meal that calls out for either mashed potatoes or cous cous. The perfect vegetable for this dish is green beans. Cous cous will be in the next recipe and mashed potato variations will be in the last chapter, Flowering of America.

GREEN BEANS: if they are not in season then buy sugar snap peas or snow peas. Look for waxy, bright green beans. If the multi colored ones are in stock, then try those out, they're even better, and remember to follow the same examinations for rich color and no blemishes. To cook the beans just bring a pot of salted water to a boil, drop them in and cook to one minute. Remove and drain, then sauté them in butter, olive, sesame, grape seed or walnut oil with a little garlic and ginger. Here again there too many variations to list, but onions, red bell peppers, almonds, and even celery root and jicama are worthy additions.

Chapter Two • MEDITERRANEAN HILLSIDES *and* BEACHES

DESSERT

TIRAMISU

Tiramisu is popular for a good reason: it satisfies the need for something sweet, creamy, cheesecake-like, and nutty. It has the bite of alcohol, and the crunch of cookies. Tiramisu is rich without making you feel as though you did eat a cheesecake. It is deceptive because it is not a light dessert, it just seems that way.

The tiramisu that we are going to make is not exactly the same as you may have had in your favorite restaurant. It is not in the shape of a cake, nor is it scooped out of a container as you would a pudding. This one will be built inside what is called a Bolla Grande, which is a red wine glass with a large, balloon shaped bottom. It's easy to make and very convenient for two to six people. This particular recipe will fill four glasses; it's too hard to make it in a batch for just two servings. After you make it, you'll agree, and you will want to eat it again the next night, or even the next morning.

At the grocery store: eggs, confectioners sugar, mascarpone cheese, espresso, milk (or semi sweet) chocolate, ladyfinger cookies or pound cake (both work). Now, go to the liquor store, or alcohol section, depending on your state of residence. You will need an orange flavored liquor, preferably Napoleon Mandarin Orange Liquor or Grande Marnier (for this recipe I am using the Mandarin Orange). You will also need Marsala. You can use any flavor of the fruited spirits that you like, but the Marsala, well....I hate to lead you away from that because it really is perfect for this recipe. Besides, I'll include a way make a classic zabaglione just to put the rest of your Marsala to culinary use.

Equipment you will need: mixing bowl, electric mixer, coffee or espresso maker, small bowl, and wooden spoon.

TIRAMISU

2	egg yolks
1½ tablespoons	confectioners' sugar
2 tablespoons	espresso
1½ tablespoons	orange liquor
1 tablespoon	Marsala
6 ounces	mascarpone cheese (if you can't find mascarpone, then blend 5 oz cream cheese with 1 oz honey. Yeah, I know it's cheating, but that's what you do in a pinch)

106 • *Ginger, Lily & Sweet Fire*

8	ladyfingers, or six thin slices pound cake
1½ ounces	grated milk chocolate

Beat the egg yolks and sugar together until it is pale and thick and forms little peaks when it is mixing. *Slowly* beat in half liquor and all of the Marsala. Add the softened mascarpone, and beat until the mixture is smooth.

In the other bowl mix the coffee and the rest of the liqueur.

Drop 3 halves of the ladyfingers in the bottom of each of the two glasses. Pour half the coffee mixture over the ladyfingers. Spoon half of the mascarpone mix on top, and then sprinkle with half the grated chocolate.

Repeat until you fill up the glasses. Sprinkle grated chocolate on top. Cover the top with plastic wrap and refrigerate for at least two hours. Easy, huh?

Chapter Two • MEDITERRANEAN HILLSIDES *and* BEACHES

• *THE FIFTH MENU* •

FIELD LETTUCES WITH TOASTED PINE NUTS, CRISPED PANCETTA, PEPPERS, AND BASIL DRESSING

BAKED EGGPLANT FILLED WITH GARBANZO BEANS, ROSEMARY AND WILD RICE, MILD GARLIC TOMATO SAUCE AND PARMESEAN

ESPRESSO CREME BRULEE

This is one of the easier menus in this chapter. The entree and dessert can be prepared ahead of time. Be warned, the preparation is time consuming. It's all rather classic and rustic, so get out your CD of Pavarotti Neapolitan songs, buy the sangria, and crank up the espresso machine. The only thing special that you may need to purchase are the baking ramekins for the crème brulee.

Gathering the ingredients: pancetta will be the hardest to find, so check around before planning to use it. If you can't find it then use your favorite salty American bacon. Pancetta is a smoked Italian bacon distinguished by the presence of allspice. Stop fretting, it is not a cookie flavored ham. The allspice takes on a peppery characteristic in this application. Remember, Pancetta in not Prosciutto. Prosciutto is air-dried and has more of an earthy flavor. Pancetta is closer to an apple-smoked bacon...but different. It is rolled and is thick. When you are ready to prepare it roll it out and cut thin slivers, and then cut the slivers into a small dice.

You can find the pine nuts (pignola) in the gourmet section of the grocery store. They come in 6 ounce jars. They are not cheap, so you will use them sparingly. It's better to buy them bulk than by the jar, and this is a good idea, especially if you plan to make a classic basil pesto (basil, pine nuts, parmesan, garlic, olive oil). Go to an international market, you will be amazed at the variety of foods. Also, a lot of health food stores carry bulk pine nuts. You will wish the pine cones in your yard were the same. They are not the same. They really are pine cone seeds from a kind of pine tree known as the nut pine, which grows in southern Europe, not southern Georgia.

In the produce section look for perfect basil, deep red sweet peppers, deep green poblano peppers and shallots. The field greens need to be dry and free of any blemishes. They are usually comprised of lambs ear, frisee, chicory, romaine, beet greens and mache. If that annoying sprinkler system starts up when you're looking for your produce just go to the produce manager and ask for greens that have not been recently sprayed. That stuff is a curse, it keeps the produce pretty and wet and kind of fresh, but remember that they charge by the pound. Get it? How much water do you want to buy?

While you're there go ahead and pick up the fresh rosemary, the waxy, firm, unbruised medium sized eggplant, and the garlic cloves. Please buy fresh garlic, please. The tomatoes for the sauce on the entree will be romas and organic red tomatoes. They can be ugly and over-ripe since you want the intense ripe flavor for the sauce.

THE SALAD

FIELD LETTUCES WITH TOASTED PINE NUTS, CRISPED PANCETTA, SWEET PEPPERS, AND BASIL DRESSING

4 ounces	mixed field greens
2 tablespoons	pine nuts
3 ounces	pancetta, diced
¼	red bell pepper, fine diced
¼	yellow bell pepper, fine diced

In a small skillet heat the pancetta on medium low. When the pancetta begins to crisp, add the pine nuts and cook until they begin to tan. The key word here is *begin*. The nuts will continue to cook when you remove them from the heat. At this stage drain the oil and save for the dressing. Set pancetta and nuts to the side.

THE DRESSING

1 teaspoon	dijon mustard
1 teaspoon	honey
1 small clove	shallot
½	roasted and peeled poblano pepper
4 ounces	extra virgin olive oil
2 ounces	balsamic vinegar
1 ounce	fresh basil leaves
pinch	salt and pepper

ROASTING THE PEPPER: We've already done this, but I'll explain again. Do it in the oven under the broiler or if you have a gas

Chapter Two • MEDITERRANEAN HILLSIDES *and* BEACHES

stove, on the flame. Turn the poblano under/on the flame until it turns black. No more no less, just at the moment it blackens. Wrap in plastic and chill. When it is cool, place the pepper in cold water and gently peel off the blackened skin, and with your fingers push out the seeds. That is roasting and peeling a pepper. The taste is mild and smoky. You can do this with any pepper. The taste is worth the trouble.

In a blender mix the mustard, honey and shallot. Puree to a smooth paste. Now, with the machine on medium speed slowly pour in the oil, then add the basil leaves and roasted pepper. It will be thick and yellow-green in color. Do not blend to very thick, just a little thick, like whipped cream. Turn the blender back on and slowly add the vinegar. Pulse in the salt and pepper. If the dressing is too thick add apple juice, if it is too thin slowly, slowly blend in more olive oil. The taste will be herby with a hint of heat from the mustard and poblano. Poblano peppers are my favorite because of their mild heat and fruity after taste. They are not as hot as jalapenos and serranos, but I do find them more complex in flavor.

In a bowl toss the salad ingredients with the dressing. If you want to garnish the salad use a slice of lime and vine ripe tomato.

Roasted Eggplant with garbanzo beans, wild rice, parmesan and tomato sauce

THE ENTREE

ROASTED EGGPLANT WITH GARBANZO BEANS, WILD RICE, PARMESAN, AND TOMATO SAUCE

It all seems simple enough, doesn't it? This is the part where I tell you that it's not as complex or hard as it seems. Now you laugh.

The beans can really be any kind that you like; they can be canned, frozen or fresh. I use garbanzo because I like the thick, meaty texture. If field peas are in season and you get them fresh off the vine, and if you shuck them yourself, go for it. Few legumes taste better than a fresh shucked bean or pea. But, forgive me, for this recipe I recommend the canned garbanzo. Were talking ease here, the same goes for the rice, use Uncle Bens Long and Wild Mix. Whenever I suggest the use of something canned or packaged I feel like I lose credibility on the hard-core front. Sometimes ease and time are more important for the home cook than the complexities of what we do in the business. If only there were time to give to ourselves as we do to our jobs. . .if only there were time. And isn't enriching that free time what this book is all about? Yes it is. And so, there are those recipes where the importance lies more in the time together than a full day in the kitchen. Authenticity and time too often battle one another. If a sacrifice must be made, make it favor of the love you build. Make the sacrifice in favor of the greater good of bringing together the attentions of two busy lives.

Ok, let's get back to the food.
You can roast the eggplant and make the sauce at the same time. Actually you can also cook the beans and rice at the same time. The real work here is in the time and coordination of that time.

STUFFED EGGPLANT

1	large, very purple, very firm eggplant
4 tablespoons	virgin olive oil
2 tablespoons	salt and pepper mix

STUFFING

1 box	Uncle Bens Long and Wild Rice
1 8 ounce can	garbanzo beans
½ teaspoon	marjoram
¼ teaspoon	basil
¼ teaspoon	rosemary

Wash and cut the eggplant in half. Without cutting into the skin, slice Xs into the flesh. Rub with olive oil, then rub in a tablespoon of salt and pepper per half. Cook in a 375° oven for forty five minutes. Remove from oven and scoop out the eggplant. Don't tear the skin. Handle carefully.

In a high-sided pot cook the rice and beans and herbs, add one cup more water than the Uncle Bens box suggests. Cook on low heat. Add the eggplant. Cook twenty minutes. After it has cooked fill the eggplant skins with the mixture. Bake again for fifteen minutes at 375°.

THE SAUCE

1 pound	roma tomatoes, chopped
2 tablespoons	garlic, chopped
½ of a	small white onion, diced
1 stalk	celery, diced
1 small	carrot, diced
2 dried	chili peppers
1 teaspoon	cilantro
1 lime	juice of 1 lime
4 ounces	canned tomato sauce
1 tablespoon	salt and pepper

Combine and heat on low for one hour. Stir frequently. Puree. See, all this can be done at the same time.

6 ounces	grated parmesan cheese…fresh!

Sprinkle cheese on top of roasted eggplant broil 30 seconds until the cheese browns. Pour six ounces sauce on each plate and set stuffed eggplant on sauce. That's it. If you are in the mood for a side use a small amount of plain pasta tossed in butter.

Start to finish this meal takes almost two hours. If you have the ability to plan ahead, then prepare the eggplant one night and the stuffing and sauce on the night you plan to eat.

DESSERT

CRÈME BRULEE

This is a popular dessert that is easier to prepare at home than you may think. And it is rich. You can vary the flavor any way you like through the use of extracts and reduced liquors, including espresso. Where I suggest vanilla extract, you may use orange blossom water, espresso, almond liquor, orange liquor, chocolate, even mango, peach, papaya and passion fruit, and fresh berries. This is where you have fun.

The recipe is for four portions. You can make two different kinds of crème brulee, that way you can have it another night of the week without actually repeating yourself. You will need a mixing bowl, whisk, four, four-ounce ceramic baking ramekins, heavy saucepan, high-sided baking pan and a wooden spoon.

1½ cups	half and half
4 tablespoons	sugar
2	whole eggs
2	egg yolks
½ teaspoon	vanilla extract
12	raspberries, for two ramekins
3 ounces	espresso boiled down to 1 ounce
2 tablespoons	confectioner's sugar

Preheat oven to 300°. Put six berries in the bottom of two of the ramekins. Make the espresso and then boil it down to 1 ounce. Set the espresso aside to cool.

Heat the half and half on medium, remove from heat just as it begins to rise in the pan. Then just leave it there while you prepare the rest. Be careful, if you boil the liquid you run the chance of curdling the milk, which will make the custard lumpy or grainy.

In the mixing bowl whisk the sugar and eggs into a light froth. Put the whisk aside and pick up the wooden spoon, now slowly stir in the cooked half and half. Pour it back into the saucepan and heat on low heat for four minutes while stirring with a wooden spoon. The wood doesn't taint the mixture with any kind of metal flavor. There's a chemical reaction that takes place with eggs and cream when heated with metal, the taste is not good. So use a wooden spoon. Move the spoon back and forth in the liquid while heating; add the vanilla extract midway through the cooking. You will do this for ten minutes, at that time the mixture will lightly coat the spoon when you lift it out of the pan.

Pour half the custard into the berry ramekins. Stir the espresso into the rest of the custard and pour that into the other two ramekins. Place the ramekins into the baking dish and fill the dish halfway with water. Cook for forty minutes at 300°. Check the custard with a thin knife or wooden skewer by inserting into the middle of the custard and slowly pulling it out. If it is clean then the custard is ready. If it is moist with custard, then cook another five minutes.

Take the custards out of the water bath and let cool on the kitchen counter. After they have come to room temperature cover with plastic wrap and poke a small hole in the plastic. This allows the moist heat to circulate out of the dish, which then allows the cold air in. If it is

Chapter Two • MEDITERRANEAN HILLSIDES *and* BEACHES

wrapped and left covered tightly then there is a chance that molds may form. Refrigerate for at least two hours at a temperature below 40 degrees.

When you are ready for dessert, sprinkle the top of each custard with a tablespoon of confectioner sugar and place under broiler for 2 to 3 minutes. Keep the door open and watch them cook. When the sugar sizzles and begins to brown they are ready to eat.

We were standing together in the kitchen talking,
the smell of tomatoes and marjoram, garlic and olive oil
rose from the stove and tangled in the air,
I was rushing to finish, I wanted to talk
and fill our time together,
and I reached out and held your wrist,
inhaled, looked into your eyes,
and suddenly forgot everything
except your silk skin and deep, deep beauty,
all I wanted was to just stand there,
hold you and hold the moment,
and I did,
and I burned the sauce....
Oh well, I guess it's a good night for fresh fruit,
and bread, and ice cream, and you,
It's always a good night to be with you.

• THE SIXTH MENU •

STEAMED ARTICHOKE WITH BASIL-LIME BUTTER

FOCCACCIA PIZZA WITH SAGE, OLIVES, TOMATO, CHICKEN AND ROASTED GARLIC SPREAD, TOPPED WITH GOAT CHEESE AND MOZZARELLA

RASPBERRY SORBET

This is a Sunday or Saturday meal, or whenever your day off may be. The artichoke is easy, basically just boil water. The bread takes a total of three hours and a bit of labor. This does not mean that you have to be with it the whole time. It's just that it takes that long. I feel that Italian breads are the best. Period. I love the yeasty taste, the thick crust, and soft texture of the triple rise. The sorbet will need time to freeze. You can make it the night before or the morning of your meal.

Artichokes are not in season during July and August. You can still buy them during these months but it's like buying tomatoes in December. Sure they're available, but is the inferior taste worth it? If you are eating for the pleasure of the food itself then buy in season. If you are eating for the trend or the habit then do what you like, just be prepared to be disappointed.

ARTICHOKE AND BASIL-LIME BUTTER

2 medium	artichokes, tight leaves, green no brown
¼ teaspoon each	basil, thyme, oregano
3	bay leaves
2 tablespoons	salt and pepper mix
3	lemons, cut in fourths
3 quarts	water

Combine all the herbs, salt and pepper, lemons and water in a deep soup pot and bring to a boil.

While the water is heating up, slice off the bottom stem a half inch from the base of the artichoke, then snip the pointy ends off of the artichoke leaves with kitchen shears. Careful, they can be sharp. Just cut off the very ends. Use a serrated knife to cut off the top half inch of the artichoke. Rub the cut ends of the artichoke with lemon to prevent discoloration.

Ginger, Lily & Sweet Fire • 115

Chapter Two • MEDITERRANEAN HILLSIDES and BEACHES

> **TO EAT THE ARTICHOKE.** Like eating oyster one wonders by whom, or how it came about that the artichoke originated as an object of affection. It isn't exactly an easily accessible food, is it? I know of no interesting legends other than the aphrodisiacal qualities of the artichoke. Aphrodisiac it is. After it is cooked and buttered you eat it by peeling the leaves off and nibbling, or sliding the tender base of the leaf across your tongue and teeth. It is a delicate flavor, and it is kind of sexy. When you reach the bottom it's as though the vegetable gods had all gotten together and created the perfect blending of the flavors of the mild oceans and exotic lands. Lastly, like all things related to the affections, as artichokes surely are, their flavor is bitter-sweet. At this point, do you understand why steamed artichokes are in so many cookbooks?
>
> Artichokes can be stuffed, eaten with butter or a mayonnaise/aioli variation, eaten cold or hot. Shrimp is a favorite stuffing, and curried mayonnaise is a favored alternative to butter sauces. They can be fried after boiling by cutting in wedges, patting dry, using a preferred batter and then frying.

Place artichokes in the boiling stock and set the lid of a smaller pot on top of the artichokes so that they will be submerged, and will cook evenly. Cook for thirty minutes. To check for doneness, lift an artichoke out of the water with a pair of kitchen tongs and tear off one of the bottom leaves. Nibble the base of the leaf. If it is tough, cook for another ten minutes. If it is soft, then immediately place the artichokes into a colander and ice them down.

When they have cooled, be gentle, open the top of the artichoke by wrapping one hand around the leaves, with the other expand your fingers outward in the top center until it opens about an inch across. There will be a cone of tender leaves, this is the heart. Open these leaves until the bottom is exposed, it will be fuzzy. Scoop out the fuzz in the bottom of the artichoke with an iced teaspoon. This is difficult, requiring lightly scraping the choke (the fuzz) off of the artichoke bottom. Or, you can just scrape off the choke during the meal when you reach it. The choke is inedible and if you leave it in it will ruin the joy of eating the artichoke bottom. If all you have ever eaten is the canned artichoke bottom or artichoke heart then you are in for one of the subtle joys of life.

BUTTER

8 ounces	unsalted butter
2	limes, juiced
A pinch	salt and pepper
2 leaves	basil, chopped

Melt the butter in a small sauce pan on low heat. When it has melted add the lime juice, salt and pepper, and basil. Heat for one minute. That's it.

FOCACCIA PIZZA WITH SAGE, OLIVES, TOMATO, CHICKEN AND, ROASTED GARLIC SPREAD, GOAT CHEESE AND MOZZARELLA

This is the hardest you are going to work on any recipe in this book, and it is a beautiful labor. In my opinion, few foods match the perfection of a well made Foccacia.

Total preparation time is three hours. This includes the rising of the dough. In those forty minute periods of waiting you can involve yourself with whatever tasks you wish, such as preparing the other parts of the meal. The most important thing about the bread is the Biga, or starter dough. Like a pet, you have to feed and water it.

BIGA

¾ teaspoon	active dry yeast
½ cup	warm water at 105
3½ cups	unbleached bread flour
1 teaspoon	granulated sugar
1¼ cups	cool water

In a small bowl dissolve the yeast in the warm water. Let is rest until creamy, but not yet foamy. It will take about 15 minutes. The water must stay at a warm temperature, so use a thermometer.

Your Biga, or starter, is the big secret. Treat it well and it will give you perfect bread every time. The one I use at the restaurant is now three years old. A Biga is yeast, water, flour and a touch of sugar. Mix all the ingredients together so that it resembles dough. Put it in a plastic container. Leave tightly covered in refrigerator for at least 24 hours. The Biga will sit patiently in your refrigerator waiting to be used and fed. Always remember that high heat kills yeast, cool does not.

Watch the temperature of the room when making the Foccacia;

Chapter Two • MEDITERRANEAN HILLSIDES *and* BEACHES

don't let it be under 80° or over 95° in there. That area of temperature is just enough to activate the rising in the yeast, if it is too cool in the room then the dough wont rise, if it is too hot then the dough quickly rises and the yeast dies.

FOCCACCIA

1 tablespoon	yeast
1 cup	warm water
1 tablespoon	sugar

Mix and let stand 15 minutes.

IN MIXER

3 cups	high gluten flour
1½ tablespoons	kosher salt
1½ cups	water
½ cup	olive oil
½ cup	Biga
6	fresh sage leaves (if fresh aren't available, then use 1 tsp dried – when revitalizing a dried herb like rubbed sage it is best to lightly toast it in a dry skillet over medium heat and then mix).
½ cup	black olives, Spanish or calamata, chopped

Focaccia Pizza with sage, olives, tomato, and chicken

Put the flour in the mixer with bread hook attachment begin spinning on low. Slowly add the water, then oil, then Biga, then salt, then sage and olives. Knead with bread hook until it is smooth. You may need to add more oil as it mixes. It will be smooth and elastic. You'll mix it slowly for twenty minutes, stopping at three minute intervals to let the bread dough rest. When you let it rest, do so for a minute each time. It will be a little sticky before it is fully kneaded, so don't be alarmed.

Rub a large mixing bowl with olive oil and transfer the dough to the bowl. Cover the dough with oil by rolling it

The Sixth Menu

> If you are making large batches and need to freeze it, then after pressing it out onto the pan, go ahead and do the dimple thing. Then wrap and stack in freezer. When it is time to bake it, take out of the freezer and let thaw for two hours. That will give it time for the last rise.

around in the bowl. Let rise ninety minutes. It will double in size. Then punch it down. Cover and let rise forty five minutes.

Dust the sheet pan with cornmeal. Roll dough out onto pan. With the palms of your hands press the dough out so that it covers the pan. Let it rise 50 minutes. Brush the top of the dough with olive oil then sprinkle with cornmeal. Using your fingertips press little dimples in the bread.

TOPPING

4 tablespoons	roasted garlic oil (see earlier recipe)
5 ounces	chopped cooked chicken breast
5	roma tomatoes, seeded and chopped
1 ounce	montrachet goat cheese, Vermont or Alabama
2 ounces	grated mozzarella cheese

After the bread has accomplished its last rise in the pan, brush the garlic oil on the top. Preheat oven to 425°. The oven must be preheated to this temperature or the bread will not rise properly and will be dry. Cook 15 minutes and then layer the other ingredients. Bake 15 minutes again. During the baking you may want to (this means yes do it) spray the oven with cool water. It helps with keeping the bread moist, while at the same time giving you a crispy crust. If you are fortunate enough to have a baking stone then by all means use it for this dish. Baking stones aide in maintaining consistent heat, and they are recommended.

As with all foods this is best eaten right out of the oven, but if you can't finish it all, that's OK, just wrap and refrigerate and eat within two days. The variations on this pizza are endless. The best thing about it is the bread, everything else is just topping.

Chapter Two • MEDITERRANEAN HILLSIDES *and* BEACHES

Raspberry sorbet

DESSERT

RASPBERRY SORBET

 Let's all sing Raspberry Beret by the Artist Formerly Known as Prince. I dare you not to. I like sorbets because you can say no fat. Of course don't look behind the curtain at all of the sugar. What a trick it is to say something's no fat. You will here learn how to make a sorbet without an ice cream maker. Who dares to do so? I do. I get tired of recipes that demand too much specialty equipment. And if you do have an ice cream maker, then use it for this dish. They are great things to have around but not all of us have the space. I've used home variations on traditional ice cream makers to a small amount of satisfaction, but not enough to suggest here. The best of course are the industrial ones for restaurants, which I've got to confess are a joy beyond description. If you have a good electric mixer at home and are inventive, then you can make ices and ice creams of anything that grows. And if you don't have one that's a problem, it just takes a little more work, but not much.

 Here's the process on how to make sorbet without an ice cream maker:

1 pint	red raspberries, fresh. If not, use whole frozen.
¾ cup	sugar
1 teaspoon	lemon juice
½ cup	water

 First we make what's called a simple syrup. This is done by mixing the sugar and water and heating them to a boil over high heat. Do not touch it while it comes to a boil or is boiling; remember that when sugar burns it sticks to the skin. When it boils turn down to a simmer and let it reduce by one third. Take it off the stove and let cool to room temperature. While it cools puree 2/3 of the raspberries and strain out the seeds. Use only the juice. Keep the other 1/3 in the refrigerator, well get to that.

Stir in the puree and lemon juice, then place the chilled mixture into a high sided metal baking pan. Cover with plastic wrap and freeze for two hours. Take it out and put the sorbet mix into a food processor and blend for ten seconds on high. It will be smooth and will fluff up. Put it back into the pan, cover and freeze. Wait two hours and do it all again. Now, put it into a plastic container, press the plastic wrap down on top of the sorbet mix and make sure that the wrap sticks to the side of the bowl. Freeze for two hours.

After two hours take out the sorbet and stir in the fresh whole raspberries. Finish freezing for another two hours. That's it, not too hard, but you do need to be at home for a while.

When you are ready to eat, take it out ten minutes or so before serving and scoop into bowls, champagne flutes, Flintstones Glasses, or Red Wine glasses.

A good garnish: roll raspberries, or grapes, or cherries, in one egg white beaten to a froth, then roll in sugar and let set for thirty minutes. If you are afraid of the egg white, then omit and just roll in the sugar and freeze the fruit until dessert time.

Sorbets are good with fruit and/or liquor sauces. Suggestions are mango puree, white chocolate sauce (melt 5 tablespoons chocolate with 1 tablespoon heavy cream), any fruit liquor sauce (1/3 cup liquor, 2 tablespoons sugar, 1 tablespoon cornstarch then bring to boil and simmer for about five minutes until it thickens. Stir with wooden spoon.)

Variations: concord grape, pear, strawberry, apple, Grand Marnier, Kahlua, mango, papaya, star fruit aka carambola, pomegranate, kiwi, orange, lemon, lime, cherry etc. Just follow the same portions and procedures.

Chapter Two • MEDITERRANEAN HILLSIDES *and* BEACHES

• THE SEVENTH MENU •

CRIMINI MUSHROOM AND BEAN SOUP

LAMB LEG STEAK WITH AVOCADO, PECANS AND RED WINE

SIDES OF SPINACH AND CITRUS ORZO

PLUM TART

The bean soup is Tuscan. The entree is fusion, and the dessert traditional. The people of Tuscany are often referred to as bean eaters, not unlike the way we southerners are thought of as squash and fried chicken eaters. Crimini mushrooms are a kind of baby portobella and are available year round. Ask the butcher at your grocery store to cut the lamb steak for you. If they don't have lamb leg then beef or chicken or pork or veal is OK, it just won't be as good. Use a Haas avocado that is not quite ripe, close, but not bursting. Buy green beans in season, if speckled are around use them. If not then use snow peas or sugar snaps. You'll find the orzo among the other pastas in the specialty section. Ahhh, plums, this again buy in season, do not use canned or frozen. <u>Do not</u>. Choices are: red beauty, black beauty, Santa Rosa or queen rosa. The Santa Rosa is the more popular, but I prefer the black for tarts because of the high sugar content and more intense flavor. The Santa Rosa is also a great eating plum.

CRIMINI MUSHROOM AND BEAN SOUP

4 ounces	large white beans (great northern or cannelloni)
2 cups	cold water for soaking the beans
¼ cup	olive oil
½	white onion, diced
1 stalk	celery, diced
½	medium carrot, peeled and diced
8	crimini mushrooms, thin sliced
¼ tablespoon	oregano, dry leaf
1	bay leaf
¼ tablespoon	marjoram, dry leaf
1 tablespoon	salt and pepper mix
½ tablespoon	ground coriander

1 tablespoon	chopped garlic
12 oz	tomato juice or even V8
1 cup	water

Soak the beans overnight. If you forget to soak them, then simmer for an hour. After the beans have soaked or simmered begin the soup. Now, this is a soup and some soups have to cook a long time. This particular soup requires an hour of simmering after all the ingredients have been put together. The cup of water at the end of the recipe is to replace any liquid that may have evaporated during the simmering process. Do not cover this soup as it cooks.

On high heat in a high sided soup pot sauté the carrots, onions and celery until they begin to crisp. Add the garlic and herbs, then add the mushrooms and cook for two minutes. Add the drained beans and then add the tomato juice. Turn heat down to simmer. Stir with wooden spoon. After it has cooked for about fifteen minutes taste for any adjustments you may need to make to the seasonings. Stir every few minutes to prevent scorching. It will be thick after forty five minutes and at this point add the extra water. This is not a crisp soup, it is a soft soup, so don't worry about over cooking the vegetables. The long simmer time allows all of the flavors to fully incorporate.

I suggest a slice of garlic bread with this soup. You can use Foccacia, ciabatta, or French as they all work rather well with this soup. Sometimes I like to make a thick rye for hearty soups. For a good reference on Italian breads look up the book *The Il Fornaio Baking Book* by Franco Galli.

NOTE: If you can't finish all the soup in one sitting, or you're just not that hungry, here's a good alternative use of leftovers: bean cakes. Chill the leftovers. When you are ready to eat your mushroom bean cakes, pour off some of the liquid, not all, let's say half. Rough blend the mix in a food processor, and please don't puree to a smooth paste, just rough. Mix in 1 tablespoon of fine bread crumbs to 3 ounces of mix. Pat the mix out into small round cakes. Flour them and sauté in olive oil on medium heat until they are crisp on the outside and hot on the inside. They go well with salsa.

Chapter Two • **MEDITERRANEAN HILLSIDES *and* BEACHES**

LAMB LEG STEAK WITH AVOCADO, PECANS AND RED WINE SIDES OF SPINACH, AND CITRUS ORZO

If you can't find the lamb leg steak, which is an economical cut of lamb, then go with lamb loin, or even thin cut lamb chops.

2 - 8 ounce	lamb leg steaks, bone-in
¼ cup	flour
2 tablespoons	olive oil
1	medium, ripe avocado, cut in 12 wedges
3 ounce	pecan halves, about a dozen
A pinch	salt and pepper mix
4 ounce	red table wine

Dust the lamb in the flour and sauté on high heat in a large skillet that will hold both steaks. Cook for two minutes on high, then turn down to medium. When they are medium rare (or however you like them) remove from pan and keep warm. Turn heat back up to high. Add avocado and pecans to skillet and sauté till the pecans begin to brown. Add salt and pepper, and then add the wine. Reduce by a third. Turn off and wait until the pasta and beans are ready.

ORZO

Orzo is a rice shaped pasta that will cook in about 10 minutes, so you can start the pasta when you turn on the pan for the lamb. The lamb takes a little under ten minutes. Usually the smaller pastas are not used with heavy dishes such as our lamb, but I suggest this one so that you can set the lamb on top of it and eat it with the lamb and the sauce. Once you do this you'll understand why. Trust me.

4 ounces	orzo
1 quart	boiling water
4 tablespoons	olive oil
¼ teaspoon	salt and pepper mix
1 teaspoon	orange zest

When the water boils add two tablespoons olive oil and the pasta, cook and stir, to keep the pasta from sticking or clumping, for seven to ten minutes. At seven minutes check for the consistency that you prefer. Drain and rinse.

In a medium sized pan heat the rinsed orzo in two tablespoons of olive oil on high heat. When the orzo is all in the pan turn down to medium. Add the salt and pepper. Stir. As it cooks add the orange zest. Total sauté time is about five minutes.

SIDE OF SPINACH

1 pound	fresh spinach
4 tablespoons	olive oil
1 tablespoon	butter
½ teaspoon	garlic, chopped
½ teaspoon	salt and pepper
¼ teaspoon	nutmeg, grated

Sauté the spinach in the oil, butter and garlic. When the spinach begins to wilt add the salt, pepper and nutmeg. Cook until it is soft, about three minutes.

THE PLATE

Everything is ready. Place the orzo on the plate and then put the lamb on top half of the orzo. Pour sauce over the meat. Set spinach next to lamb. That's it.

This is a variation of the classic lamb with artichoke hearts and pine nuts. If you feel like going more authentic then do everything the same, except use artichoke and pine nuts in place of avocado and pecans.

DESSERT

PLUM TART

First, the tart shell, a daunting and grandmotherly thing, the tart shell. For some it is pure mystery, a thing you buy. For others it is a puff pastry. For you, now, it is something to be proud of. Also, there are a lot of recipes for tart shells out there. If this one isn't your particular favorite then try one that uses egg as binder. The ones with egg are not as buttery and have a small sponge texture to it. Take heed: a tart is not a pie. Pie shells are soft, tart shells stand on their own.

If the plums are not quite full flavored enough for you, then add a few fresh blueberries. If the plums are out of season then don't use them, use blueberries or strawberries, or raspberries instead. A tart is another one of those things that once you know how to make a basic tart, you can make any kind you please. This recipe is for a full sized pan. Sorry, I just can't do the little individual shells here. You'll thank me.

TART SHELL
Use a 1¾ inch high ruffled tart tin 11-inch round

1½ cups	unbleached all purpose flour
1 tablespoon	granulated sugar
¼ tablespoon	salt, regular
12 tablespoons	unsalted cold butter cut into 18 pieces
4 tablespoons	cold, cold water
¼ tablespoon	ground cinnamon

In the food processor: put flour, sugar, salt and butter and pulse until the mixture looks like oatmeal. Sprinkle ice water over mix. Pulse again for about ten seconds or so until the dough holds together. Soft is good, crumbly is bad. Dust a cutting board with flour and roll the dough into a ball. Then roll it out with a rolling pin into a thirteen inch circle. Sprinkle a little more water on top. Lift an edge and fold it over to the center and roll again. Keep the underneath dusted with flour, not a lot, just dust. Roll and fold until you have done this to the entire circumference of the circle. It will still be thirteen inches. Rub the tart pan with butter, no need to flour. Place shell in pan with 1 inch overhanging all around the pan. Cut the excess so that it is eve with the edge of the pan. Fold in the edge dough and press around the edge so that it doesn't fall when it bakes. Now, take a fork and prick the pastry all over, not ragged, just little holes.

Preheat your oven to 425°. Fill shell with dried beans and bake fifteen minutes. Remove and discard beans. Brush shell with butter. Let cool.

PLUM FILLING

15	ripe plums cut into small quarters
5 tablespoons	sugar
2 tablespoons	brown sugar
2 tablespoons	cornstarch
¼ cup	water
¼ cup	sweet vermouth

The Seventh Menu

Mix all the ingredients and cook on medium heat until it thickens. This will take about twenty minutes. When it is done let it cool. Then pour the mixture into the cooked tart shell. Let it set for an hour.

Cut into wedges. Jams and whipped creams go well with tarts. Sometimes a glaze is just the thing to finish off a tart. To make a glaze for the plum tart, heat 4 tablespoons damson plum preserves until it is almost liquid, then spread it evenly over the top of the tart and chill until it settles into a glaze. Crushed cashews are good on this tart as well.

*Did Mister Polo know that when he crossed the desert
food would change forever in the West?
Did he even dream of the rich palates and alchemies
that we take so for granted today?
Today we do look at it all as so ordinary,
but it's not, no, nothing is really ordinary.
Today a soup, tomorrow bean cakes,
maybe we'll even bread fish with couscous,
maybe tomorrow we'll just eat fried bread...
Do this, hold your hands high over the steaming pot,
place your hands upon your cheeks,
close your eyes and feel the warmth,
close your eyes and think of what is ordinary.*

SALT AND SEE WHAT TASTES CAN BE

Salting and salted. Brined and cured. Seasoned and seasoning. Iodized. Sea salt. Kosher, pickling, rock and granulated. Alumino-calcuim silicate and trace elements are added for free flowing anti-caking salt. High in minerals and sometime odd flavors, sea salt has become a table and kitchen favorite here in the early 21st century. So what about this dandy device that cures, preserves, seasons and open up our taste buds in miraculous ways but a few grains too many and a dish is destroyed? What about salt? Why is it on my mind? Why should it be on your mind?

We crave salt and oil. Shanghai cuisine is based upon this craving. Our memory is jogged by salt and oil. The devil in the details of chain restaurants is salt and oil. Salt. Pretty demon, a siren on the rocks just sitting and singing, luring passersby with smell and memory alone. MSG, one molecule moved over and made to tenderize our tongues, bad in large amounts, but is it really such a bad guy?

Well, we all agree that yes, MSG is monosodium glutamate is bad because of headaches and other unsavory reactions. The lurid question is if it is used in proper quantities is it really so bad? I have no answer.

Salt has reemerged as a featured ingredient in the cooking of today. Salt is center stage in many ways. It is pretty cool how many different salts have become available; the new is the old. The slow food movement was supposed to make the food itself the center, not the chef and not the salt, but the food. Slow food is about cooking fresh food. We have at our hands foods fresher than ever before, foods of the world. We have been given the choice to cook whatever we want to cook because everything is within hands reach. You can find anything you need at farmers markets and specialized grocery stores. So why are chefs and cooks suddenly forgetting that we want to taste the food, not the salt? What happened? Let's first look at a few things about salt.

Salt (sodium chloride) is a device. It is an ingredient. It does things, it transforms proteins, greens, vegetables, fruits, liquids (soy sauce, fish sauce), and then even makes our mouth water to allow more flavor into our thousands of taste buds. Sea salt is a member of umami fifth flavor group. It translates as "delicious". Too much salt and delicious becomes inedible. Because salt can be thought of as a device it has many applications. Flip the salt switch on nasty bits and you end up with tasty tarts.

My most memorable meal from childhood, and my siblings agree to this, was green beans and mashed potatoes that my Mother had over salted. Imagine, of all the meals this is remembered. Of course there are those pot roast Sundays and Fried Chicken Fridays, BBQ Saturdays and all the family meals of mid-week, but mention salt and all three of us agree that the green beans are our Proustian Madeleine of perfect recall. Childhood emerges in all of its speckled glory from this one taste memory, too much salt. Think back, of course our memory is often food filled and food directed, but what of life around the meal? Why would too much salt be what we remembered?

Salt is passive aggressive. If regarded as an emotional reagent we see how salt acts out if mishandled. Salt can destroy and preserve in the wave of a measuring spoon. Iodine is added to help prevent various thyroid diseases. This is a good thing. Too much salt in the diet results in hypertension and heart ailments. Passive aggressive in that it cools the body one day and the next it is acting out and burning us up from the inside.

Brining preserves and seasons at the same time. Salt brines using Kosher salt (coarse either sea or cave) are wonderful for turkey, pork roasts, ocean fish that needs to be held for a few days and for vegetables to set them up for pickling. Too much salt in the brine and the skin on your turkey becomes a crisp salt crust rather than a seasoning. It is a thin line between seasoning and seasoned. Seasoning is what we do while cooking or eating, and seasoned is what takes place prior to cooking; it is a preparation and a curing. You're not supposed to really taste the salt when properly brined, cured or seasoned, the salt brings our the natural flavors and preserves them just beneath the surface of the food. I like brining.

The array of salts available to us today is fantastic. I love it. Who would not get a kick out of developing recipes to match up with *Irish black sea salt* for an omelet on the one hand and for salt curing a side of salmon on the other? This salt is both salty, smoky and has a slight fermentation aroma. How about *apple wood smoked sea salt* for grilled pork? Bacon salt, for Tom sake! Bacon Salt!

Smoked salts though are a very different beast that when used in pinches and as an aromatic are feasible, but overall there are few that really are attractive on our foods. And I'll tell you why. Alder coarse, apple, hickory, alea fine Hawaiian, Yakima, Cyprus flake Mediterranean (white crystals), Durango (brown fine), Salish fine alder are just a few salts I recently sampled. I felt like I was in a commercial for BIG FLAVORS!!! But thankfully I was not all big and bold; I was examining what they **did** to my tongue and what my physical reaction was to them. Once the body set the pace I could then examine how to use them. Salish fine alder was the best of the bunch because of how light it was, and that makes it perfect as a final garnish to a plate. These salts are dominate, they have attitudes and the last impression that I had was that they were the sort of salts used to cure meats for fast casual chains and hence not so much an attraction for me. They have a place, true, but not for me.

Himalayan pink coarse salt for extra virgin olive oil and then brushed over fresh baked focaccia is heavenly. Take this salt and set it on top of lamb chop and as it melts into the meat it totally takes over the flesh and kills all flavor except that of watery salt.

Salt is a mineral, it never goes stale, keep this in mind and you will begin to understand that the lamb needed the salt while it was cooking, not after. Why? It helps the meat to brown on the outside and to keep the juices in the meat, not running out into the flames. Salt enhances. Minerals are forever so why rush it?

Gray salt comes from France. This is a table salt and preparation salt. It is applied after cooking and the aromas of low tide gently coat the outer shell of the dish. *Gray salt, sel de gris,* is famed for its use with seafood and waterfowl. Duck and goose become more flavorful with this; their natural fats are loosed from the meat and flow out in a rivulet of deliciousness from medium rare duck and all day slow roast goose. Douse it on the skin after cooking and it is as if the rich meat was cured for days, but no, just for a moment and the gentleness of salt of is revealed. There is no taste difference between fresh ground salt and already ground salt. The only thing that a salt mill at the table will do is release it into the air so that you have a scant amount in your nostrils as well as on the food. It makes your mouth water. Salt makes your mouth water, but it will also dry you out if you use too much.

Mediterranean sea salt offers such a nice and slight aroma of the sea, but it can be misapplied in the quietest of moments, just when you think the wild caught striped bass is ready, the grassy and salty flavor of the fish is coaxed up off of the plate with a sprinkle of salt. Perfection. Give this same moment to a ruined tongue, to a lapsed chef or ill trained cook and the fish gave its life for nothing more than to be a receptacle, a thing upon which to set a mound of once subtle salt. Subtlety is the thing. The subtle use of a salt exposes the dish. Taste. If a chef/cook doesn't taste then how could they possibly know that they just destroyed a great meal because of their misunderstanding of salt itself.

Sea salts offer sublime appreciations of the waves from which they are harvested. We must respect this precious mineral. Once upon a time such salt was money. It was commodity and exchange. If we think of salt as money then understanding how it works is easier. Understanding why it was money gives us the key to its importance as a preservative. Salt is necessary for us to live. One tablespoon coarse kosher sea salt equals two teaspoons granulated salt. This tablespoon was a dollar. We did not evolve over the centuries because foods were covered in salt, we evolved because food was preserved and seasoned with an ingredient necessary to our staying alive. Too much of a good thing is not a good thing. Heart attacks are different than salving a basic need.

Salt crust makes a baked halibut a food for kings. Whipped with egg whites and poured over the fish, put into a 400°oven and baked for twenty minutes. Take it out, crack it with the back of a chef knife and lift the fish from this shell. Don't let it touch the shell. Brush the salt off of the fish. Serve. Here we have a moment that chefs and guests adore. This is the use of salt as a device for cooking; kind of like an instant Dutch oven. If the fish is just encased in the salt it is on a level of salt cod that has not been soaked free of the salt. Salting and salted. The egg white salt case is best made with *Hawaiian pink salt* that has an earthy hint to the saltiness. Pink from the clay and a soft flavor that permeates into the sweet fish.

There is also a *black Hawaiian salt* made from waters meeting the lava fields. This black salt and shellfish is a perfect match because the salt has a mussel and clam scent. Very low tide, but in a good way like, think of the soft sulfur of Indian foods, of Thai and Vietnamese and there you have good applications of black sea salt. The Hawaiian black salt is also called *Sanchal* in recipes from the subcontinent. It reduces bitterness and sourness, acidity.

So we have the basic salts: iodized table salt which is for the table, kosher salt for cooking and the various sea salts for seasoning our foods. Further away from this is rock salt for ice cream, for freezing things as well as thawing them. We use rock salt on the driveway to clear away the ice, but if this same rock salt is poured over ice cubes for making ice cream it freezes the cream faster. Dual purpose again, even for dried salt lake salt there are two uses found by varying the amount of salt.

Salt dehydrates food for curing. It preserves by guarding, or fighting off bacteria and moisture. I guess you could say that salt cures and preserves by being hostile to anything outside the salt itself, hostile in such a way that bacteria cannot live so that the meat is able to age and gain concentrated flavors without any risk of poisoning. When used for curing and preserving you can think of it as a firewall. Too much and it becomes the focus and is in fact a poison to the body by the way that if eaten it will cure and dehydrate inside the body. Hypertension doesn't just happen; it is brought on by a diet too rich in salts.

There are salt lakes in China going back between 4000 and 6000 years. Think about it, the Chinese have been manipulating and working with food on the high level of salt before the West even had forks and knives. And then they found MSG, the bad side of salt, the rowdy neighbor kids who stole your bicycle but then returned it with new spokes. Salt gives and it takes away. MSG is just mean. MSG and salt open the taste buds to more flavors, but too much and all we taste is the invasive salt. Salty food dehydrates, but it also manipulates the meat in such a way that we can salt and preserve so that it is good for months on end. How do you think our ancestors survived the long winters or seasons when fresh seafood (salmon) or meats could not be found? By salting, and by smoking which is just a short stick of hickory away from salt curing. How do you think that Gravlax came into being? By cold salt, sugar and herb cures because this was what was there for them to use, and by the wondrous nature of life it just so happened that this presence was a need. A very true physical need, not a yearning to mask flavors, it was a use of what was present in the world that was realized by being both tasty and essential.

Korean bamboo salt, jook yeom, is cured and roasted inside of bamboo so that it takes on a mineral-ly taste, and there is even a variation of this where mugwort leaves are used in the salt as part of the drying process. I use this one for late stage in my cooking, a little at the very end of a wok cooked dish brings out the five flavors in a very bold way. I find these more elaborate salts satisfying to my need to intellectualize cuisine. Once understood it makes it easier to accept what the body already knew.

We NEED salt in order to live. Salt is necessary to our existence. Dig that. We have searched for salt from the very beginning of our life as homosapiens. Salt has always been there, like a guardian, killing bacteria, sealing meats, seasoning our salads, soups and vegetables. No salt…no live. So why are chefs today forgetting the way that salt is to be used? What is so bad about enhancing?

Hot, sour, salty, sweet and delicious: earth, water, air, wood and metal. The five flavors are enhanced by the use of sea salt. Sea salt is metal or delicious, or umami. A substitute would be dried kelp or dried mushroom. Citrus zest will preserve in small amounts for ceviche in ways similar to how salt reacts on meats.

Again: Why are chefs over-salting food today? I hear this a lot. I believe it is ignorance to the qualities that are inside the various salts. Too many chefs/cooks do not taste the food that they prepare. In one mind there may be a need to enhance a grilled rib eye with a lot of salt after the fact of the fire/heat but on the plate it becomes another thing altogether, it kills the taste buds rather than enticing them to taste. Making salt the feature of a dish distorts not only the tongue, but it is so brash a statement against the flavor of the dish that you might as well toss off the protein and eat that spoon of salt and corn/vegetable oil. Salt is an ingredient. We have all killed a magnificent porterhouse or strip loin on the grill with that foolish last dash and the hardest thing for a cook is to let the food be itself, and this is where experience and **tasting** your food comes in handy.

We learn not to over salt, and yet our vanity, our emotions will lift that nefarious little touch of coarse bacon smoked salt and there it goes, down into the sizzling fat and it rests, it stays right there on top of the meat. The salt remains poised and ready to open the follicles of our taste buds, to do it's job of preparing the body to taste the meat, and then, then it happens, another layer of salt crushes all the efforts of the first and we are lost to the cause. Remember this, hold back, and let the food itself express, not the salt.

Fresh red drum on the plate with Cajun seasoning is a complex and delicious dish, so why hide it with too much salt? Does fear increase the volume? Is it insecurity? I would hope not because the slow food movement and the very elements of good training will show a cook that salt enhances, it is not the entree, it is not the focal point of the dish. If we keep this to the front of our thinking, which salt enhances we are in good shape. You there with your hand full of French coarse sea salt over that New York strip, stop, hold back, don't do it, turn that hand into a pinch. That's the key, hold back. Just because it is there does not mean you have to use it to excess. Salt is money in more ways than one. We crave sea salt, oil/butter/fat, sugars and all things umami. Memory is key here; they must leave with a balanced impression of the food itself. A salty memory will be just that, the memories of a salty dog, roaming, looking for another restaurant.

CHAPTER THREE

ISLAND and OASIS

*Now she stood alone
in the darkened room,
silently gesturing
towards rosemary wreaths
and strands of fresh garlic,
her chestnut hair fell
in swirls of pure drama,
pulling it back, looking down
into the book one more time,
she swore she would get it right,
it's just food,
and the pile of fresh shrimp and calamari
just sat and taunted,
waiting for her hands,
waiting for the moment
this little scene would begin.*

*I*SLAND AND OASIS. HOT AND DRY, hot and lush, sometimes it rains; sometimes it rains a lot. The food's that way too, sometimes a little spicy, sometimes a little dramatic, but never too much one or the other. All cuisines seek a balance of the available resources. This is both nutritional (as the body dictates) and a matter of developed tastes for what is presented. We crave sugar and salt, high fat meats and the energy consuming acids of peppers and exotic fruits. Although the chapter is largely devoted to the American side of Caribbean flavours; guava, passion fruit, star fruit, mahi mahi, wreckfish, duck, macadamia nuts, plantains, and calamari, we will touch a bit of the East with the use of grape leaves, cous cous, olives, dates, apricots, mascarpone and sambal oelek. Why? Islands are an oasis, and an oasis is an island. There are similarities with what is done with available foods that I just can't ignore, and besides, this is all about regions of romance and how we consume that romance. Island and Oasis. Or perhaps how romance consumes us.

If you have the fortune of an international farmer's market in your area this is the time to explore the bounty of these Disneylands of possible dining. These are the places where if you can't find the exact fish or fruit that I mention, you can bet there will be something close to it. Otherwise continue on your pursuit of being the pesky shopper at your local grocers. There will be those occasions of the impossible where buying frozen is the only alternative. Don't feel ashamed, and don't think that I'm ripping you off on the idea of what is available. Calamari is a good example of the impossible. Otherwise, make those requests, make friends with the clerk in the seafood section, chat with the produce manager. It works.

Chapter Three • ISLAND *and* OASIS

• *THE FIRST MENU* •

SHRIMP, CALIMARI, AND PLANTAINS SAUTÉED AND GLAZED WITH PEPPERS, GINGER BEER, MINT AND COCONUT CREAM

BABY BACK PORK RIBS WITH MANGO BARBECUE

CHILLED PASSION FRUIT WITH CASHEW CRISPS

Your first questions will be about calamari, ginger beer, and passion fruit. Calamari is a mollusk found in tropical waters, they have elaborate, wide conical shells. The meat must be sliced thin. If the meat is cut too thick or cooked too long it will be tough and chewy. It is purchased frozen here on the mainland. Fresh calamari, like fresh abalone is a true delicacy.

Ginger beer is a kissing cousin to ginger ale. Ginger beer is spicier, heavier, and has more ginger. The most readily available is Red Rock. (Here's how fast our culinary world changes: I wrote the last sentence two days ago, today at the grocers there was a row of imported ginger beers in the international section.) Do not drink ginger beer with hot spicy food, you'll just get hotter. I made that mistake on my first encounter with a true ginger beer while eating a jalapeno heavy salsa with chips, and I couldn't taste anything except ginger and pepper. Ginger beer is good iced with a slightly sweet meal, or just by itself. Ginger beer is non-alcoholic. It is good with dark or black rum, and to that, Ahoy Matey

Passion fruit is best purchased when the skin is wrinkled, and when you shake it you should hear the pulp slosh around inside. Eat the pulp and seeds only. More on passion fruit during dessert.

The plantains for the appetiser must be ripe and soft; otherwise the alum taste will overwhelm the other ingredients. If you purchase green plantains just let them sit out on the counter for two or three days. Plantains ripen fast so don't worry about planning too far ahead. If you are rushed put them in a paper bag and they will ripen overnight.

Remember that plantains look like bananas, are starchy, and taste like citrus-sweet potatoes. Plantains can be fried, stewed, sautéed, or roasted with other dishes. Plantains are best known as a fried chip here in the States, while in equatorial regions they are generally sautéed or roasted. They are particularly good in tomato sauces for lasagne.

Plantains adapt well to the inventive cook. Be inventive. They're not really something you peel and eat...don't try, you'll just be disappointed. We are in this for the pleasure.

SHRIMP, CALIMARI, AND PLANTAINS SAUTEED AND GLAZED WITH PEPPERS, GINGER BEER, MINT AND COCONUT CREAM

3 teaspoons	butter, yes real UNSWEETENED butter
½ cup	all purpose flour
6 large	shrimp, peeled and deveined
8 oz	calamari, very thin sliced
1	plantain, peeled and sliced thin on a diagonal
3 strips each	red, green and yellow bell pepper
6 oz	ginger beer, warm
10 leaves	spearmint
4 oz	coconut cream, open can, scoop top part

SPICE MIX:

¾ teaspoon	oregano
¾ teaspoon	cumin
¼ teaspoon	rock salt
1/5 teaspoon	ground red pepper
½ teaspoon	ground bay leaves

This dish cooks best in a wok, if you don't have one use a high sided sauté skillet at least two inches high and 14 inches round. If you haven't bought a wok by this point in the book then you aren't paying attention!

Set the following on separate plates: Clean the shrimp, thaw the calamari and sprinkle them with half of the spice. Slice the plantain and peppers. Pick the mint. Open the coconut milk, and do not shake the can, you want only the thick top part, this is the cream. Pour the ginger beer into a glass and let it go flat before use. This allows it to settle and it won't be as foamy when you add it to the sauté. Sift the flour onto a plate.

This will sound wrong, but go with me on this: put the butter in the pan and cook on high until it foams, add the plantains and Sauté until they begin to tan. Add the peppers and cook till the edges darken, almost to a black, but not burnt.

Turn heat down and flour the calamari and shrimp. Add to pan and stir two minutes. Turn heat back up to high. Add coconut cream

Chapter Three • ISLAND and OASIS

and bring to boil. When it boils add the ginger beer and the rest of the spice mix. Cook until it reduces to a thin syrup. It should reduce by two thirds. At this time add the mint, stir and remove from heat.

Divide onto two oval plates. Garnish with fresh cut lime and sprinkle rock salt over the food. Not much, just a quarter teaspoon.

This appetiser is good with jasmine rice, mixed greens or even pasta it you want to prepare it as an entree.

If you want to go vegetarian use firm tofu and Japanese eggplant instead of shrimp and calamari. If you don't have calamari, then scallops or even a different meat like chicken.

NOTE: The reason we flour at the last second is to avoid any kind of clumping or over-saturation of the meat with the flour. The longer flour sits on a meat the more the meat absorbs the flour and becomes "thick" rather than "dusted". You want to sauté with a light flour dusting for these kinds of dishes. Thick is for traditional Southern frying. And what we are doing is anything but traditional.

THE ENTRÉE

BABY BACK PORK RIBS WITH MANGO BARBECUE SAUCE

All ribs are good. My favorites are country ribs, 3 inch cut short ribs and baby back ribs. For this recipe you can use either country ribs or baby back ribs. The flavor is in the fat, but so is the waistline! Country ribs take longer to cook but the reward is in fall off the rib bone deliciousness. The baby back ribs are all meat and bone and do have a natural sweetness. Use a 14 bone rack of baby back ribs if you are eating light, two racks for a big meal with leftovers. Besides, if you can't eat it all, cold ribs are a nifty snack.

MARINADE

3 cups	red wine vinegar
3 cups	peach juice, or 1½ cups papaya juice & 1½ cups apple juice
1 cups	molasses
1 cups	brown sugar
1 cups	soy sauce
3 tablespoons	coarse ground black pepper

Mix seasoning, and marinade ribs overnight.
Some people like to par boil their ribs before roasting or grilling.

Boiling is only necessary if you are using the larger American style ribs. We will slow roast.

Set oven at 275°. Remove ribs from marinade and discard the marinade. The possibility of bacteria forming is too high to risk using the marinade liquid for a baste or sauce.

Place ribs in roasting pan and set in oven. During the first thirty minutes make the sauce. Total roasting time is two hours.

THE SAUCE

2 cups	mango puree (you can buy this or puree 4 very ripe mangoes)
3 cups	ketchup (yes, use what you like)
3 tablespoon	sambal oelek (Vietnamese chilli)
1 t each	cumin, paprika, curry, oregano, rock salt, ginger
½ cups	soy sauce
1 cups	molasses
½ cups	brown sugar

Option: puree 3 ripe bananas and add to sauce. You can also use any of your favourite exotic fruits for this BBQ: papaya or guava.

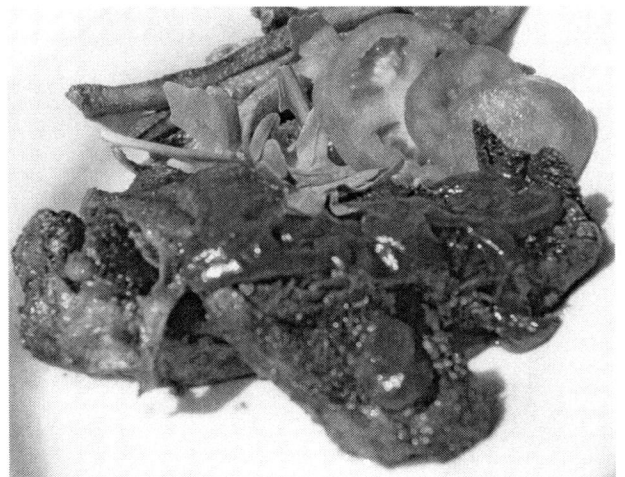

Baby Back Pork Ribs with Mango Barbeque Sauce

Mix ingredients together and heat on stove in high sided sauce pot on medium low for at least thirty minutes, and as much as an hour. Stir frequently.

After thirty minutes brush the ribs with sauce. Let cook fifteen minutes and turn ribs over, and sauce again. Cook thirty minutes and do the same again. Then again for fifteen minutes. Then again, and then turn oven up to 300° and cook another fifteen minutes. Remove from oven and eat.

The sides for this dish are up to you. Ribs are such a subjective experience that I am hesitant to go into too much detail on the matter.

Friends, family, neighbours, please forgive me for presenting a BBQ in such short terms.

Chapter Three • ISLAND *and* OASIS

Sunday, feasting on the powers of Georgia BBQ,
revelling in the glory of a lakeside fish fry,
rib roast, corn roast and potato salad,
small talk, a little bit of Hegel and MLK,
buckets of sweet tea and a grove of lemons.
Bit of a fight over the better voice,
Haggard or Yoakum, nobody won.
Talk about the sauce, my lips are sealed.
My mother tells a story about my Grandfather
during the Great Depression.
Arrested jumping trains stopping in Tucker, GA,
when they slowed he tossed sacks
of corn and flour to his friends in the woods.
He served time for being hungry,
for feeding people when there was no food,
and sure, it's against the law,
and he was a renegade, but what can you say?
Tipped Fedora and Lucky Strike cigarettes,
something of a rascal, a colorful guy,

The First Menu

taught me how to drink coffee and milk.
I still think about him twenty years later,
and I tip the cup into the saucer,
swirl the pale brew around,
pour it back into the cup, and toast my Papaw,
a colorful man in a colorful land.
And the barbecue tastes better as she tells
the story and I think about the coffee,
and everybody's talking about their family
heroes, and yeah, the skeletons in the closet
are all coming out now, they can smell
the cookout from a hundred years away.
And I'm glad for the life all families have
when the food is rich and the talk is long.

Chapter Three • ISLAND *and* OASIS

DESSERT

CHILLED PASSION FRUIT WITH CASHEW CRISPS AND GINGER VANILLA CREAM

THE CRISPS

1 tablespoon	unsalted butter, soft
2½ tablespoons	sugar
1	egg white, small
2 tablespoons	ground cashew, size after grinding
1	zest of half an orange, lemon or lime
2 tablespoons	cake flour

Preheat oven to 425°. Beat sugar and butter together in mixing bowl until creamy. Beat in egg white. With a rubber spatula, or your clean hand, fold in the ground nuts and orange rind. Gently stir in the flour with the spatula.

Rub a baking sheet with butter, or baking spray, and with a tablespoon drop small rounds of the batter on the tray. Make sure you leave about three inches of space around each cookie. Flatten each cookie into a circle with a cold, wet knife; this keeps it from sticking to the batter.

This will yield eight to 10 cookies.

Bake 10 minutes, they will be golden. Cool on wire rack.

If you don't like cashews, any nut will suffice, i.e. almonds, walnuts, pecans or hazelnuts. Set aside until it's time for dessert.

VANILLA CREAM

¼ teaspoon	vanilla
¼ teaspoon	ground ginger
½ cup	heavy cream
1 teaspoon	fruit flower honey: orange or blueberry

You need a medium metal mixing bowl and a flexible wire whisk.

Pour the cream into the bowl. Begin whisking at a slow rate and increase your speed as the cream thickens. When the cream is at a soft peak add the vanilla. Whisk just to firm. Add the honey and blend to firm peak. Refrigerate. Make this just before dinner. It will not stay firm for a long time. If it does fall, just whisk it a little and it will come right back to form.

The First Menu

> Passion fruit is a small purplish fruit that is related to our native maypop. It is grown primarily in the tropics. Passion fruit is also known as granadilla, which is the edible fruit of the passion flower. Although it's fun to think of the fruit as being "passion" inducing, it really gets its name from the Spaniards who settled in Brazil. They saw the symbol of the cross in the purple and white flowers. The flowers are edible as well and are often used in herb tea blends.

You will need four passion fruit; refrigerate, but don't get them below 40 degrees. Anything below would be too cold and the fruit flavor would be obscured. If you can't find them, which would be a shame, then use papaya. Pomegranate seeds are a good garnish for this dish. Thin sliced, ripe star fruit (carambola) is also a worthy accompaniment. And hey, why not? To eat the passion fruit, cut it in half and scoop out the bitter-sweet red seeds, juice and pulp. You also can use the pulp as a topping for ice cream.

In the center of the plate mound the whipped cream. Arrange the cashew crisps and passion fruit around the cream. Dip the crisp into the fruit, scoop and eat. If you have access to any kind of edible sweet flowers then by all means use them. Just sprinkle around the plate. If it's spring and the tiger lilies are blooming, and the honey suckle is in bloom and you just by chance happen to pick a few....well, let the love of delicate dining begin.

Chapter Three • ISLAND *and* OASIS

• *SECOND MENU* •

SCALLOPS WITH JALAPENO AND PEARS

TOMATO AND BASIL COUS COUS WITH VEGETABLES AND CHICKEN

WHITE CHOCOLATE MERINGUES POACHED IN ORANGE WATER

This is one of the easiest menus in the book. You get to Sauté, roast, steam, and poach! What more could you ask for when you want to show off while working together? The tastes range from spicy, to hearty, to sweet-tart. There's a lot of hand washing and cutting board cleaning involved in this menu, divide your chores equally so one doesn't feel like the chef and the other the scullion. We are working together, as equals. Being equal is one of the most difficult challenges present to any relationship; balance must occur in all things in order for the outcome to be uniform and satisfying: relationships and food alike are all about balance.

SAUTEED SEA SCALLOPS WITH JALAPENO AND PEARS

Scallops cook really fast, so be careful as to not overcook them. If you have to check them, then just cut one in half, the color will be two thirds white with the middle third being shiny and glassy. This dish takes about seven to ten minutes from start to finish. If you cannot find karchai then use fresh ginger or dried galanga (another kind of ginger that is earthier tasting).

8	large sea scallops
¼ cup	peanut oil (good for high heat and flavor)
1/4 cup	flour
1	jalapeno pepper, seeded and cut in thin strips
1	Asian pear, or Bartlett, cut in thin half circles
¼ cup	coconut milk

1 teaspoon	karchai, aka baby ginger, this will be two thin slices (it's more pungent than regular ginger and is regularly used in Thai cuisine)
¼ cup	thin soy sauce, it's made from yellow rather than black soy beans and has a fruitier taste
1 tablespoon	rough chopped parsley
1	lime, cut in quarters
14	large spinach leaves, washed and stemmed.

Pick the "stem" off of the scallops. Heat medium sauté pan or wok on high until peanut oil begins to turn clear. Flour scallops. Add scallops and jalapeno to pan and agitate skillet, or just toss with a pair of long metal tongs. When scallops turn tan, about one minute, add pear and karchai. Keep heat on high, you just have to go fast. Add coconut milk and reduce by a third. Add soy and parsley. Squeeze in juice of two lime wedges. You are done.

Scallops with Jalapeno and Pears

To serve: lay out seven to ten spinach leaves per plate and pour scallops over the center of the leaves. Garnish with lime wedge.

This dish can easily be adapted to an entree by the use of rice noodles, soba noodles (a Japanese pasta made from buckwheat flour and yams), jasmine rice, or even served over steamed vegetables such as crimini mushrooms, broccoli, red peppers and asparagus.

Chapter Three • ISLAND *and* OASIS

THE ENTREE

TOMATO AND BASIL COUSCOUS WITH VEGETABLES AND CHICKEN

First, couscous is not rice, as has been suggested by many a friend and customer. Cous cous is granular durum wheat semolina. Couscous is a rice-like pasta if you will. The name 'couscous' also signifies the completed preparation. So, you need couscous to make couscous. It first appears in a thirteenth century Spanish cookbook by a man named Ibn Razin Al-Tubjibi-Al-Andalusi. So as far as we know couscous has its origins in the Moor occupied regions of Spain. And that's your history lesson for today.

Talking about cous cous can get me in trouble, like Asian rice, Italian pasta, and Southern barbecue there is a lot of history and attitude about what is the perfect preparation. I am no authority; I just like to eat and cook what best suits my tastes. But you have that figured out by now. Say these words and let your imagination roam: *Algeria, Morocco, Tunisia.....Senegal...*Get the picture?

You are welcome to use traditional couscous or the instant kind. The recipe here is for straight cous cous. Be careful, couscous, if not properly cooked, i.e. long enough, will continue to expand in your stomach. Instant cous cous does this; two cups dried can end up being twelve if you keep on cooking it.

Steaming is the best and most recommended method. You can boil seasoned broth/water, add the grains, cover, turn off heat and let it set for 10 minutes covered, and you will have edible couscous. If you are a hard-core addict to all things "gadget" for your kitchen, and it does help, then buy a Couscousier, which is a kind of double boiler with very, very fine holes. If you have a regular American kitchen, then use a double boiler or vegetable steamer. You know the ones; they are a thin stainless steel and open and close with flower like sections. When using a standard double boiler, stretch a damp piece of cheesecloth around the rim of the steamer section so that the steam only goes through the holes, not up around the edges. Don't worry about the couscous falling through the cracks, the steam will keep it up as the grains cook and expand.

Also, you can use a bamboo steamer. Bamboo is my favourite steamer method but that is a purely personal and affected choice.

The Second Menu

COOKING THE COUSCOUS: 1½ CUPS DRY COUSCOUS

Place the grains in a fine sieve and rinse under cold water. Drain and put it in a large bowl. Let it set and swell for five minutes or so. Break up any and all clumps with your hands.

Fill the bottom of the steamer with water or highly seasoned broth.

10	anatto seeds
10 fronds	saffron
½ teaspoon	allspice
½ teaspoon	cardamom
2	bay leaves
1 teaspoon	dried basil leaves
1 tablespoon	crushed garlic
1 tablespoon	kosher salt
1 teaspoon	cracked black pepper
4 cups	water

You can even put the vegetables and chicken in the water and have everything prepared at the same time. We're going to do that. Bring to boil with steamer section firmly in place. Then add:

8 oz	diced chicken, dark and white mix
½ cup each	diced zucchini, eggplant, yellow onion, celery, and carrots
2	large ripe tomatoes, diced

Put the couscous in the steamer, cover and steam for thirty to forty five minutes.

Dump couscous into large serving dish. Fluff. Moisten with broth. Cover and let stand for ten more minutes. It's ready for the rest of the good stuff.

Taste the stew for seasoning. Adjust to your tastes. Place a big mound of couscous on a plate and pour the stem over the couscous. Eat.

So, as your experience shows, couscous just sounds and tastes exotic, cooking it is easy.

So, do you think I'm just going to give you a quick recipe for something as rich in history and romance as this and move on? You're right. I am. The rest of the experimentation is up to you. Follow your tastes, and of course read more cookbooks on the subject.

Let's explore more of the world.

Anyway, we have meringues to make.

Chapter Three • ISLAND and OASIS

DESSERT

WHITE CHOCOLATE MERINGUES POACHED IN ORANGE WATER WITH CHOCOLATE WHIPPED CREAM

If you are lucky enough to find orange blossom water, use it. This is a Middle Eastern water made with orange blossoms. It is light and fragrant. Once you have used orange blossom water you will find it difficult to use the heavier orange juice for this and similar dishes. I have found a good standby by making a tea of lime and orange blossoms, which can be found at most health food stores.

THE MERINGUES

2	large egg whites
2 teaspoons	water
½ teaspoon	cream of tartar
¼ cup	fine sugar (process granulated sugar in your food mill for two minutes until fine)
A dash!	of salt, this is barely the tip of a teaspoon
2 ounces	finely grated white chocolate
1 teaspoon	fresh orange juice

Here's a rule: beat egg whites from slow to medium fast; beat egg yolks from fast to slow. Why? Egg whites must not be foamy for meringues and mousses. Egg yolks create a tighter bond when beaten from fast to slow, also keeps from beating them too thick at the end. It has to do with proteins combining with oxygen and the ingredients to the dish.

In order to prevent any formation of the bacteria *salmonella* we will cook the whites as they whip over boiling water. The egg whites, when formed into meringue will be a temperature of 160°. So, keep that thermometer handy. To check for accuracy just dip the thermometer into crushed ice and a little water, it will read 32°, if not then get a new thermometer. Ice, no matter the sea level will be 32°. Since water boils at different temperatures depending on your sea level it isn't as accurate to check for the old reliable 212° of boiling water.

Put the egg whites, cream of tartar, orange juice, salt and sugar in a high sided mixing bowl. Lightly whisk with wire whisk to mix the ingredients.

Bring water to boil in saucepan. Place mixing bowl in water, hold it with one pot holder protected hand. Begin your whisking. Slow to fast. Do not beat it so fast that it becomes foamy. It must remain intact. Beat until it reaches 160°. Remove from heat and continue beating until thick peaks form in the meringue.

You have thick peaks. Gently whisk in the finely grated white chocolate.

In another pot: boil 3 cups water and one cup fresh orange juice. Turn down to simmer. With a large serving spoon (holds about 3 ounces) form little egg shaped ovals. Do this by dipping the spoon in the hot water and then into the meringue, turn the spoon around in your palm and slide the oval into the poaching water. Repeat until you have used all the meringue.

Simmer for two minutes per side. Turn the ovals over with a slotted spoon. Poach until firm. Remove from poach water with your slotted spoon and drain on paper towels.

CHOCOLATE WHIPPED CREAM

½ cup	40% fat whipping cream (the higher fat content makes for a richer sauce, you can go as low as 36% for whipping)
2 tablespoons	finely grated dark sweetened chocolate
1 tablespoon	maple syrup or molasses

Whip all ingredients together in a mixing bowl to a very light cream.

Pour onto serving plate. Set meringues in cream with the point of the ovals touching in the middle. Garnish with peeled tangerine wedges. These go well with cookies. Any cookie.

Chapter Three • ISLAND *and* OASIS

• *THE THIRD MENU* •

CHICKEN BREAST POACHED IN TAMARIND AND SOY WITH MOLASSES AND RUM GLAZE OVER MIXED GREENS

SAUTÉED LOBSTER MEDALLIONS WITH A SAMBAL OELEK WHIPPED MASCARPONE

MANGO NAPOLEON

The only thing hard here is working with phyllo (or filo) dough for the napoleon. By now you know what mascarpone is and what sambal oelek is, and they are even better together than you may at first think. Poaching chicken is easy as long as you let the broth do the work, all you have to do is keep from boiling the chicken. If you cannot find tamarind pulp for the poaching liquid, then use tamarind juice, which can be found in any Asian or Latin grocery. Lobster is only a choice, you may use any favourite shell fish...of course it wouldn't be as good as cold water lobster. Stress, cold water lobster, not warm water, please. The flavor is as many miles apart as the oceans. The only dish here that can be made ahead is the assembly of the mango napoleon, everything else is cook and serve.

CHICKEN BREAST POACHED IN TAMARIND AND SOY WITH MOLASSES AND RUM GLAZE OVER MIXED GREENS

8 oz	chicken breast, skinned and defatted
6 oz	tamarind juice from 4 oz tamarind paste
3 oz	mushroom soy sauce
3 oz	molasses
2 oz	brown sugar
3 oz	dark rum
½ teaspoon	Chinese 5 spice powder
5 oz	fresh, mixed greens (the kind with kale, chicory, romaine, green leaf, lambs ear, mache)

First, cure the tamarind pulp by pouring one cup boiling water over the pulp. Mash it up and let it rest for at least thirty minutes.
Strain the liquid and throw away the pulp.
Trim any fat, skin and bone off of the chicken breast and rub with 5 Spice Powder. Set aside.

Pour liquid and soy into poaching pan. The pan can be any pan or skillet that is at least three inches deep. Bring to boil and turn heat down to simmer. Add chicken breast. Cook five minutes and then turn the breast over. Add rum, molasses, and brown sugar. Continue cooking for ten minutes. Remove breast from broth and make a small cut in the thickest part to see if it is cooked. The meat will be white to tan, not pink to red.

Sauteed lobster medallions in olive oil and butter

It will also be plump from the poaching, not thin and flat.

If the chicken is not done then return to broth and cook another five minutes. Remove from broth and set in warm place, like in another pan on the stove. Turn heat up and bring broth back to a boil. Reduce down to a glaze, now this isn't a tricky thing, but you can burn the pan if you leave it alone during the reduction process. Stay nearby and keep an eye on it while you work on the preparations for the rest of the meal.

The broth is reduced to a glaze when it coats a spoon. Just stir a regular silver or stainless steel spoon around in the sauce (it's a sauce now) and if the sauce coats the spoon, then it is a glaze and it is ready.

Arrange mixed greens in a mound in center of plate. Thin slice chicken into ten to twelve slices. Set the slices in fan design over greens. Drizzle sauce over the whole thing, greens, chicken, and the plate.

A nice garnish for this would be mild green olives and cocktail wafers. If you want something different and tasty, find Korean or Japanese preserved plums. They are tart and have a "bite" similar to the milder olives. I think they make a better accompaniment, but they may not be readily available in some areas as Asian preserved fruits and vegetables are not yet high on the American tastes chart. They should be, but they're not. If trends continue this will soon no longer be the case.

Chapter Three • ISLAND *and* OASIS

SAUTEED LOBSTER MEDALLIONS WITH RED BELLS, ONIONS, ARTICHOKE HEARTS AND A SAMBAL OELEK MARSCAPONE CREAM

3 med	new potatoes, sliced thin
5 oz	lobster tail meat
5 oz	sea scallops
¼ cup	flour, to dust lobster and scallops
1 med	red bell pepper, diced
½	yellow onion, diced
5	artichoke hearts, quartered
1 teaspoon	salt and pepper mix
½ teaspoon	grated ginger
½ teaspoon	grated garlic
6	large fresh basil leaves
3 tablespoons	butter
4 tablespoons	olive oil

Sauté potatoes in oil until they are light brown. Add butter. Add garlic, ginger, peppers and onions and cook on medium high until they are soft. Add artichoke hearts and cook one minute. Add scallops and cook till outer flesh turns white, then add the lobster and turn heat back up to high. Salt and pepper. Cook two minutes. Pour off excess liquid into cream mixture.

In a separate pan prepare the

CREAM SAUCE

1 tablespoon	sambal oelek, or Cholula (if you want it milder)
½ cup	mascarpone cheese
½ cup	heavy cream
1 tablespoon	juice of half a lime

Pour cream into a saucepan and heat to warm, then add cheese and stir so that it melts. Add sambal. Add lime juice. Should be lightly thick. Pour into sauté. Stir in. Add basil leaves and cook until it thickens.

This dish works well with wide rice noodles, which can be prepared by simply softening in hot water and stirring and heating with the cream mixture.

NOODLES

5 oz	dry weight, wide rice noodles or rice sticks
1 quart	hot water to soften noodles

Put noodles in the very hot water. After they begin to soften, about three minutes, stir them around so that they are completely exposed to the water. They will soften enough to eat within ten minutes. Drain and stir into the sauce, continue to heat on low. When they are completely warm and the sauce is thick, pour onto serving platters and have a good meal.

Alternate additions to this sauté are broccoli and wild mushrooms, or even a medley of exotic fruits such as carambola, guava and papaya. If you want to do it with fruit and the exotics are not available, then oranges or tangerines, sweet apples or Bosc pears. The fun for this dish is the combination of heat and sweet.

DESSERT

MANGO NAPOLEON

Here we go, phyllo. Phyllo dough is a very, very thin flour pastry that can be difficult to work with without tearing the delicate sheets. It is important to keep it cold, moist and smooth. Buy a commercial brand in the freezer section of the grocery store. If you want to make it then refer to Julia Child or Marcella Hazan. Puff and phyllo pastry doughs are things that I prepared during my apprentice years, and are best kept as fond memories of well wrought labors. I like them best as memories. Today we have the great convenience of doughs made by professionals that rival, and in my case, surpass what can be made at home. I've never been that good at dessert pastries anyway, I think it requires a certain touch sort of like making Southern biscuits or chicken and dumplings as only a grandmother can. Besides, there are some things that one must be unashamed about, and for me, this is a lesser sin of omission.

If you are in it for the authenticity and satisfaction of making your own then do it, the gratifications of this task rival that of the legendary climb on Everest. "Because it's there." Again, refer to cookbooks that specifically detail pastries as prepared in their home country or region. Most of the recent cookbooks I've been reading don't even use phyllo, they substitute puff pastry, which is acceptable, but a Napoleon is phyllo. And that's where I stick to tradition. I've got enough hard stuff for you to do in here anyway.

The recipe we will make is similar to a Moroccan "kteffa". This is a phyllo pastry covered with a custard cream, and garnished with fresh berries. We use mango. You will need a fine bristled, soft pastry brush.

PREPARING THE PASTRY

8	sheets phyllo dough
¼ cup	graham cracker crumbs (yep!)
¼ cup	melted butter

Thaw the pastry at room temperature with a damp cloth covering the dough. Gently (I will use this word a lot here) unroll the cylinder of dough. Gently lift the dough from each side. Pull the sheet back towards you...slowly pull the sheet. If it sticks, and some will, then lift and pull from the other side. Lay the sheet down and brush with butter and sprinkle with cracker crumbs. This helps the dough layers "puff" when it bakes.

Repeat this procedure three times. Set aside with a damp cloth covering the pastry. Do it again so that you have two pastries.

MANGO CREAM CHEESE

1	mango, very small dice
½ cup	cream cheese
1 tablespoon	granulated sugar
1/5 teaspoon	cinnamon
1 tablespoon	all purpose flour
1 tablespoon	cold unsweetened butter
¼ cup	crushed, toasted almonds

In a bowl mix mango, cream cheese, cinnamon and sugar together.

Cut the pastries into six squares each, this will be twelve total. Rub a baking sheet with cold butter and sprinkle with flour. Shake off excess flour.

Lay two squares next to each other on the pan. Spread one teaspoon mango mix. Lay next sheet on top of that and sprinkle one teaspoon almonds on that sheet. Do it again until you have six layers for each Napoleon. Now, cup your hands around the Napoleons and gently fold the edges down. Brush each with melted butter.

Heat oven to 350°. Bake on center rack for twenty minutes.

While the pastries bake, prepare the custard.

The Third Menu

CUSTARD

2 teaspoons	powdered sugar
¼ teaspoon	rum extract
1	cinnamon stick
1 cup	milk
1	egg yolk
1 teaspoon	cornstarch
¼ cup	heavy cream

Heat sugar, rum, cinnamon, egg yolk and milk in medium saucepan on medium heat. Stirring all the time, bring to a simmer. Mix cornstarch and cream so that it is smooth. Slowly pour into simmering milk with one hand, whisking steadily with the other hand Simmer until it is lightly thickened. This means that it will coat a spoon. The total time to make this is ten minutes.

When the pastries have cooked to a golden brown remove from oven and place on dessert plates. Pour custard over the pastries. There you have it, a creamy, crispy, fruity, nutty dessert. Garnish with fresh berries (your choice), or candied flowers. I prefer candied violets, which can be purchased in gourmet kitchen shops.

Chapter Three • ISLAND *and* OASIS

Beside me here in the kitchen today,
your long fingers lifting pastries
and cut fruit with all the tenderness
of one who can only love, and well,
it's that way for me,
in this room so full with the aromas
of sweat and salt,
of honey and rose water,
of herbs and quick kisses caught
between the chopping and reading and hunting...
and that's what it's like when we cook together,
the food seems to lift itself for you,
just like me, here for you.

• THE FOURTH MENU •

MIXED PEPPERCORN, ALLSPICE AND CORIANDER CRUSTED TUNA WITH WASABI FRUIT SALSA

JERK CHICKEN WITH PLANTAINS AND PINEAPPLE-CUCUMBER SLAW

WARM DATES STUFFED WITH PISTACHIOS, SERVED WITH TAMARIND

"LEMONADE"

This menu is all about marinating, rubbing, stuffing and mixing. Every bit of it can be made ahead and then cooked when you are ready to eat. Tuna must be sushi grade yellowfin or big eye, accept no substitute, and this is an absolute. If you want to grill the chicken, do it, it tastes best that way **if** you are an experienced back yard grill person. For the sake of simplicity we will roast, and that is a good thing to do, i.e. roast and, at times be simple.

THE APPETIZER

MIXED PEPPERCORN, ALLSPICE AND CORIANDER CRUSTED TUNA with wasabi fruit salsa

8 oz	1½ inch thick sashimi grade tuna loin 'saku block'
2 oz	grapeseed or corn oil
1 teaspoon	Sichuan peppercorns
½ teaspoon	whole allspice
1 teaspoon	dried seaweed (nori)
½ teaspoon	green tea leaves
½ teaspoon	coarse pink sea salt (Hawaiian)

Grind spices, salt, nori and tea leaves to coarse grind in spice mill or coffee grinder. Rub the tuna with the oil. Rub the spices into the tuna so that they are both into the meat and as a crust. Wrap in plastic wrap and refrigerate over night.

Another choice of seasoning for this dish is to add sesame seeds instead of the coriander and allspice. Feel free to use sesame one time, and then this recipe the next, just to see which you like best.

Chapter Three • ISLAND and OASIS

FRUIT SALSA

5	strawberries, stemmed, quartered
1	tangerine, peeled, use the wedges
1	golden delicious apple, small dice
½	papaya, peeled, seeded and diced
4 stalks	green onion, thin slice all
¼	poblano pepper, seeded and small dice
½	mango, firm, peeled and diced
4 ounces	pineapple juice
5 leaves	fresh mint
10 leaves	fresh cilantro
¼ teaspoon	wasabi powder.

If you can find fresh wasabi, then buy it, it will be expensive but try it at least once in your life. You will be very, very happy with your new delicacy. Wasabi is now being farmed in the US so only time and market demand will determine the future price. Powdered wasabi often contains a lot of extra ingredients, so I do recommend that you research and read the labels of the varieties offered. Some pastes and wasabi powders are flowery while others taste of pure horseradish and dry mustard. What you prefer is a matter of tastes, as always, experiment.

Toss all ingredients together in a glass bowl. Refrigerate for at least an hour. It will hold overnight, but it isn't too good if you try to keep it much longer than a day or two: the fruit looses it's vitality and individuality after a while.

Now you are ready:

In a very, very hot skillet with a tablespoon of corn oil sear the tuna.

Take it easy when you put the tuna in the skillet, you do not want to burn yourself, and you do not want to lose any of the coating. Cook one minute all around the tuna. The coating will be crisp, the edges of the meat will be white and the inner section of the flesh will be a deep red.

You can eat it two ways: let the meat rest for fifteen minutes at room temperature, or refrigerate for an hour. I prefer it chilled.

When you are ready to serve the tuna hold your hand around the tuna, then with a very sharp knife you will make smooth, thin slices, and I do mean thin, as in paper thin. If you are good you will yield about 15 to 20 slices.

Spread the salsa out on a plate and fan the tuna slices over the salsa. You may want to have a little sweet soy sauce and pickled ginger slices as a garnish. This is a nice fresh and spicy dish. Think champagne.

THE ENTRÉE

JERK CHICKEN WITH PLANTAINS AND PINEAPPLE-CUCUMBER SLAW

This is sort of a county island dish. Jerk seasoning serves many purposes besides just being sweet and hot. It preserves the meat. The peppers make you sweat so you cool off. It tastes good. I like jerk spices better than the cayenne and paprika blackening because the jerk seasonings bring out more of the combination of tastes, rather than a dominant thrust of char and heat that is the blackened signature. Blackened is a great method, and many heavier fish invite the process, like amberjack, red fish, all the drums, and large mahi mahi fillets. It's just that I like the flavor of brown sugar, scallions, onions, nutmeg, cinnamon, thyme, allspice, and bird chilli peppers (Scotch bonnet pepper is the island way). If you don't want to make the jerk seasoning there are commercial blends available, as always avoid the ones with salt as the first or second ingredient. It's best to avoid the ones with salt altogether. You want control of your intake of salt, don't always leave it up to the provider.

Jerk Chicken with plantains and pineapple-cucumber slaw

JERK SEASONING

2 tablespoons	light brown sugar, sifted
½ teaspoon	nutmeg
½ teaspoon	allspice
½ teaspoon	cinnamon
1 tablespoon	dried thyme leave
1 tablespoon	crushed chilli peppers
1 tablespoon	kosher salt

Chapter Three • ISLAND *and* OASIS

Optional: (this is a personal addition)
½ teaspoon	coriander
½ teaspoon	cardamom
½ teaspoon	ginger

Mix the spices together. Set aside two tablespoons of the mix.

½	diced yellow onion
5 stalks	scallion, diced
1 cup	blend oil
3 tablespoons	lime juice

In a plastic bowl mix with the jerk spice blend.

1 whole	chicken, cut into breast, leg and thigh sections, bone included.

If you don't like all the chicken, then use your favourite section in the way you prefer, i.e. boneless breast, leg only, thigh only.

Submerge the chicken in the jerk marinade. Refrigerate overnight.

When it's time to cook, lift the chicken out of the marinade and set on a plate. Rub the remaining dry two tablespoons of seasoning on the chicken.

Roast in 375° oven for 45 minutes. When you insert a knife into the

---

This of you with a grill: grill. Use wood and briquettes to match the meats you are grilling. Pecan, hickory, mesquite, apple, cherry, Jack Daniels, coconut and alder are all favorites. My grills are: the Big Green Egg, Weber Kettle and Brinkman Smoke 'N Grill. They are efficient and highly effective for any kind of smoking, grilling or barbecuing for home use. Big Green Egg is hands down the best of the best. To smoke/grill the chicken use a 1 to 3 mix of apple and pecan. Temperature when you start should be 250 degrees. Place chicken on the grill, lower the lid and cook for 30 minutes. Do not lift the lid during this time unless the temperature goes over 300 degrees. After 30 minutes add 5 ounces pecan chips that have soaked in water. Smoke another 30 minutes. Beer can chicken is a thing of legend. Open a can of beer, Dr. Pepper or ginger ale and put it inside the cavity of a whole chicken. Put it on a hot grill, 400 degrees, lower the lid, set baffles so that the temperature maintains at 350 degrees and cook for one hour.

thickest part of the meat and the juices run clear the chicken is done. If you have a thermometer, and you should, the dark meat will register 165° and the white meat will be 150°. Below these temperatures you invite the presence of bacteria; above these temperatures you have dry, tough chicken.

PINEAPPLE-CUCUMBER COLE SLAW

1	seedless cucumber, peeled, cut in half and sliced thin
¼ head	green cabbage, cored and sliced thin
½ cup	pineapple, diced...come on, use fresh. You can roast or grill the rest with the chicken
¼	red onion, diced
2 stalks	scallion, diced
1 teaspoon	mix of white and black sesame seeds
1 teaspoon	salt and pepper blend
1 teaspoon	crushed and chopped fresh garlic
2 tablespoon	corn oil
1 tablespoon	apple cider vinegar

Mix all together in plastic bowl and refrigerate overnight, or at a minimum of three hours.

PLANTAINS

2	ripe, yellow plantains, peeled, sliced thin
1 cup	corn oil

Heat oil to 335° in high sided pan or wok. Gently submerge the chips one by one into the oil. This keeps the temperature from dropping too fast to fry. Fry until they are crisp, 3 minutes. Stir as they fry. Drain on paper towel. Plantain chips are good with a thin apple and curry aioli, or whatever you like to dip in like traditional salsa, ketchup or blue cheese. You can also sprinkle them with any of the following: salt and pepper, jerk seasoning, sugar, cayenne and sugar, or just eat them plain.

The chicken is cooked, pineapple is cooked, the plantains are fried, and the slaw is ready. This is a simple, country meal; so for what it's worth you have everything you need for a nice foray into the easier side of the islands. Hey, there's nothing wrong with loaf bread when it's like this.

If you must have a sauce, I recommend a mango barbecue, or even a little of the fruit salsa from the tuna appetiser. Thickened passion fruit juice works wonders.

DESSERT

WARM DATES STUFFED WITH PISTACHIOS, SERVED WITH TAMARIND "LEMONADE"

10	whole, seeded medjool dates
1 ounce	crushed pistachios
1 ounce	crushed hazelnuts
1/3 teaspoon	garam masala spice mix
2 ounces	creamy goat cheese (chevre)

Roast the nuts and spice in 350 degree oven for 15 minutes. Remove from oven, and in a mixing bowl combine by hand the nuts and chevre so they make a coarse paste. Remove the seed from the dates. Stuff each date with the cheese/nut paste. Place the dates on a baking dish and bake at 400 degrees for 8 minutes. Serve on a platter so that you share this while sipping the Tamarind lemonade.

TAMARIND LEMONADE

8 ounces	tamarind paste
4 cups	boiling water
½ cup	sugar or light brown sugar, or honey (if using honey make it a full cup)
2	lemons, just the juice

Pour the boiling water over the tamarind paste. Stir with a long wooden spoon. Cover and let it sit for at least an hour. After an hour stir in the honey and lemon juice. Strain the juice through a fine strainer so that you get only liquid. Throw away the pulp. Refrigerate until chilled. Serve over crushed ice. This is very similar to a limeade kind of drink. Tamarind is more tart and has a deeper flavor. The color will be a dark tan. If it is too strong just cut it with cold water. Now if you have a taste for dark or spiced rum now is the time to spike your drink.

You've had a nice fiery island meal. You sit back in front of the air conditioner or on the porch, nibble the stuffed dates and sip the tamarind nectar. Relaxing. Tamarind is good for settling the stomach after a rich meal. Maybe listen to a little Papa Wembe, Cesaire Evoria, or even a bit of vintage Bob Marley...Get the picture?

• THE FIFTH MENU •

CRAB CAKES MIXED WITH CHEDDAR AND MESQUITE SEASONING, SERVED WITH A CURRY AIOLI

GRILLED MAHI-MAHI WITH CARAMBOLA AND BUTTER

BANANA CREAM CHEESE EGG ROLLS WITH PAPAYA PUREE, CRYSTALLISED GINGER CREAM AND PAPAYA SLICES

The hardest parts of this menu are the egg rolls. The rest is just easy mixing, sautéing and grilling. Mahi mahi loves the grill like no other fish.

I have grilled fresh mahi mahi with a garlic aioli and it was wonderful. Mahi mahi (also known as dolphin fish or Dorado, and it is not a mammal) is a light and firm fish that swims with tuna, and the mammals, dolphin and porpoise. Mahi mahi does not require a lot of sauce or seasoning. It combines best with fruit sauces.

There are two aiolis in this chapter because I like aioli. Knowing how to make the various aiolis is a great asset to the kitchen. You must get away from the typical mayonnaise and mustards. Experiment. It's a big world.

CRAB CAKES MIXED WITH CHEDDAR AND MESQUITE SEASONING, WITH CURRY AIOLI

CRAB CAKES

8 ounces	fresh lump crab meat
1/3 teaspoon	mesquite seasoning
½ teaspoon	Old Bay Seasoning
2 ounces	grated sharp cheddar cheese
1 stalk	green onion, diced
1 stalk	celery, fine dice
1 tablespoon	poblano pepper, fine dice
1/3	avocado, diced
	(reserve the rest of the avocado for garnish)
½	fresh lime, juice only, will equal a teaspoon
1 tablespoon	panko bread crumbs
1	egg yolk, extra large

Chapter Three • ISLAND and OASIS

> It is best to use either pasteurised eggs or follow the method of beating the eggs over low heat to a temperature of 160 in order to prevent the formation of any bacteria. You must follow safe handling practices with eggs and poultry, more people poison themselves at home than when going out to eat in restaurants. I don't have a strict statistic on that, but the home cook tends to take far less precautions than health code and chef directed restaurants.

Pick through the crab meat to remove any shell fragments. There will always be shell fragments no matter what the label says. With very clean hands mix all the ingredients together. Pat out into four cakes. Refrigerate until you are ready to cook.

CURRY AIOLI

2	egg yolks
1 teaspoon	curry powder (recommend madras unless you are making your own)
4 ounces	virgin olive oil
2 ounces	rice wine vinegar
1 ounce	cold water
¼ teaspoon	kosher salt
1 teaspoon	fresh chopped garlic

In your food processor or by hand in a mixing bowl with a whisk: Beat the egg yolks until they begin to turn a light yellow. Add the garlic, curry and salt. While still mixing, slowly pour in the olive oil, when it becomes thick slowly add the vinegar. Then add the water. It will be a very light yellow and thick.

COOKING THE CRAB CAKES

2 ounces	corn oil

In a skillet heat the oil on medium heat to 335°, until it begins to turn clear. Place the crab cakes in the oil and cook on medium for three minutes per side. Agitate the pan as they cook so that they do not stick. Each side will be a little brown and crisp. When they have cooked drain on paper towels.

The Fifth Menu

Spread the aioli in a thin layer on the serving plate, and set the crab cakes on the aioli. A good garnish is a lemon wedge, diced onion, pickled okra or a gherkin, and a sprig of cilantro.

If you are out to impress: puree three tablespoons of roasted red bell pepper with 1 tablespoon of cream. Dot the aioli with the puree. Pull the point of a knife through the center of each dot into the aioli. See? It makes little commas.

GRILLED MAHI-MAHI WITH CARAMBOLA AND BUTTER

Again with the grill, now if you don't have a grill or the weather isn't right then broil in the oven. Carambola is another name for star fruit. It grows like the weed it is in equatorial regions and in Florida. Carambola has become popular, and instead of the price going down, it has gone up. The shape and the tart pineapple/banana taste are worth the price.

Crab Cakes mixed with cheddar and mesquite seasoning

2 - 7 to 8 ounce	mahi mahi fillets
2 (16 slices)	star fruit thick sliced (buy yellow, not green, like all fruit green is not ripe. If you cannot buy it ripe, then let it ripen in a paper bag over night. If that doesn't work you can always slice and marinade in pineapple juice)
2 tablespoons	unsalted butter
A pinch	salt and pepper mix

Grill over hot coals 10 minutes per inch thickness of the fish. This is the Canadian Method, which is rather fool proof. On the second turn, place the fruit slices on top of the fish. Sprinkle with

Ginger, Lily & Sweet Fire

Chapter Three • ISLAND and OASIS

salt and pepper. When it is done remove from grill and set on plate. Immediately put slices of butter on top of the fish so that it melts. This is as simple as I get.

This is great served on a salad of mixed greens with a drizzle of ginger and garlic, oil and vinegar dressing poured over the greens.

DESSERT

PAPAYA AND CREAM CHEESE EGG ROLLS WITH YOUR FAVORITE ICE CREAM

4	egg roll wrappers
½	ripe papaya, small dice
½	banana, small dice
3 oz	cream cheese
2 tablespoons	brown sugar
1	egg, beaten
1 cup	peanut oil

Dice and mix fruit with cream cheese. Sprinkle board with one tablespoon brown sugar. Lay out the egg roll wrappers. With one point of the wrapper facing you, place a fourth of the mix in the center of each. Fold the front tip over the mix and tighten. Brush the egg roll around the edges with the beaten egg. Fold in the two opposing edges over the center roll. Now roll it over until you have a smooth cylinder. Brush with egg and roll over in brown sugar.

Papaya and cream cheese egg rolls

Heat oil to 335°. Gently, very gently add the egg rolls one by one to the oil and fry for five minutes. Turning them over once a minute.

Remove from oil and place on paper towel to drain excess oil.

Cut each egg roll in the center at a 45 degree angle. Set on plate with pointy ends facing each other. Scoop ice cream in middle. That's it.

The Fifth Menu

GOODNIGHT

Hear the rain in the bamboo glade?
It taps like talking drums
telling of the feast we had tonight,
and the air moistens and cools,
and the heavy dessert seems light now,
and sleep rests with us for a while...
I wish it were always like this,
gentle into the house of dreams.
Gentle into your arms.

Chapter Three • ISLAND *and* OASIS

• *THE SIXTH MENU* •

GRILLED CILANTRO FLATBREAD WITH AMFISI OLIVES AND TOMATO

MACADAMIA AND COCONUT CRUSTED WRECKFISH WITH LIME SAUCE

PINK GUAVA MOUSSE

GRILLED CILANTRO FLATBREAD WITH AMFISI OLIVES

This is something of an afternoon dish and goes well with a classic Chablis, or even sparkling water with peach.

CILANTRO FLAT BREAD

THIS IS A 2 LOAF BATCH. Don't over work the dough, when it has mixed stop. It works best after having been frozen. If you don't have time to freeze, then be sure the oil or the grill is hot enough to force it to crisp before falling out of shape. Traditionally it was cooked on hot rocks. We will cook in oil. You can also bake it and then transfer to the grill.

Don't let the bread making thing here intimidate you. Making bread is very relaxing and it's a good workout for the triceps.

1 tablespoon	sesame seeds
1 tablespoon	black sesame seeds

Toast until crisped. Remember that they cook after you remove from heat.
Set aside. This is a later stage of mixing.

BATTER

2 cups	high gluten flour
2 cups	boiling water, it must be this hot

Blend together with bread hook in mixer. Or, do it by hand on a marble or well floured cutting board. When it has mixed, stop.

Cover with damp towel and let the dough rest for at least 15 minutes. After that, cut it into 2 equal portions. Flour table and roll dough into half inch thick circles.

Ginger, Lily & Sweet Fire

SEASONING

1 teaspoon	kosher salt
½ cup	minced cilantro
3 stalks	minced scallion = 2 tablespoons per loaf of bread
2 tablespoons	sesame oil = 1 tablespoon per loaf of bread

Now, rub each circle the sesame oil and then with the salt, cilantro and scallion. Then press down on the dough with the palms of your hands to secure the seeds and herbs. Roll dough into cigar shape. Pinch edges. Twist dough a 3/4 turn. Fold dough over end to end to the center. Flatten the dough. Sprinkle with 1 tablespoon sesame seeds for each loaf. Roll out into 10 inch circles. Place wax paper between each loaf of bread and wrap in plastic wrap, and then freeze. Stack carefully so that they don't bend out of shape. It takes at least twelve hours for these to freeze

COOKING THE BREAD
3 METHODS

Heat a half cup of blend oil in a large skillet. Medium heat. Place one bread circle in and cook 4 minutes per side. Remove and drain on towel.

Second method: Bake at 450° for twenty minutes.

Third method: cook on grill by brushing grill and bread with corn oil. Place on grill and let cook about 10 minutes per side depending on grill temperature. Usually you grill at around 325° to 375°.

The outside of the bread will be crispy. The inside will be moist and somewhere between a description of fluffy and thick.

OLIVES AND TOMATO

12	pitted amfisi or Greek olives
2	vine ripe very red tomato, chopped, save juice
2 leaves	leaf lettuce
1	orange, peeled and cut into wedges

Chop up the tomato and save it all. Shred the leaf lettuce and place the tomato on top of the lettuce. Cut the bread into triangles and set around the plate. Set the olives all around, same for orange wedges. Eat by spreading tomato on the bread, eat an olive, eat some bread, eat orange.

This is a dish that is great with a puree of roasted garlic. Grated Parmesan is also a nice addition. Fresh buffalo mozzarella takes this to another level. If you like Korean sour plums, they also are an interesting addition to this classic Italian snack.

MACADAMIA AND COCONUT CRUSTED WRECKFISH WITH LIME SAUCE

2 - 6 ounce	wreckfish fillets
1 cup	rice flour
4	eggs, beaten with 2 tablespoons water
½ cup	crushed, toasted macadamia nuts
3 ounces	dry, unsweetened flaked coconut

Here you learn the wet hand dry hand way of crusting, or breading. Left hand flour and egg, right hand nuts, this way you don't get your hands gummed up with flour, egg and nuts. And even better, nothing is wasted by sticking to your fingers, which you would have to wash off into the depths of the sink.

With your right hand roll the fish in the flour so that the fish is completely covered. We use rice flour here for the light contrast on the surface of the fish to the heavier nut coating. You must coat the meat in flour in order for the egg wash to hold to the flesh; otherwise the coating will fall off during the cooking process. After flouring place fish in egg wash, make sure it is submerged using your left hand, and that the egg adheres to the surface of the meat. Lift the fish out

Macadamia and coconut crusted Wreckfish with lime sauce

with your left hand and roll the fish around in the nut mixture with your right hand. Press down as you go. It must be evenly coated.

The fish is breaded; I like to say crusted. Put it in the refrigerator. This further seals the breading to the meat. One to two hours ahead is plenty of time. You can keep it there as long as you like, two days at the most, unless you like stinky fish. And you don't like old fish.

COOKING THE ENTREE:

4 ounces   blend oil: 30 percent olive to 70 percent corn

Preheat oven to 450°.

Heat sauté skillet with oil in it on high. When the oil is clear add the fish and shake the skillet to keep the fish from sticking to the pan. Cook two minutes and turn the fish over. Turn heat down to medium. Shake pan.

Cook four minutes, and then turn the fish over again, and place in hot oven. Cook about ten minutes in oven.

To check the fish just pierce the flesh with a sharp knife, the liquid should come out clear. Try to avoid the whole cooking till dry thing; fish is so much better when it is cooked to a medium or even medium rare range. Temperature? 145° maximum. Temperatures can tell you many things but it cannot tell you when the fish is perfect. This comes through practice. Not all fish cook the same way at the same temperatures. Some, like yellowfin or bluefin tuna need only the quickest and highest amount of heat and should be stopped at rare to medium rare. It's a personal affair, some people are afraid of undercooked fish because of bacteria and the like. You know for yourself if you are this type of person. Think sushi.

Other fish like sea bass and halibut like to be cooked slowly to a medium temperature. Snapper and it's relations are fine on medium to high heat. Trout likes high fast heat. Salmon is the grill fish, and that's a slow, smoky, 10 to fifteen minute cook time.

The fish is cooked.

Chapter Three • ISLAND and OASIS

> **TUBERS:** What are they and how come they're not all used? Sweet potatoes, yams, red potatoes, yellow potatoes, russet potatoes, boniato, yucca, taro, malanga are all tubers, or potatoes as we commonly call them. Like so many vegetables and fruits today we use what is most easily grown. Also we use what the market demands. It is a good thing to ask for little known fruits and vegetables, as this helps to encourage the small farmers to broaden their base and hence prevent being taken over by commercial farms. We all need work, and we all need a wide variety of foods. The more various your diet, the more the need for those things to be produced. Always look for the little known, this is a place where inspiration is often born. A thing about tubers, we seem to always find a way of describing them in terms of nutty and citrus. (SEE GLOSSARY)

LIME SAUCE

This is simple.

1 cup	coconut milk
4	juice of four limes
1 cup	apple juice
¼ teaspoon	salt
1 teaspoon	honey
1 teaspoon	shredded fresh ginger
2 teaspoons	cornstarch
4 teaspoons	cold water

Heat coconut milk in sauce pan. When it begins to boil add juices, salt, honey and ginger. Bring to a boil. Mix cornstarch and cold water together. As the sauce boils stir in the cornstarch thickener. It will be a thin sauce so don't fret if it isn't thick.

Pour over fish.

This is a hearty entree, so your best sides will be light. Snow peas are a favourite. Just plain sautéed or steamed snow peas with a little salt and pepper. If you want to stay exotic and yet a little heavy, then use fried or boiled malanga and taro as the starch. They whip well, like mashed potatoes, but are not as bulky.

WHIPPED MALANGA AND TARO

1 pound	equal of malanga and tarot
4 oz	butter
1 teaspoon	salt and cracked black pepper mix
2 teaspoon	crushed garlic

Cut the tubers into small wedges. Place in three quarts of water and bring to a boil. Cook till tender, about twenty minutes. Drain. With a heavy wire whisk beat the roots till smooth, add butter, salt and pepper, and garlic.

THE PLATE

Put a mound of the whipped malanga in the center of the plate. Set the fish at an angle on the malanga. Circle plate with snow peas. Cut thin slices of lemon and arrange around plate on top of snow peas. Sauce over middle of fish.

DESSERT

PINK GUAVA MOUSSE

Guava is a small, green skinned, egg shaped fruit that has a million seeds, a flavor encompassing honey, melon and strawberry. It's easiest to work with in the paste, nectar or jelly form. Fresh guava is sometimes hard to come by, it you see it, buy it, peel it, scoop out and discard the seeds, eat the pulp. This recipe calls for guava nectar that can be found in the import section of the grocery store, or in the canned fruits section of a Latin market. Guava isn't a terribly popular fruit because it's so hard to eat, but that's not a problem here since we will be using the nectar.

I have used guava as a base for barbecue to great success. But I am prejudiced, I like all tropical fruits, and think that they should be used wherever possible.

MOUSSE

1	egg white
¼ teaspoon	cream of tartar
1 teaspoon	granulated sugar
1 tablespoon	juice of half a lime

Chapter Three • ISLAND and OASIS

Beat the egg white, tartar, sugar and lime together in a mixing bowl over boiling water to a temperature of 160°. Remove from heat and continue beating until you have semi-firm peaks. Refrigerate.

3 ounces	pink guava nectar
1½ cups	40% whipping cream
2 tablespoons	granulated sugar

Combine ingredients. In mixer, begin whipping at high and turn to low as peaks begin to form. By hand do the same in a mixing bowl. Continue beating until firm peaks have formed.

Using a rubber spatula, fold the beaten egg white into the thickened cream. Scoop into champagne flutes, or into frozen orange halves, and refrigerate at least an hour, or until it is time to eat.

Garnish with mint leaf.

You can add grated white chocolate or dark chocolate to make it a bit thicker and richer. Fresh berries sliced and layered in the mousse give the dessert a bit more of a flare. Sugar cookies, graham crackers, lemon crisps are all worthy additions.

If you want to go for a dramatic presentation: Buy puff pastry sheets from the frozen pastry section of the grocery store. Cut the shape of two swans in the pastry, or whatever you're good at, and brush the pastry with a mix of one beaten egg, 1 teaspoon sugar and 1 tablespoon water. Bake at 450° for ten minutes until it is brown and rises in puffy layers. Remove from oven and let cool.

With a knife and your fingers: separate the pastry in the middle layers from the bottom of the shape. Scoop the mousse onto a plate. Set the pastry like a tent over the mousse. Garnish with slices of fresh fruit or berries.

The Sixth Menu

*The summer night sets as a seal
on my eyes, stars the color of holy basil
seep into waves of fading light,
a cloud of hissing bees rise
from a clutch of Cherokee rose,
nesting cardinals knitting ivy
in the trees rustle and whistle,
thick kitchen smells wrap around the house,
and like an old Chuck Jones cartoon
they gesture back towards an open door,
an open door where she stands...
And I think about the Song of Songs
and the gates to the city
and the fertile plains where she
would wander searching for me...
and I would search for her...
And you call me in to dinner,
and I feel a little guilty
about not helping with the food tonight,
so I smile and tell you the clean up's on me,
and tomorrow you will be
my Shulamite in the garden playing,
and I in the kitchen cooking whatever you desire.*

Chapter Three • ISLAND and OASIS

• THE SEVENTH MENU •

STEAMED ASPARAGUS WITH PROSCUITTO AND APPLE AIOLI

SWEET SOY, CAYENNE AND GINGER BEER ROASTED DUCKLING

GINGERBREAD WITH APRICOT

This menu is a hybrid of the Mediterranean, Caribbean and then a bit of the entire world. If you can't find prosciutto then use Washington State Westphalia ham, which is a worthy American substitute. The aioli is eggless, so you learn a new method of making a condiment. Whole duck and other whole game birds just aren't used enough anymore, and they should be, so let this recipe be a springboard for exploring birds that have more flavor than the white and yellow stuff now sold as chicken. Free range chicken is good, and is recommended if you are into chicken for the taste, and not just because it's considered low fat.

STEAMED ASPARAGUS WITH PROSCUITTO AND APPLE AIOLI

10	asparagus
5	thin slices of prosciutto
1 cup	apple juice
1 frond	tiger lily

Steam asparagus in apple juice and tiger lily to a firm "crisp." This will only take about two minutes. Chill.

Wrap one slice prosciutto around two asparagus spears so that you have five wraps. Chill.

AIOLI

1	apple, peeled and chopped, granny smith
3	crushed garlic cloves
¼ teaspoon	cardamom
½ teaspoon	salt and pepper mix
1 cup	virgin olive oil
1	juice of one lemon

In food processor, puree apple with garlic, cardamom, and s/p mix. Slowly, in thin stream pour in olive oil. When it is thick add the lemon juice. Chill.

2 tablespoons	diced red bell pepper
2 tablespoons	diced mango or papaya

The plate: Set the prosciutto wrapped asparagus on the appetiser plate. Place a tablespoon of the aioli in the center of the asparagus with a little falling over onto the plate. Sprinkle the diced pepper and mango around the plate.

SWEET SOY, CAYENNE AND GINGER BEER ROASTED DUCKLING

1	whole duck, preferably 3 pound, no more than 4
1 cup	Indonesian sweet soy sauce
1 ounce	mix of jasmine and oolong tea leaves
1 teaspoon	cayenne pepper
1 tablespoon	grated garlic
1 tablespoon	ground allspice
12 ounces	ginger beer

Remove any neck or gizzards from the cavity of the duck. Thoroughly wash the duck under cold water. Pat dry inside and out. Cut off any tail fat from the end of the duck cavity between the legs.

Mix all of the ingredients except for the soy and ginger beer.

Rub the whole duck with the sweet soy sauce. Then rub in the spices.

Refrigerate and marinade overnight.

STUFFING

1 stalk	celery, diced
1	white onion, diced
1	boniato or taro root, diced
½ cup	chopped cashews
1 tablespoon	whole butter
1 cup	bread crumbs
1 tablespoon	Caribbean jerk seasoning mix
2	whole eggs, beaten

Chapter Three • ISLAND *and* OASIS

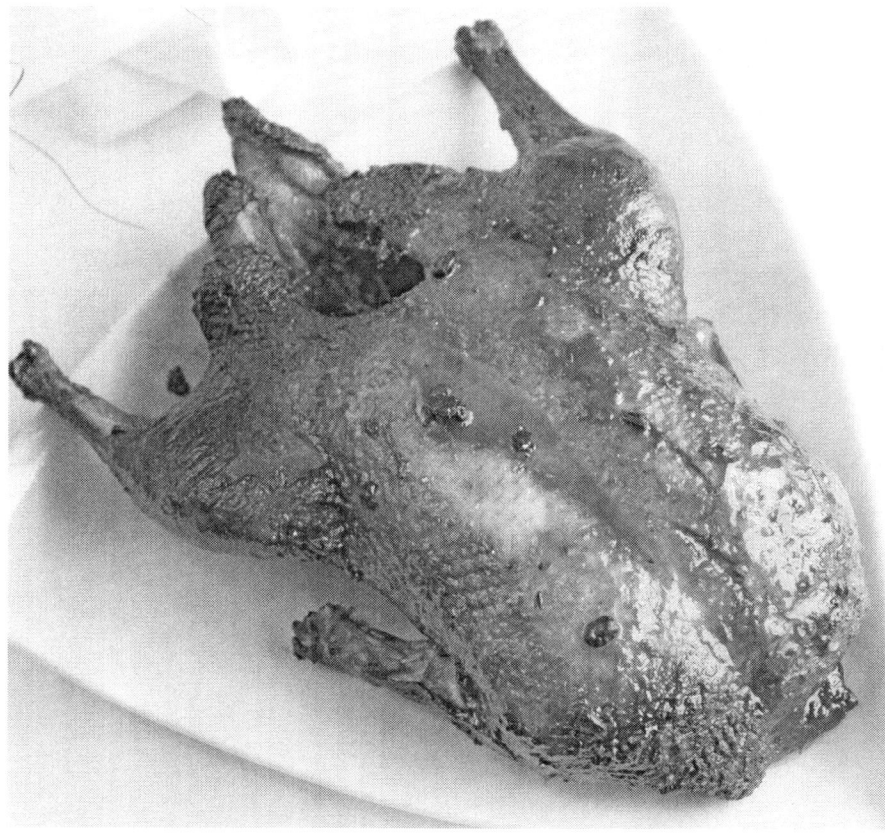
Sweet Soy, Cayennes and Ginger Beer Roasted Duckling

Sauté the celery, onion, boniato and cashews in the butter until crisped. Chill.

Mix the sauté with bread crumbs, jerk and egg. Refrigerate.

Remove duck from refrigerator and fill the cavity with stuffing.

Preheat oven to 375°. Place duck on roasting pan breast down. Roast for thirty minutes. Turn duck over so that breasts and legs are facing up.

As the duck roasts pour ginger beer over and into the duck every few minutes for the first thirty minutes. The duck is done when the skin is moist and slightly crisp (odd distinction, but you will notice this as it cooks), the internal temperature is 165°, and the juices run clear when you pierce the thickest part of the thigh.

Remove from oven and let the duck rest for 20 minutes. This resting time allows the meat to shrink back together and also lets the juices settle. When meat is cut too soon after coming out of the oven it will tear apart, rather than slice.

While the duck is resting skim the fat off of the remaining cooking liquid in the pan. Put the pan back into the stove and let the juices cook for fifteen minutes.

Mix 2 tablespoons of melted butter with 1 tablespoon of flour. Stir this into the cooking juices while they are very hot. Return to oven. Cook for fifteen minutes. It will be a little thick, and bursting with flavor. This is your sauce.

Remove stuffing and set it aside.

Cut the duck in half. Cut the thigh and leg section away from the breast. Put the duck back into the sauce and turn it around until all of it has been coated with the sauce. Return the duck pan to the oven with the oven turned down to 300°. Heat for fifteen minutes.

Now, what goes good with duck? How about fried fresh corn kernels and steamed bok choy? You bet!

FRIED CORN

2	ears fresh corn, cut the kernels off
1 tablespoon	minced fresh ginger
½	small jalapeno pepper, seeded and minced
1 tablespoon	dark soy sauce
2 tablespoons	blend oil

In a high sided skillet or wok, heat the oil on high, add ginger and jalapeno, stir and add corn kernels, keep it on high as this is fast cooking, you know stir fry, add soy sauce and continue cooking for one minute. Total cooking time is about three minutes.

STEAMED BOK CHOY

Don't forget to get out your bamboo steamer, or steamer fan, or basket for this.

1 pound	baby bok choy
1 tablespoon	minced scallion
1 tablespoon	Chinese black vinegar, or red wine vinegar
1 teaspoon	dried chilli flakes

Toss all of this together in a bowl and let it set for 10 minutes.

Your steaming water should have 1 bay leaf in it. Bring the water to a boil and set the steamer in place. Steam for 5 minutes. Remove, drain.

1 teaspoon	sugar

Toss the bok choy with the sugar and set on plate. Arrange duck over the bok choy. Spoon the fried corn around the duck. Spoon the stuffing between the breast and thigh/leg portions. Pour a couple of ounces of the sauce over the duck.

Eat! Guess you didn't think duck could be this tender, did you? As an aside, most American duck is raised on Long Island, and are descended from three ducks and a drake imported from China in the late eighteenth century.

This is not the neatest meal, so be prepared to be a little sloppy.

DESSERT

You will need a 9 x 5 x 2 ¾ inch loaf pan for this bread. As a helpful hint here, measure out all your ingredients before starting the mixing stage. You can put the flour, baking powder, salt, ginger, cinnamon, allspice, and cloves together. You can also premix the butter, brown sugar, molasses and honey. Put them aside until you are ready to begin. Total time for this dish including baking is about 90 minutes

GINGERBREAD WITH APRICOT

2 cups	all purpose flour
1 teaspoon	baking powder
½ teaspoon	salt
1½ teaspoon	ground ginger
½ teaspoon	allspice
½ teaspoon	ground clove

Sift and set aside

4 ounces	softened unsalted butter
½ cup	light brown sugar
½ cup	unsulfured molasses
¼ cup	honey

Mash together and set aside

2	large eggs
½ cup	sour cream
1 cup	peeled, chopped and mashed apricots

(If you can't get fresh apricots, use preserves. It'll just be a little sweeter)

Preheat oven to 350°. Grease the loaf pan with butter and flour, shake out excess flour.

In a mixing bowl cream the butter, brown sugar, molasses and honey with a hand held electric mixer. You have more control this way as opposed to doing it directly in an electric mixer. Blend until smooth.

Add the eggs, one at a time, and mix well before adding the second egg. Mix some more. Now add the sour cream, mix. Add the mashed apricots and mix until it is all combined.

Add the dry ingredients and continue mixing for about two minutes until it is relatively smooth and blended.

Scrape into the loaf pan and bake in center of oven for one hour.

Do the regular test of sticking a toothpick in the center of the bread; it will come out clean when the bread is baked.

Let bread cool for 10 minutes or so. Run a knife around the edges of the pan to loosen the bread. Tap the pan around the edges, turn it over onto a wire rack and shake out the bread. Let it cool just a little, about 15 minutes. You want to serve it warm.

Now you just slice and eat like a cake. If you want to you can add a scoop of ice cream, or whipped cream and fresh fruit.

Chapter Three • ISLAND *and* OASIS

*Together in a rocking chair
on a porch at sunrise,
watching moths and fireflies
lay down to sleep,
singing birthday songs
to the God unseen inside
the orange she holds and smells,
and so he watches her,
watches the colors change,
her bare feet curling, pushing,
rocking, rocking,
rocking their lives into the day.
He reaches over to hold
her hand, tells of a walk
through lemon groves
and a white sand road,
by the sea he travelled,
in awe, in search,
downtown to a store*

where all the great mysteries
of kites and wind,
of ginger and coconuts,
of mango and gin
joined together at the whim
of the old shopkeeper.
So together, so yearning,
and they felt the lure,
they felt the movement
of voices adored,
of sea shores and late meals...
Hours later, still hungry,
still rocking and holding hands,
still singing to the God
in oranges and Chinese kites,
still dreaming of the path to the store
that's always there...

CHAPTER FOUR

FLOWERING of AMERICA

*Behind the hedges
in the backyard
we kissed.
In the kitchen
by the stove we kissed.
After work
in the grocery store
we lingered
by the boxes
of ripening guava.
Thick tropical
scent griped us,
and we kissed.
It seemed the fruit
was beginning
to rot.*

*I remember every
place we've been
by the times
we touched,
by the love when
you pressed your
lips to mine.
It's too sweet
but I really don't care
life tastes better
with this to share.*

Chapter Four • FLOWERING *of* AMERICA

*T*HIS IS THE FINAL CHAPTER of our journey....for now. We explore our home, the most mystifying and ordinary of places where all the world is there waiting for us to come to them. Yet we cannot go to all the parts of the map, so we bring the map to us, here, in the kitchen where love and the expression of love is experienced through the senses. The rest is there between you, in the center, over the table where the love thought and, the love felt creates the being we call us and we.

By this point of the book you should have learned to share and cook together in the kitchen. You should know how to shop together, how to compare and agree upon the best vegetable, cut of meat, and fruit. Hopefully, you will have found even greater treasures not mentioned here in the grocery stores and markets.

There are four grilled entrees. I hope you have a grill. If you do not own a grill I have included alternate recipes for oven roasting and broiling. Grilling is tricky, but it really is a lot of fun, and you will ask yourself after a successful meal why you don't grill out more often. I do every time. We all too frequently associate the outdoor barbecue and grill (Grilling and barbecuing are different) as something for parties and larger gatherings, and they are worthy affairs. But, this is still about romance and the feelings of an early moon, citronella candles, smoky aromatics filling the breezes, and learning to work together in the kitchen. Simply sitting and chatting do more to meld the spirits of two people than all the finest restaurants in the world. Think relaxed and free.

In case you haven't noticed by now, I use a lot of cream. Can't help it. No matter what changes occur in health and food I cannot get away from a love of cream. You can of course eliminate it in some dishes by using a no-cream cream recipe included in this chapter. As far as dessert goes, there are soy products, coconut cream, and the non-dairy products in the grocery store. I personally find soy products quite tasty. So, as with all things we decide to include in our lives, the choice is yours. I just choose to take the cholesterol risk in favor of flavor. The point is don't eat cream and dairy products all the time, balance the way you eat on a daily and life basis, not by the occasional splurge on an extravagant meal.

As an aside, my concern with California cuisine is located primarily in the late 1970s and early 1980s during the reign of Northern California cookery in the hands of Alice Waters, John Ash, Jeremiah Tower, Mendocino Cafe, a few lamented and long gone bistros in the Mendocino and Sonoma Valleys, the food writings of Lukins and Rosso, and the good people I worked with at St. Orres on the Mendocino Coast, notably the beautifully souled Naomi, Rosemary, Gretchen, Ted, Kim Cheen, and Kiko. If only they knew: It was during my time there that my love of the new cuisines of America and Hong Kong was first nourished. Every meal was memorable and every conversation imbedded into my life. And yes, I associate the food with the people I was fortunate enough to work and dine with during those early days of my courtship with the East and West. Every time I throw a flower on a plate or drink a fruit laced sparkling water I think of them all.

One of my favorite afternoons was spent at the St Jean winery with the staff of St. Orres, and the owners, wine master and staff of the winery. We ate traditional cassoulet with hard French bread, we drank the vintner's choice of wines, and we sat at a long picnic table under the shade of what I recall as a magnolia. I was in Eden for those two hours. And for all that were there I may not remember your names, but I do remember the feelings of love and companionship. Proustian? Yeah.

And today, new feelings, new foods, new explorations into the palate and the heart. The former grandiosity of the banquet is replaced by the picture perfect, life humming moment of sharing an appetizer plate and tasting the same tastes, the same inspirations and secrets. And when you take that first bite and look at each other, taste, smile and nod, and perhaps reach over to her hand, you know a new memory has been created. The love may or may not last forever, but the perfect moment will (and this is for my beloved of black halters and ginger scented skin), and then again live as a sense of love, a moment encased in in food and beauty, it will last forever.

Chapter Four • FLOWERING *of* AMERICA

• *THE FIRST MENU* •

SPINACH AND ROSE PETAL SALAD, DRUNKEN RAISINS, ALMONDS

RICE VINEGAR, CARDAMOM, AND SICHUAN PEPPER.

GRILLED SALMON STUFFED WITH POBLANO PEPPERS, ASIAN PEAR AND THYME, SIDES OF GRILLED CORN AND POTATOES

KIWI WHITE CHOCOLATE MOUSSE WITH CRÈME DE CASSIS

THE SALAD

Spinach and Rose Petal Salad, Drunken Raisins, Almonds

This is a romantic salad with a sharp contrast of delicate and bold. The roses must be organic, as it isn't good to eat pesticides, so when purchasing please be certain of their origins. If roses are not available then use lilies or violets, even honeysuckle will do in a pinch. Use the small leaf spinach. Golden raisins only. Black raisins are too intense, and with the wine marinade you want the subtlety to come through, and here the kind of wine you use does make a difference. If possible use a Riesling for the light sweetness to balance the sharper flavor of the golden raisins.

The vinegar, oil, cardamom and Sichuan pepper add a light and spicy aromatic sense to the salad. This all sounds complicated, doesn't it? Well, sometimes a salad has many faces, and this is one that with a few carefully chosen ingredients is able to portray the Asian, American, Italian and California side of our culinary heritage.

SPINACH AND ROSE PETAL SALAD, DRUNKEN RAISINS, ALMONDS, RICE VINEGAR, CARDAMOM, AND SICHUAN PEPPER.

20 leaves	washed and stemmed spinach
2	roses, organic grown, no pesticides
1 tablespoon	white raisins soaked in white wine for 36 hours
1 tablespoon	toasted, sliced almonds
4 tablespoons	rice vinegar
4 tablespoons	walnut oil
6 seeds	cardamom, crushed
6 seeds	Sichuan peppercorns, crushed

Lay the spinach in a spiral around the plate. Sprinkle raisins and almonds over spinach leaves. Mix vinegar, oil, cardamom and Sichuan peppercorns by whisking in mixing bowl. Pour over spinach. Pick rose petals and scatter over the salad. That's it, you've got it made and ready to eat. This is a salad you eat slowly, with warm lime scented spring water.

GRILLED SALMON STUFFED WITH POBLANO PEPPERS, ASIAN PEAR AND THYME, SIDES OF GRILLED CORN AND POTATOES

Asian pears look a little like a large green-orange apple, the taste is super sweet and crunchy, when real ripe they are soft, but at this stage the flavor is a bit bitter. Go for the crisp ones. The flesh looks like a pear. The shape like an apple. They are sometimes called apple-pears. Go figure.

SALMON

2 - 1½ inch thick	7 oz salmon, center cut fillet
2 tablespoons	poblano, diced, half a pepper
2 tablespoons	Asian pear, quarter of a pear
1 teaspoon	fresh thyme leaves, please only fresh

Chapter Four • FLOWERING of AMERICA

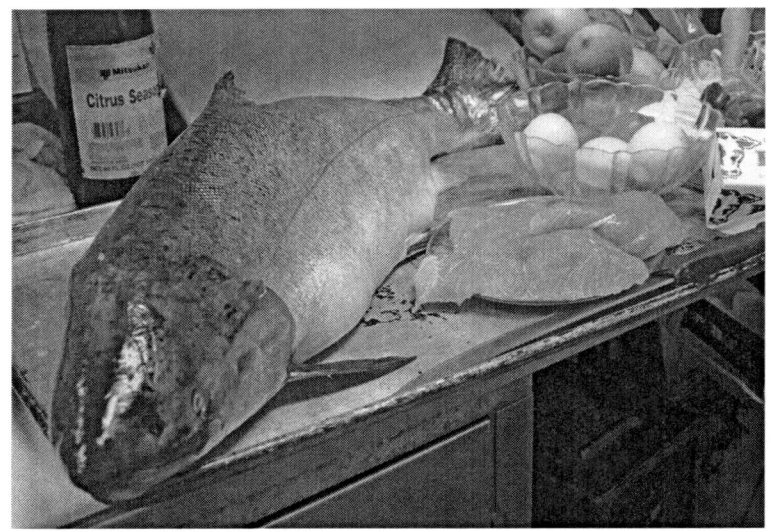

Grilled Salmon stuffed with poblano peppers, Asian pear and thyme, sides of grilled corn and potatoes

Make an incision across the thickest front part of the salmon about an inch and a half across and two thirds into the meat. Mix the other ingredients and stuff the salmon.

1 tablespoon	olive oil
1	lemon zested, use the zest
1 teaspoon	salt and pepper mix

Rub the salmon with olive oil, lemon zest and salt and pepper. Refrigerate for one hour.

2 ears	yellow corn, husk, brush and wrap the husk back around the corn
8	red potatoes, or taro cut into half inch slices

As always, if you do not have a grill or if the weather is not quite right then bake in the oven.

Grill: Use apple wood chips with your charcoal briquettes. Sometimes salmon is best grilled on high fast heat, but for this one you need to slow grill in order for the flavor of the stuffing to cook and permeate the flesh.

After the charcoal has turned gray place the corn and potatoes on the grill. Cook ten minutes. Add apple chip to coals. Cook five minutes.

Put the salmon on the grill. Put lid on grill.

Grill the fish at least six inches above the coals. Cook 10 minutes per side.

Remember that I prefer to use a Smoke and Grill type grill. It helps to put the lid on and let the smoke do its job.

The First Menu

OVEN

Cover the salmon with Asian pear slices and bay leaves, 3 leaves and a half a pear for each salmon.

Roast the corn and potatoes at 400° for 10 minutes before putting salmon into oven. Then cook them all together for the remainder of the time at 325° for fifteen minutes.

Now I rarely use any kind of sauce or extra butter with a meal like this, it just seems superfluous. But a bread sure is a nice touch:

FRIED SWEET POTATO BREAD
for 8 puffs:

1 cup	pureed sweet potato (cooked)
½ teaspoon	mix of clove, cinnamon and allspice
1 tablespoon	peanut oil
2¼ cups	all purpose flour

Mix spice, potato, oil and flour in bowl, sprinkle with water as you knead until it comes together without being sticky. Knead till smooth, dust with flour as you knead. Food processor: flour, potato, spice, oil and mix, add water until a ball of dough forms on the blade. Process thirty seconds while turning machine on and off every five seconds as you go. Remove and cover with a moist towel. Let rest ten minutes.

Cut dough in fourths, or halves if doing smaller amount. Shape into ropes and cut into eight equal portions. Cover with moist towel and let the dough rest for five minutes.

Roll into three inch balls. Remember to dust with flour to prevent sticking. Don't stack, but do keep covered with that wet towel.

Fry 1 at a time at 375°. It will sink then rise, push it down with a slotted spoon and cook until the bread puffs, about thirty seconds. Turn it over and cook another fifteen seconds. Lightly browned. It'll puff up like a balloon. Serve immediately.

Variation: *Cilantro and green peas, pumpkin, white potato, basil. Or you can just make a simple by the book cornbread. Ok, I do like that hillbilly cornbread mix that comes in the little foil packets. There. I said it. Just mix with milk, egg and bake, that stuff's great at times.*

Chapter Four • **FLOWERING** *of* **AMERICA**

DESSERT

This mousse is going to be a little different from the one in the last chapter; here we will not use whipped egg whites. The chocolate will be liquid and warm when whipped in with the cream.

It will still be light and mousse-like, just creamy not fluffy. My reason for doing this is so that you learn another method in case you have an aversion to eggs, also just for the hell of it because it tastes good.

KIWI WHITE CHOCOLATE MOUSSE WITH CREME DE CASSIS

2	ripe kiwi, peeled and diced
3 oz	white chocolate
10 oz	whipping cream
4 tablespoons	granulated sugar
¼ teaspoon	vanilla extract
2 oz	crème de cassis

Melt the white chocolate with one ounce of cream over very low heat, or in the microwave oven. Stir so that it is smooth. Set in warm place.

In a metal bowl, Whip the cream to soft peak and add sugar and vanilla.

Stir Crème de Cassis into the chocolate. And then begin whipping the cream again. As you whisk, at a moderate speed and in a thin stream, pour in the blended chocolate and liquor. When you have thick peaks in the cream you are finished.

Now, fold in the kiwi. If it seems delicate at this point, that is OK, when you refrigerate the mousse it will firm up. Refrigerate for at least an hour, but not more that a day in advance. The kiwi will become bitter, so it is best to make this dish close to the time you will be eating.

Divide the mousse into old-fashioned champagne glasses, martini glasses, or sherbet dishes. Top with grated white chocolate, mint and whatever fruit you have handy, like blueberry, peach, kiwi, raspberry or strawberry.

The First Menu

A MAN ALONE
Opening and closing the cabinets
and refrigerator, staring at the spices,
pacing the room,
shrugging my shoulders,
nothing looks good, but still I'm hungry.
You're at work and I miss you.
I want to talk, I want to do something,
anything together right now.
Ritz crackers and peanut butter,
a slice of fresh peach,
and then a cup of blueberry yogurt,
a mug of iced coffee,
I start to fill up, but still...
Funny how it works, this whole thing
about becoming a man,
and becoming whole and independent,
and yet I like needing you,
I like desiring you,
I just wish I could eat a full meal
without you...
I don't know, food comes alive with you,
it surely does, and always will.
I wish you would get home soon.

Ginger, Lily & Sweet Fire

Chapter Four • **FLOWERING** *of* **AMERICA**

• *THE SECOND MENU* •
PORTOBELLA MUSHROOM PIZZA STUFFED WITH MANGO, JALAPENO, YELLOW PEAR TOMATO, RED PEPPER, CILANTRO AND FETA

BASMATI RICE WITH LEMON, BASIL AND ROSEMARY ROASTED VEGETABLES

PISTACHIO BISCOTTI WITH AN ICED LATTE

APPETIZER

Yellow pear tomatoes are very small tomatoes that are yellow and are shaped like pears. The taste is sweet and a touch fruity, but still distinctly tomato. They are a treat. Pear tomatoes are also red, and tiger striped, and when placed together on a plate they do make for a nice presentation, and best of all, all you have to do is put them next to complimentary colors and flavors. If you can't find the yellow pear tomato, then look for yellow tomatoes, and the taste is close, but more tomatoey. Available in late summer.

PORTABELLO MUSHROOM PIZZA

2	portobella mushrooms large, at least two to
three inches	across
1 tablespoon	extra virgin olive oil
2 tablespoons	diced mango
1 teaspoon	diced and seeded jalapeno
1 each	yellow pear tomato, quartered
1 teaspoon	red bell pepper, diced fine
½ teaspoon	chopped, fresh cilantro
2 tablespoons	grated firm feta cheese
½ teaspoon	salt and pepper mix
1 cup	boiling water
1 ounce	red wine, or red wine vinegar

Blanch the mushroom caps in a boiling water and red wine for one minute. Remove and drain. Sprinkle inside of mushrooms with salt and pepper mix. Pour extra virgin olive oil in cap and rub in as well. Mix mango, peppers, jalapeno, cilantro and feta together and put equal portions in each mushroom cap.

Bake in 400° oven for fifteen minutes. That's it.

BASMATI RICE WITH LEMON, BASIL AND ROSEMARY ROASTED VEGETABLES

If you have a rice cooker this is the place to use it. They cost under $20 and are worth four times the price. Otherwise, you can cook this on the stove top in a sauce pot or in a wok. Basmati rice is one of my favorite rices; it is a full flavored rice that has a slight popcorn smell while it is cooking.

THE RICE

1½ cups	Dry weight basmati rice
3 cups	Water
3 tablespoons	Olive oil
1 tablespoon	Lemon zest
½ teaspoon	Salt and pepper mix
10 leaves	Fresh rosemary (pretend there is no such thing as dried rosemary).

Combine and cook. Bring to boil, turn down to simmer. Cover pot and cook on low for twenty minutes.

While the rice is cooking roast the vegetables. You will use the lesser used vegetables called patty pan, Japanese eggplant, and bok choy, leeks and sugar snap peas. The seasonings are slight, just butter, soy and garlic.

ROASTED VEGETABLES

¼ cup each	diced: patty pan squash, Japanese eggplant, baby bok choy, celery root, leeks
5	sugar snap peas, sliced in half
4 tablespoons	whole unsalted butter
4 tablespoons	mushroom soy sauce

Preheat oven to 375°. Dice the vegetables and mix with the soy sauce. You need aluminum foil here, so roll out a piece about two feet long. Lay the vegetables in the foil, and roll them up into a tight cylinder. Pinch the ends so that they are tightly closed. Cook for the twenty minutes that it takes for the rice to cook.

When everything is cooked:

Divide the rice between two plates. Carefully unroll the vegetables, using a kitchen towel or tongs helps. Divide the vegetables over the two

Chapter Four • FLOWERING of AMERICA

rice plates. That's all you do. This has to be the easiest thing I've ever suggested.

DESSERT

PISTACHIO BISCOTTI WITH AN ICED LATTE

This is a cookie. This is an old school Italian crisp cookie that goes with either wine or coffee. Take your pick. Here we will make espresso with brown sugar and cream, refrigerate and enjoy. You will need it, making the biscotti is work, but it is work that can be shared. Forgive me the indulgence of giving a recipe here that goes far beyond the meal for two. It is for 4 dozen, cookies, yep, 48 cookies. You will thank me after you eat a few. They keep well in a sealed container and are great with yogurt for breakfast, as well as being a nice finish to a light meal.

The recipe is based on the Cantucci Di Prato from the Il Fornaio Baking Book by Franco Galli. Read it. It's one of the best professional Italian bread books I've read and used.

Things to know before you begin: you <u>must</u> bake in the top two thirds of your oven. Do not overwork the dough. When it is mixed it is mixed. When you have rolled it into a cylinder it is rolled. Do no more. The more you work dough the tougher it gets. For some dough this is OK, but not here.

Pistachio biscotti

You will have to do this without an electric mixer, unless you have a professional model it will burn out. You see, this is a rather bulky dough. If you must use a mixer stop after the texture is kind of rough, then mix the rest of the way with floured hands.

It is best to go ahead and measure everything out and set aside in small containers around the cutting/mixing board. If you are doing this together then one can mix and the other measure. Marble is the best breadboard to use. If you don't have marble use a highly finished wooden board. You also need two mixing bowls, a stiff wire whisk, the cutting board, two baking pans, parchment paper, a measuring cup, measuring spoons, a fork, a sharp knife and a little extra butter to grease the pan. And probably a shot of espresso before you start. I suggest a Cubano, which is espresso with a teaspoon of brown sugar.

PISTACHIO BISCOTTI

½ cup	pistachio halves, raw, green, not the bleached white ones
1 cup	all purpose flour
¼ cup	sugar
¼ teaspoon	baking soda
1/8 teaspoon	salt
1½ tablespoons	unsalted, soft butter
1	whole egg, large
1	small egg yolk, it has to be small or the dough will be too elastic
½ teaspoon	vanilla extract
1 teaspoon	fresh grated orange zest

NOTE: You will also need a little extra flour to dust the breadboard with, so keep a small pile at the edge of the board.

Toast half the pistachios, and then crush them, not powder, just crush. Set aside.

In one mixing bowl mix the pistachios, flour, sugar, baking powered, salt and butter. In the other bowl combine the eggs, vanilla, and orange zest, and whisk with the fork until blended.

Now, one person holds the flour bowl and a stiff whisk while the other pours in the egg mixture into the flour. Beat the mix the whole time it is being poured in, and continue to beat until a rather rough and granular dough forms. You have to mix kind of fast for this to happen.

Flour the board. Lay the dough on the board. Knead until everything is almost smooth. Stop. Let the dough rest for fifteen minutes. Cover it with a damp cloth.

Divide the dough into two foot long portions one inch round.

Place the parchment paper on the baking pan and grease it with the extra butter. Set the dough cylinders on the pan about two to three inches apart.

Chapter Four • **FLOWERING** *of* **AMERICA**

Dust your hand with flour and flatten the dough down until it is a half-inch thick.

Bake at 350° for 20 minutes. The cookie dough will be golden brown, any darker and it's burnt. Take it out and let cool a while, 10 to 20 minutes. Put the cylinders on the cutting board. Slice the cookies on a diagonal: / a half-inch thick.

Line the two baking pans with parchment paper and grease again. Place the cookies on the pans. Bake again at 350° for 10 minutes. They will be a light tan color. Remove and let cool.

You're there. They will keep in a sealed container for at least two weeks.

ICED LATTE

Sounds cool, tastes cool, is cool. For those who don't drink alcohol a good latte is like a Romanèe Conti to a wine connoisseur. (SEE GLOSSARY for a list and explanation of coffees.)

6 tablespoons	fine grind espresso
4 cups	water
3 tablespoons	unrefined sugar
4 ounces	heavy cream, lightly whipped
2 cups	crushed ice

Make the coffee in your preferred coffee brewer. Stir in 3 tablespoons of unrefined sugar, also known as Sugar in the Raw. After it has brewed let it set at room temperature. Refrigerate.

When it's time for dessert pour the coffee into a glass packed with crushed ice and top with the cream. That's it. Sit back, nibble the biscotti and sip your iced latte. Take your time. Savor.

The Third Menu

• THE THIRD MENU •

BOSTON LETTUCE WITH NASTURTIUM FLOWERS, RED HOTS, RED ONION AND WASABI VINAIGRETTE

SAUTÉED WAHOO/ONO WITH POMEGRANATE AND TOASTED CASHEW VELOUTE

PORT WINE CHEESE, GRAHAM CRACKERS, GOLDEN DELICIOUS APPLES AND FRESH FIGS

This is a good menu for an easy night. The salad is a mix of whimsy, California gardens and Japanese fire. Nasturtiums have a slight peppery flavor, are pretty and are easy to grow. The flower and the leaves are edible. Red hots are red hots, the kind you see in corner quickie marts. Sure it's candy, but it's candy that has eye appeal as well as a nice tang. I serve this salad whenever the flowers are available, and when I'm just feeling a little silly. It will put a smile on your face from both the look and the taste, and you can't beat that. The wasabi dressing is not pure fire, so don't fret about it, the orange and amount used make it an interesting and complex dressing. Boston lettuce is a soft textured, lime green lettuce with a delicate watery flavor.

Ono/wahoo is a tropical fish that is in the mackerel family. It is mild, light and slightly salty depending on the waters it is caught in. I like it a lot and if it's ever in your market, or if any restaurant you eat at has it as a special be sure to order it, you will be pleased. As far as the sauce goes, yes here we are again with the fruit and nut combinations. They work and the end results are always surprising, and sometimes even operatic.

The dessert is simple. Just buy the highest quality cheese and fruit, and you will feel your evening slide from the vibrant flare of the salad and entree into a mellow sense of a night well lived.

SALAD

BOSTON LETTUCE WITH RED HOTS, RED ONION, NASTURTIUM FLOWERS AND WASABI VINAIGRETTE

1	head Boston, pull whole leaves off base
1 tablespoon	red hots, the kind you get at fast food stores
½	thin sliced red onion
10	nasturtium flowers

Chapter Four • **FLOWERING** *of* **AMERICA**

WASABI VINAIGRETTE

1 bulb	shallot, this will equal a tablespoon
1 tablespoon	wasabi powder
½ cup	blend oil
2 cups	orange juice
2 tablespoons	equal black and white sesame seeds
3 tablespoons	honey
3 tablespoons	apple cider vinegar
2 tablespoons	soy sauce

Place chopped shallot and wasabi powder in blender. Turn machine on and slowly add oil. After the oil, add each one at a time with the machine running: Honey, then orange juice, soy, and vinegar. Blend until it is emulsified. Chill.

If you prefer the dressing to be thicker just add a tablespoon of sour cream or soft cooked sushi rice. For the sushi rice all you have to do for is add two tablespoon of cooked sushi rice to the blender, and then add the other ingredients in the order they are written in the recipe. For the sour cream add at the end.

Pull the root end out of the lettuce and break off the first half-inch of leaf connecting to the root. No knife here, it'll bruise the leaves. Lay the whole leaves out in a circle on the plates. Large leaves on the bottom, and then go from there to the smallest so that it looks like an opening flower. Are you with me?

Drizzle three ounces of the vinaigrette over the leaves.

Arrange the flowers randomly on the leaves. Lay the red onion slices under the flowers to give the appearance of a stem. Sprinkle the red hots over the salad. Pretty, isn't it?

THE ENTRÉE

Wahoo/ono is just one of those fish who you wish was more available A member of the mackerel family, it has a good oil content, has spiral white flesh, mild and a bit salty. Rockfish is good, it's just important to sell it as rockfish. Unless you are familiar with the fish charts, and it's a good thing to know, then you are at the mercy of the grocer. Buy what is freshest.

As all the books say, it is best to buy the whole fish. Check the eyes for glassy-ness, firm red gills, flesh that bounces back, and most important: no smell. Truly fresh fish does not have a dominant odor. It will smell of the sea. I like the smell. If you have ever spent time on the ocean you know the seductive aroma of high tide. Store the fish between 34° and 42°. You must keep it cold, not frozen, just cold. Also, as mentioned in chapter One, if you must freeze the fish or buy it frozen: it cooks better if you do not thaw it out. You don't lose any of the valuable flavors by cooking directly from a frozen state. This is an important point to remember.

If you can't find a good fresh wahoo, then small wreckfish or even tilapia will do just as well. White sea bass and striped bass are also recommended. White sea bass (true bass, not Patagonian tooth fish: sea bass), one of the best tasting fish along with Opah and Mong Chong, is becoming over fished, so let your conscience be your guide. Striped bass and tilapia are farm raised fish. The taste and texture will not be the same, but diversity is a plus in this world.

ABOUT POMEGRANATES:

You will prepare this dish during the winter months when pomegranates are available. November is the best. Remember the Greek myth about Persephone and Hades? She was kidnapped and was bound to stay in the underworld if she ate or drank anything. She refused up to the last minute when she ate six pomegranate seeds. She had to return to Hades for six months every year. Hence, her mother, Demeter, the goddess of corn mourned her absence for those six months: Winter. The pomegranate (some say quince, others apple) is also placed in the Garden of Eden. It is a fertility symbol. When you open the fruit there are at least a hundred bright red seeds exposed. In classical myth it also represents the womb. Hence, it is also considered an aphrodisiac, and that's a good thing. That's your lesson in symbolism for the day.

Do this over a plate: To seed a pomegranate cut the top off and insert your fingers into the opening, with your other hand pull the fruit apart. You will see a lot of juicy red seeds; this is the edible part. You can't eat the flesh. Gently remove the seeds by breaking the rest of the body of the fruit apart, and then with your fingertips push the seeds out onto the plate. They will taste tart and sweet, and have a slight crunch to the bite. If they are at all bitter then the fruit is not ripe, or you are eating some of the skin. You will get a lot of red around the kitchen if you are not careful, as you will find out the seeds will stain just about any cloth they come in contact with.

Chapter Four • FLOWERING of AMERICA

Oh yeah, grenadine was originally made from pomegranate juice. Grenadine is now sort of a red sugar water, but if you ever have to go for a substitute for a sauce then a mix of grenadine, cranberry juice and black currant juice will come close to the deep flavor of pomegranate. If you must, there is nothing wrong with doing this for a sauce.

Now, to the cooking:

SAUTEED WAHOO WITH A POMEGRANATE AND TOASTED CASHEW VELOUTE

2 7 ounce	wahoo fillets, boned and skinned
¼ cup	all purpose flour
2 ounces	blend oil (70% corn, 30% olive)
3 tablespoons	pomegranate seeds
24	whole cashew halves
¼ cup	cranberry juice
¼ cup	black currant juice
¼ cup	pear juice (apple if you can't find it)
2 tablespoons	whole unsalted butter
¼ teaspoon	salt
½ teaspoon	Vietnamese chili paste (sambal oelek)

Dust the snapper in the flour by quickly rolling it around in the flour and then shaking off any excess flour. In a sauté pan heated on high with the blend oil just beginning to smoke, slide the fish into the pan. Agitate the pan (yeah, yeah, call it names) and sauté for three minutes. Turn the fish over and turn the heat down to medium. Sauté another three minutes. Pour the oil off into a metal container. Throw the used oil away when it has cooled down.

Now, you must act quickly for the following steps: add the cashews and cook until they begin to tan, then add the pomegranate seeds, cook one minute. Remove the fish and hold in a warm oven, 225° degrees.

Add the juices and scrape the bottom of the pan to lift up any flour that may have stuck to the pan. Don't worry, this is good stuff.

Turn heat back up to high. Add the sambal oelek and the salt. Let the liquid boil, this is the stage where all the flavors come together. It's the magic part of cooking where you begin to understand how flavors combine.

When the sauce has reduced to 2/3 cup, turn the heat off and stir in the whole butter. Don't let it get too hot at this part of the process, as the sauce will break. It breaks when the butter's fat separate from the juices. If this happens, return to the heat and add a couple of tablespoons of cream and stir it in until the sauce is smooth. The butter cream softens the tartness of the sauce. To see for yourself, taste before and after adding the butter...Big change, huh? That's the magic. The beauty is how fruit combines with the gentle creaminess of butter and coats the tongue just enough to impart the essences of the flavors of the chili, pomegranate and cashew.

Remove the fish from the oven and set on serving plates. Pour the sauce over the fish.

It's OK to eat roasted new potatoes or even a hearty baked potato with this dish.

Now for the classic side vegetable, and I mean classic, as in right out of Escoffier, the man whose methods all Western chefs must master before moving on to the other parts of the world, the father of Haute Cuisine.

GINGER CARROTS AND BLACK GRAPES

14	peeled baby carrots
¼	onion, minced
1 tablespoon	whole unsalted butter
1 tablespoon	fresh ginger, minced, must be fresh
1 cup	orange juice
1 cup	water
10	black grapes
4 tablespoons	honey
1 tablespoon	brown sugar
1 tablespoon	cornstarch mixed with 2 tablespoons cold water for thickening the liquid
1 teaspoon	salt

Chapter Four • FLOWERING *of* AMERICA

Sauté the ginger and onion in the butter. Add the carrots and stir in with the sauté. Add the liquid, honey, brown sugar and salt.

Bring to boil and cook five minutes. Add the black grapes (seedless, Concord if you can) and fold in with the carrots. Continue to boil for another five minutes on a medium bubble of a boil. This is medium heat. Stir in the cornstarch and water mix (it's called slurry). The liquid will lightly thicken. That's it. It will have reduced by more than half and will have a rather mellow flavor.

I hope you enjoy this; it is one of my favorite meals.

DESSERT

PORT WINE CHEESE, GRAHAM CRACKERS, GOLDEN DELICIOUS APPLES AND FRESH FIGS

If you can't find fresh figs use Japanese Persimmons. Fear not, figs and persimmons are good food, they are sweet and succulent and much too over looked in our dining experience.

4 ounces	port wine cheese
10	graham crackers
1	golden delicious apple, 10 slices
4	figs, quartered

The beauty is in the eating. Put the cheese in the center of a large oval platter. Fan the apple slices around the cheese. Fan the crackers around the apple. Lay the figs out around the crackers with the pulp side up. Eat, and chat the cherished moments away into the night.

The Third Menu

What of quiet meals in quiet gardens,
as if we were first man and woman,
sitting, dining, smelling the smoke
and rose and apple rise up
into the uncharted skies.
I would hold this moment
as my time in heaven,
as the one moment to feel
throughout all time.
Now, always now.
Eating fire and wood
and earth and water,
consuming the elements,
living inside our senses only
without a thought of work or task,
just us together at the table
being who are, seeing
that the heart of the trinity
involves a you, a me and an us.

Chapter Four • FLOWERING *of* AMERICA

• *THE FOURTH MENU* •
CORN CHOWDER

GRILLED BEEF FILET STUFFED WITH SMOKED GOUDA, ONION, SWEET SAUSAGE AND SPINACH

STRAWBERRY CHOCOLATE SHORTCAKE WITH WILD BERRIES

THE SOUP

This is a soup that I have tried to get away from for the last few years, and yet everyone seems to want it. It's easy, takes about forty-five minutes total to make, and is hearty and rich. Corn, it doesn't get more Western Hemisphere than that.

Corn Chowder

CORN CHOWDER

1 ear	yellow corn
1 ear	white corn
½	yellow onion, diced
¼	poblano pepper, diced
¼	green bell pepper, diced
2 cups	chicken stock
2 cup	heavy cream
4 ounces	jack cheese, shredded
2 tablespoon	corn oil
1 tablespoon	salt and pepper
1 tablespoon	chopped garlic

Combine cream and stock and simmer in a one gallon high-sided pot. Cut corn off of cob. Scrape juice out of cob into cream/stock. Heat oil in medium skillet. Add garlic, onions, peppers and corn and sauté three minutes. Cook vegetables till crisp. Pour off the oil and add vegetables to stock. Bring to boil for one minute. Reduce to simmer and add cheese and, salt and pepper. Stir and simmer two minutes.

At this stage be very careful not to scorch the soup. When making cream based soups it is important to stir by not touching the bottom of the pan. If you scrape any solids up into the soup it will affect the taste. You run the risk of a scorch taste. This is a sage and experienced caution, so please take note, especially after stirring in the cheese.

If necessary, thicken with a blond roux (butter flour mix). You now have a simple corn chowder.

Not satisfied with a simple corn chowder? Need something more? Here it is:

CORN AND CRAB CHOWDER:
Take the corn chowder from the above recipe and before the cheese:

1 cup	clam stock
1 cup	cooked crabmeat, bluefin is the best
1/3 cup	king mushrooms, thick sliced
¼ cup	fresh only cilantro, this is 12 leaves
1 teaspoon	white wine
2 teaspoons	fresh ginger, peeled and minced
½ cup	soy sauce
2 teaspoons	rice vinegar

Add above ingredients to chowder. Simmer. Garnish with chevre toast. Chevre toast is ciabatta bread or French bread spread with a soft Vermont goat cheese and then toasted in the oven for about two minutes on 375° degrees.

THE ENTRÉE

We are going back to the grill for this one. Your best wood chip will be hickory. If you don't have a grill, then you will sear the stuffed filet in a skillet and finish in a 350° oven for fifteen minutes, which will give you a medium rare. If you have a grill section to your stove, well...grill it there, you just won't have the wood smoke flavor.

GRILLED BEEF FILET STUFFED WITH SMOKED GOUDA, ONION, SWEET SAUSAGE AND SPINACH
Also including recipe for grill smoked pork loin in case you are in the mood for something other than a heavy beef dish.

2 - 7 ounce	center cut beef tenderloin filets
1 ounce	smoked gouda, grated
2 stalks	green onion, diced

Chapter Four • FLOWERING of AMERICA

Grilled Beef Filet stuffed with smoked gouda, onion, sweet sausage and spinach

2 ounces	sweet Italian sausage, cooked and chopped
4 leaves	fresh spinach, chopped
½ teaspoon	salt and pepper mix

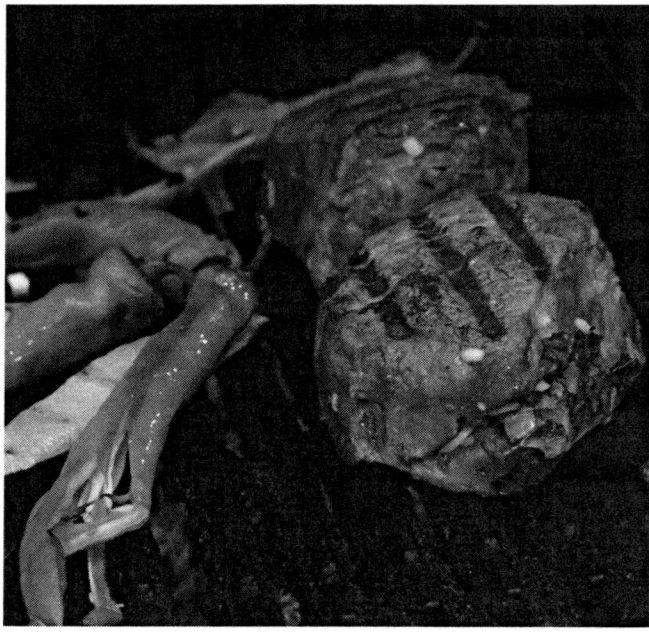

Chop and mix the gouda, scallion, sausage, spinach and, salt and pepper blend. Cut a one-inch opening in the side of each filet, with the knife inside the meat cut two thirds of the way in and cut a semi circle cavern. Divide the stuffing and fill each filet.

Grill on medium hot coals about four inches above the coals. Cook five minutes, turn it over, cook five minutes turn it over again, and try to make an **X** in the meat with the grill marks. It looks like you know what you are doing when you

MEAT TEMPERATURES AND SAFE HANDLING OF MEAT:

Although I find the recommended temperatures to be a little high with the USDA, I do understand that their choices are for health reasons.

So here are the two beef temperatures. You make the choice; it all depends on how you handle the meat (sanitation and refrigeration) and your physical constitution. It is best to wear food safety gloves when handling meats. If you don't have the gloves, wash your hands with anti-bacterial soap. Wash often, especially when going from meat to vegetable. Keep your cutting boards and work surfaces clean with bleach and then wash with hot soapy water, and then wash again with hot water.

Some people are more sensitive to existent bacteria than others, as stated in the previous chapter. Don't be afraid, it is a simple truth that there are bacteria in all foods and that cooking and proper handling will kill the harmful ones. Yet, and this is a big yet, this does not guarantee safety, nothing does. Thankfully our risks are few. Protecting our health with make the **X**. Usually the meat will be fully cooked to a good medium rare in less than fifteen minutes on a hot grill. But this is where the thermometer or the cheating cut in the beef comes in handy. Medium rare will be 130°. I prefer it at 120°. If you are serving an unstuffed filet, 117° to 120° for a red rare. A digital instant read thermometer is the best of all possible choices for a thermometer.

RED WINE BUTTER SAUCE OR BUERRE ROUGE

1 cup	decent red wine, the kind is your choice
2 tablespoons	red wine vinegar, or balsamic vinegar (preferred)
2 bulbs	shallot, minced i.e. fine dice
1 clove	garlic, minced
6 ounces	cold butter cut in quarter ounce slices
½ teaspoon	salt and pepper blend

Put the shallot, garlic, vinegar and wine in a high-sided sauce pan. Turn heat on high and boil the wine down to almost four tablespoons of liquid. You have to watch this, don't go anywhere away from the stove.

NOW, use a flexible wire whisk to stir. Remove from heat and quickly stir in the butter one slice at a time. You may have to return to the heat halfway through, but only do so if the sauce begins to congeal

strict laws concerning the growing, raising, harvesting, butchering, and preparation of our foods is one area of the government that we should all give our full support.

ME	USDA SAYS:
VERY RARE: 115° TO 120°	Not recommended.
RARE: 120° TO 130°	140°
MED. RARE: 130° TO 135°	150°
MEDIUM: 135° TO 150°	160°
MED. WELL: 150° TO 165°	170°
WELL: WHY?	STILL, WHY?

Also, beef and all other meats will cook during their resting period after you remove them from the direct heat. If you are cooking large cuts of beef or pork the time for the meat to come together is about fifteen minutes. During this fifteen minutes the temperature will rise anywhere between three and eight degrees. Keep that in mind. Roasts will rise a minimum of ten degrees.

Chapter Four • FLOWERING of AMERICA

and not just thicken. WHISK FAST. Do so until all the butter is incorporated into the wine shallots. Add salt and pepper.

There, you have made a classic French Beurre Rouge. The taste is will be rich and a little tart. Use immediately.

Variations: make it with white wine; add beef stock; use a touch of cream to enrich it even more, and to stretch the sauce; any kind of fresh herbs at the end of whisking, a little bourbon to give it a Kentucky feel, it can also be made with sake or vodka added to the wine.

What kind of sides would be good with this? How about a Caesar salad. You can go two ways, do it with the traditional Caesar dressing, or with a Raspberry Vinaigrette. Guess which one I want?

You can buy the raspberry mustard or make it. To make the mustard just blend together:

RASPBERRY MUSTARD
- 2 tablespoons   French dijon seed mustard
- 4 tablespoons   raspberry puree

SIMPLE RASPBERRY VINAIGRETTE
- 3 tablespoons   raspberry mustard
- ½ cup   olive oil
- 1 teaspoon   sugar

Whisk together.

Arrange lettuce on plate in circular fan. Drizzle sauce over lettuce. Sprinkle salad with onion, red hots, and flowers.

- heart plus
- 4 leaves   romaine lettuce, shredded by hand
- 1 tablespoon   toasted pine nuts
- 2   roma tomatoes, quartered

In a big salad bowl mix the lettuce, nuts and tomato with the vinaigrette. Serve yourselves from the bowl at the table.

ADDITIONAL RECIPE FOR QUICK SMOKED JERK PORK LOIN

This takes one and a half hours grill time. You need mesquite chips, but don't soak them in water overnight; you will use them dry.

The charcoal you will use is hickory.

1	3 pound pork loin with chop bones
4 ounces	olive oil
2 ounces	dark soy sauce
4 tablespoons	jerk seasoning
1 tablespoon	powdered ginger
3 tablespoons	light brown sugar
2 tablespoons	cardamom
1 teaspoon	cinnamon

Rub the loin with the soy, work it into the flesh. Let it rest for a couple of minutes. Rub the oil into the flesh. Let it rest and soak in for a couple of minutes. Mix the spices together and rub them into the meat. Be vigorous about it, you want the taste to get into the meat. Refrigerate for at least two hours, overnight is best.

Prepare the coals. When they have turned a fiery gray set the loin on the grill screen six to seven inches above the heat. Cover the grill. Turn the loin over after thirty minutes. After an additional fifteen minutes take the lid off of the grill and add eight ounces of mesquite chips to the coals. It will smoke like hell, but that's OK. Cover the grill. Cook another fifteen minutes. Turn the loin back over and cover, and let it finish this way. Internal temperature will be 165°. I like this best with smoked corn on the cob and smoked French bread. Place the cooked bread in the smoker for the last fifteen minutes. Corn takes twenty minutes in the husk.

DESSERT

STRAWBERRY CHOCOLATE SHORTCAKES

Don't you dare buy the pound cake imitation shortcake in the frozen food section. I know, it tastes cheap and sinful, and reminds you of school food when you were a kid, but: Make the shortcake yourself. There's a reason strawberry shortcake is a classic and it's not because of the luxury of freezing. Sometimes I wonder where this century would be without Freon, cigarettes and cars.

SHORTCAKES

¼ cup	unsweetened cocoa
1 cup	flour
¼ cup	sugar
1 teaspoon	baking powder
A pinch	salt
3 ounces	cold butter, cut in bits
½ cup	cream

Preheat oven to 425° degrees.

Sift all but cream and butter. Cut butter into mixture and mix until it is rough, like oatmeal. And the cream and stir with fork until it forms a dough. Divide and cut into four equal pieces, and cut them into circles. Bake for twelve minutes.

Remove from oven and let cool on wire rack.

STRAWBERRIES AND CREAM

6	large, ripe strawberries, sliced
5 ounces	whipping cream
2 tablespoons	granulated sugar

Whip the cream and sugar to a stiff peak. Cut the shortcakes in half. Fill with whipped cream and strawberries.

If your tastes and the market will it, use any kind of berry, or combination of berries. *TRY NEW THINGS.*

• THE FIFTH MENU •

SHIITAKE EGG ROLLS WITH MISO VINAIGRETTE AND WASABI

SICHUAN AND CORIANDER GRILLED TURKEY STEAK WITH ROSE HIPS AND ZINFANDEL SAUCE

BREAD PUDDING WITH ROSEMARY SYRUP AND CHERRY CREAM

Here we have a little bit of the new and the old. The egg rolls are of the new cuisines, the grilled turkey steak combines the old, the East and the West, and the bread pudding is from the birth of history. The bread pudding takes a little bit of planning the day ahead. Rose hips can be purchased at any health food store. Miso and wasabi can be found in the import section at the grocers, at a health food store, or at any large scale international farmers market.

THE APPETIZER

SHIITAKE EGG ROLLS WITH MISO VINAIGRETTE AND WASABI

Directions on how to roll egg rolls are in the first chapter. Miso is made from fermented soy paste. The one we use here is the red miso, which is a bit stronger than the white. Miso is salty, so you do not need to use any extra salt with the recipe.

SHIITAKE EGG ROLL

4 ounces	sliced shiitake mushroom
4 ounces	sliced crimini mushroom
2 ounces	crunchy sprouts: kidney and lima
2 tablespoons	equal diced red and green peppers
2 tablespoons	diced onion
1 tablespoon	mushroom soy sauce
2 tablespoons	Mirin, Japanese cooking wine, if you don't have any substitute sherry
½ teaspoon	cracked black pepper
1 teaspoon	chopped fresh parsley
1 teaspoon	chopped fresh basil

Chapter Four • FLOWERING of AMERICA

1 teaspoon	chopped fresh garlic
4	egg roll skins, fresh if you can.
1	small egg, beaten with teaspoon water
2 tablespoons	yellow corn meal
1 cup	corn oil

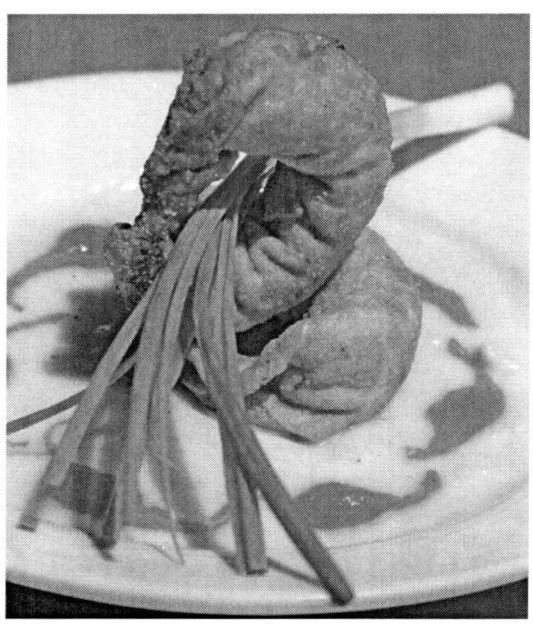

Shitake Egg Rolls with miso vinaigrette and wasabi

Combine all ingredients except egg roll, egg, corn meal and corn oil, of course. Sauté in olive oil until the mushrooms just begin to soften. This is two minutes on high heat. Stir fast as you sauté. Wok is best. Drain all excess liquid out of the pan, and discard the liquid.

Chill the vegetables.

Sprinkle the corn meal on a cutting board. Lay out the egg roll skins on the cornmeal. Brush with some of the egg wash. Lay the egg rolls with a corner pointing towards you. Divide the vegetables between the four skins; this will be one and a half tablespoons per skin, in the upper third of the skin closest to you. Roll the corner over the vegetable so that they are wrapped in the first roll. Fold the two opposing ends over to close the edges of the egg roll on the first roll. With both hands, all your fingers, finish rolling the egg roll into a cylinder. Brush the last bit of exposed skin with egg wash and roll the egg roll into a tight cylinder. Sprinkle with corn meal.

Do the same for all the rest of the egg roll skins.

Pour the oil into a deep skillet or wok. Heat to 335°. Place the egg rolls into the oil one at a time. Fry two minutes per side, turn them as they cook with a pair of tongs. Drain on paper towels.

MISO VINAIGRETTE

½ cup	olive oil
1 tablespoon	ginger, grated
1 tablespoon	whole garlic
2 tablespoons	Japanese Mirin, a sweet white rice wine
1 tablespoon	rice vinegar, to balance flavor
1 tablespoon	red miso

Put ginger and garlic in blender. Slowly pour in half the olive oil. Add miso and blend. Slowly add the rest of the olive oil. Mix the Mirin and vinegar together and pour in while still blending. The vinaigrette will be sweet, a little sour and very rich with the flavor of the miso.

WASABI PASTE
You can buy the tube of wasabi paste or you can buy the powder and adjust the intensity to your own liking. If using the powder stir gently, when the powder gets in the air and in your nostrils and lungs it really burns...Really.

Spread a thin layer of the miso vinaigrette on each serving plate. Drizzle a teaspoon per plate of the wasabi over the miso. Cut the egg rolls in four slices per roll. Arrange on plates. Hey, let's eat.

THE ENTREE
As with so many legends, the Sichuan peppercorn isn't exactly a pepper, it comes from what is called an ash bush. They are flowery and spicy. Best used crushed for dishes such as this one. Coriander is the seed of the cilantro. The flavor is quick and intense like the smell of fresh cut cilantro. Rose hips have a lot of history and are best understood for their medicinal heritage of being high in vitamin C. The flavor is like the smell of roses and lemons.

The turkey steak is cut from the breast. It should be at least seven ounces. A good substitute is smoked turkey breast if you can't find any suitable fresh, or if you just want the flavor without the process of grilling out. If using smoked breast then cook under the broiler in your oven.

SICHUAN AND CORIANDER GRILLED TURKEY STEAK WITH ROSE HIPS AND ZINFANDEL SAUCE

2 - 7-ounce	turkey breast steaks, half inch thick.
1 tablespoon	dijon grain mustard
1 teaspoon	honey
½ teaspoon	crushed Sichuan peppercorns
½ teaspoon	crushed coriander seeds

Mix the mustard and honey. Brush both sides of the steaks with the honey mustard. Sprinkle the peppercorns and seeds over both sides of the steaks. Press them into the meat. Refrigerate an hour.

Chapter Four • FLOWERING of AMERICA

Prepare the grill. The coals should be medium hot, not a red hot. You want to cook this slowly. An equal mix of apple and hickory chips is good for this kind of grilling. Mesquite is too much of a fast high heat.

Oil the grill rack before cooking the steaks. Grill eight minutes per side for two turns. Then it is done.

NO CREAM, CREAM *(or you could use soy milk, but it's not as rich)*

Because not every one is able to consume the amounts of cream and dairy that I keep suggesting, here is a recipe for a no cream, cream:

2 tablespoons	olive oil
½ cup	yellow onion
1/3 cup	glutinous white rice, like sushi rice
2 cups	chicken or vegetable stock (no fat)
1 cup	white wine
½ tablespoon	salt and pepper

Sauté onions, add rice and cook two minutes. Add 3/4 cup of stock and the wine, cover and simmer twenty five minutes. Cool and puree. Add the rest of the stock until desired thickness.

You can also use soy milk. It has a nice earthy taste, is healthy, and is creamy.

THE SAUCE

1 cup	zinfandel wine
2 tablespoons	rose hips
1	bay leaf
¼ cup	Worcestershire sauce
1 cup	rice cream from above recipe

Put everything together in a sauce pan and reduce by half on medium heat. It will take about fifteen minutes.

Neat flavor, huh? Bet you didn't think a no cream could taste like that. You can also buy soy milk and use it in place of either cream or rice cream.

Serve on a bed of Japanese soba noodles. You will use the brown ones that are made of buckwheat and yams. They are six inches long and round like spaghetti. They cook quickly, so don't leave the pot when you put them in the boiling water. Soba means noodle in

Japanese. The white ones are what you are probably more familiar with, and they are a chow mein noodle. The brown is more often used for cold dishes. Here we will toss with fresh spinach leaves.

BUCKWHEAT SOBA NOODLES

4 ounces	dry weight buckwheat soba noodles
2 quarts	salted boiling water
20 leaves	fresh spinach, small leaves
10 thin slices	red bell pepper
10 pods	sugar snap peas cut in half on diagonal: /
1 tablespoon	sesame oil

Cook the noodles until soft, about five minutes. Drain under cold water.

Sauté the spinach, pepper and peas in sesame oil with the drained soba. Divide on two plates. Set the Turkey steaks on top of the soba. Pour equal amounts of the sauce on each. YUM!

The recipe works just as well with very firm tofu instead of the turkey breast. Don't grill, cook under the broiler in your oven.

BREAD PUDDING

8 ounces	sliced Krispy Kreme donuts dry overnight
½ cup	milk
½ cup	half and half
3 tablespoons	golden raisins
3 tablespoons	apricot preserves
3	eggs
¼ cup	sugar
1 teaspoon	vanilla extract

Bread Pudding

Tear the donuts into half inch pieces and put in a bowl. Add milk and half and half. Mix well and let stand an hour, toss occasionally. Mix raisins and preserves into the bead.

Whisk eggs, sugar and vanilla in mixing bowl. Then combine all ingredients.

Bake in buttered baking pan on 325° for forty-five minutes to an hour.

Chapter Four • **FLOWERING** *of* **AMERICA**

When it is done it will be moist but not runny. Serve it warm, so you want to make the cream and syrup ahead of time.

ROSEMARY SYRUP

10 leaves	fresh rosemary
½ cup	maple syrup

Heat the syrup until it just begins to simmer with small bubbles. Add the rosemary and turn off the heat. Set aside to let cool.

CHERRY CREAM

¼ cup	coconut cream
6	cherries crushed

Whip the coconut cream and cherries together so that it is a light pink color. Chill.

Divide the warm bread pudding between two serving plates. Try to make it look nice by molding it with your hands into a nice square shape. Pour half the cherry cream over each pudding, and then pour half the syrup over each pudding. This is a rich dessert, so a chamomile and mint tea is a good beverage. Champagne works as well.

The Fifth Menu

*Equal across the table,
hands flighty and animated,
she sets them
next to the cup of chili salsa,
her Chopin fingers lift and point,
fold and punctuate
the tales of her siblings and her life.
Responding in kind
my own hands orchestrate
the verses of my life,
the one before manhood
before insight.
And the conversation moves to
a study of sex and the sensual,
of voyeurs and lovers
in world history,
my confusion over roles and needs
of civilization can only carve,
scratch and question,*

Chapter Four • FLOWERING *of* AMERICA

I can't reach a conclusion.
Sex: She knows she has the power,
the flexed presence of womanhood,
it commands and controls
the simpler natures of men.
Sensual: Me, I'm so found in her,
all I want is to hold her hand,
to talk on into the distance
where dialogs never end.
And there's one thing I know
about all this:
sensuality, language and relating
teach more, drive more,
satisfy more
than any night of passion can.
And I keep humming to myself
that song from The King and I:
Getting to know you....

• *THE SIXTH MENU* •

SHREDDED DUCKLING AND VEGETABLES BAKED IN RICE PAPER

SEARED TUNA WITH GOLDEN PEPPER AND HONEY COULIS

PRALINE TULIP WITH ESPRESSO CREAM

This menu also represents the East West cuisine at its finest. Rice paper is made with rice flour, salt and water. It is very delicate, so handle with care. We will fold the duck in little boxes. The tuna must be of the highest grade. If you can't find tuna use marlin, Opah, wahoo (a kind of mackerel, but tasting nothing like common mackerel), or halibut, each of which must be sushi grade as we are searing medium rare.

The new thing we will use here is rice flour. Rice flour is finer than cornstarch, has almost no taste and just lightly fluffs the coating around the meat. It is also used as a thickener instead of wheat flour. It has fewer calories, and I am finding it to be a new favorite. You can also use water chestnut flour, lotus flour and even tapioca flour each of which seems an obscene extravagance, but they are not, they are just different. Each offers a subtle and light flavor unlike flour any other I have ever used. If you see these in the store, buy them and use wherever conventional flour is required, except for baking. You will be as pleased and surprised as I have been with the results.

But do not use wheat flour for the appetizer. You must use rice or tapioca flour. Wheat flour makes it way too gummy to be any good, and it obscures the other flavors.

THE APPETIZER

SHREDDED DUCKLING AND VEGETABLES IN WONTON SHELL

1	8 to 10 ounce skinless duck breast
1 stalk	thin sliced asparagus
1 tablespoon	each: red bell, green bell, zucchini, onion, carrot and celery

Chapter Four • FLOWERING of AMERICA

2 tablespoons	sweet soy
1 tablespoon	Chinese sweet bean chili paste (if you can't find this then use tom choy paste)
1 teaspoon	ground galanga, or ginger and miso mixed
1 teaspoon	rice vinegar
¼ teaspoon	ground cinnamon
3 tablespoons	rice flour
2 teaspoons	chili oil
1 teaspoon	sesame oil
6	sheets round rice paper
2 tablespoons	Mirin

THIN SLICE the skinned duck breast. I mean thin slice, paper thin if you can. Mix duck, vegetables, flour and spices. Refrigerate for an hour.

Heat large skillet with the oils. Sauté the duck mix until it is cooked medium rare. Drain and chill.

Soak the rice paper is hot water for five minutes. They will be soft and pliable. Lift out of water and set on cloth towel. Put a tablespoon of duck mixture in center of each paper. Fold opposing corners of paper over to the center of the paper. Press closed. Sprinkle with Mirin.

Bake in 450° oven for 15 minutes. You can also steam or fry these won tons.

Also, if you don't like duck you can substitute firm tofu, eggplant, or chicken.

DIPPING SAUCE

¼ cup	sweet soy sauce
3 tablespoons	rice vinegar
¼ teaspoon	white sesame seeds
1 stalk	diced scallion
¼ teaspoon	minced ginger
¼ teaspoon	red pepper flakes

Combine and refrigerate one hour.

Serve by placing won tons on serving plates and pour dipping sauce into small bowls. Eat with your fingers, or with chopsticks.

THE ENTREE

If you cannot find a suitable tuna use Marlin, Wahoo, White or Striped Sea Bass, Mong Chong, Opah, or Tombo.

Infusing the oil is easy, it just sounds fancy. Bring a cup of medium grade olive oil to 125° in a deep skillet. Add the zest of three lemons and heat for ten minutes. Let cool. Pour into glass container and seal it air tight. Set in dark cool place, not refrigerator, for a week. There, it's infused. You can do this with anything you want to flavor the oil, don't be bemused by the infusion hype. Stuff like this is for everybody, so let's share the good.

SEARED TUNA WITH GOLDEN PEPPER AND HONEY COULIS

2, 7 ounce	tuna loin steaks
2 ounces	lemon infused olive oil
2 tablespoons	sweet rice flour for dusting the tuna

Heat sauté skillet with lemon olive oil. Dust the steaks with rice flour. Sauté for three minutes per side. Remove from heat and immediately serve.

Seared Tuna with golden pepper and honey coulis

Chapter Four • FLOWERING of AMERICA

THE SAUCE
Easy, easy, easy, just puree in a blender.

GOLDEN PEPPER AND POBLANO HONEY COULIS

1	golden pepper
½	poblano pepper
1/3 cup	honey

Chop peppers and put in blender with honey. Puree till smooth. Set aside.

This will go good with a daikon and cabbage slaw. Daikon is a kind of radish but is not as hot as horseradish, hotter that radishes, and a little more pungent. Instead of a regular starch, sauté Asian pear and slices of sweet potato.

DAIKON AND CABBAGE SLAW (QUICK KIM CHEE)

1 cup	shredded daikon
1 cup	shredded Napa cabbage
½ cup	thin sliced yellow onion
1 tablespoon	golden fish sauce
¼ cup	sugar
¼ cup	rice vinegar
¼ cup	extra virgin olive oil
2 tablespoons	garlic
3 ounces	arugula (mild chicory tasting green)

Combine ingredients and refrigerate in a sealed plastic container for a week. When it is time to eat drain off the liquid and reserve for another marinade.

To my Korean friends and loves, please don't hate me for this Americanized and simplified version.

SAUTEED ASIAN PEAR AND SWEET POTATO

1	Asian pear cut into thin slices
8 ounces	peeled sweet potato cut in thin slices
4 tablespoons	butter
½ teaspoon	salt and pepper mix
¼ teaspoon	fenugreek (an herb used in making curry)

Heat a large sauté skillet or wok on high. Add butter and melt till it begins to froth. Add the pear and potato. Cook five minutes and add the salt, pepper and fenugreek during last minute. Remove and drain.

Everything is cooked. Set a pool of the sauce at front of plate. Place tuna on top of sauce. Arrange starch at top right of plate. Slaw at top left. These are your left and right with the tuna closest to you. Garnish with shredded green papaya. Yes, shredded green papaya. The flavors will come alive.

DESSERT

PRALINE TULIP CUP WITH CHOCOLATE ESPRESSO WHIPPED CREAM AND STRAWBERRIES.

PRALINE CUP

1 cup	pecans, crushed fine
6 oz	all purpose flour
5 oz	light brown sugar
4 oz	corn syrup
5 oz	butter
Spray	pan release or just cooking oil

Praline Tulip Cup with chocolate espresso whipped cream and strawberries

EQUIPMENT NEEDED: Food processor, two 1 cup measuring cups, high sided one gallon pot, wooden spoon, mixing bowl, whisk, sheet pan, six small bowled soup bowls, thin metal spatula.

Pre-heat oven to 375°.
Blend pecans to coarse. Mix with flour. Set aside.

Add sugar, syrup and whole unsalted butter to pot and cook on medium heat to a boil. Stir with wooden spoon. When it has melted and cooked up so that it froths stir in the pecan and flour mix and stir, at the moment it is mixed remove from heat. Let it rest one minute.

Spray or grease your sheet pans. Spoon the mix in six equal circles on two sheet pans (3 per pan). They will be four inches around. Wet your hands and pat them down just a little. Immediately place in oven and cook for fifteen minutes. Remove from oven and let rest thirty seconds, or until the bubbles in the pralines appear dry. Test by gently lifting the sides of the pralines, if they tear then wait.

Lift and set each one on a bowl, you may need to hold your hand on it to prevent tearing. Let them harden.

WHIP CREAM AND ESPRESSO

1½ cups	heavy cream
2 tablespoons	espresso
2 tablespoons	sweet chocolate
2 tablespoons	XXX sugar (confectioner sugar)
12	strawberries, sliced

Make a small amount of very strong espresso, or coffee and let cool. Mix with chocolate and sugar. It will be a syrup.

Wash, stem and cut strawberries into fourths. Set aside.

Whip very cold cream by hand with a whisk in mixing bowl. When it forms firm peaks stir in syrup. Place thickened cream in praline cups with strawberries.

Any fruit puree is good poured over this, like raspberry or mango. If you don't want to use the cream just use your favorite ice cream.

• THE SEVENTH MENU •

PAN-FRIED TOFU WITH TORTILLA AND TOMATILLO SALSA

SAUTÉED LAMB LOIN MEDALLIONS WITH APPLE MINT VELOUTE AND SAFFRON CREAM

CHOCOLATE DECADENCE

APPETIZER
Use extra firm tofu for this dish. Again, we have a good mix of the East and the West.

PAN FRIED TOFU WITH TORTILLA AND TOMATILLO SALSA

6 ounces	extra firm tofu
½ teaspoon	ginger, peeled and minced
½ teaspoon	garlic, minced
1 ounce	powdered nori (toasted seaweed)
¼ teaspoon	salt and pepper mix
4 tablespoons	walnut oil
2 tablespoons	rice flour

Cut the tofu into eight small squares and combine with all ingredients except the flour and walnut oil. Marinade two hours. Bake 20 minutes at 350°. Chill.

Heat the oil in a wok or skillet. Sauté the tofu five minutes. Drain on paper towel. Chill.

TORTILLA AND TOMATILLO SALSA
Use raw yellow corn tortilla for this dish. Tomatillo is an equatorial tomato like vegetable that is green with a leafy coat. Remove the leaves under running hot water, this keeps them from sticking. Tomatillo is tart like a lime but meaty like a roma tomato.

1	shredded yellow corn tortilla
4	tomatillo
2	roma tomato
¼	green pepper
¼	red onion

Chapter Four • **FLOWERING** *of* **AMERICA**

1 stalk	celery
20 leaves	cilantro
10 leaves	opal basil, or strong mint
1 teaspoon	chipotle chili sauce (use the thick kind)
1 tablespoon	molasses

Note: chipotle is roasted jalapeno pepper. The roasting mellows and gives it a smoky flavor. Raw jalapeno has a great flavor when very fresh. Be careful with the seeds. Dry them to use as seasoning for other dishes.

Combine ingredients except the tortilla, and coarsely chop in food processor. Add shredded tortilla. Chill until ready for use.

Place a tablespoon of walnut oil in a hot skillet and again sauté the tofu, add salsa after one minute. Cook for one more minute.

Divide on two plates. Serve with tortilla chips, or really any of your favorite or unfamiliar chips, such as tomato, taro, malanga, or even fried shrimp chips.

THE ENTRÉE

SAUTEED LAMB LOIN MEDALLIONS WITH APPLE MINT VELOUTE AND SAFFRON CREAM. SERVED WITH SIDE OF ANGEL HAIR PASTA, TOSSED WITH VIRGIN OLIVE OIL AND SPRING VEGETABLES.

EQUIPMENT NEEDED: 2 high sided small sauce pans for the sauce. One 4 quart pot for the pasta water. Strainer for the pasta. 1 sauté skillet for the lamb. Cheese or vegetable grater for the vegetables.

THE SAUCES:
Apple-Mint Veloute:

1 small	jalapeno pepper: fine dice
1 teaspoon	olive oil
1	granny smith apple: fine dice
½ cup	apple cider
10 fresh	mint leaves. Note: save the stems to use for a seasoned olive oil.
¼ teaspoon	salt and pepper mix

Sauté the minced jalapenos in olive oil over medium high heat. When it is crisp add the apple, and cook twenty seconds. Move pan off of the heat and add the apple cider, and then return to heat. Boil and reduce the liquid by 1/3. This should take about three minutes at high heat.

At this point it may be necessary to thicken with a slurry:

Mix 2 tablespoons cornstarch with 2 tablespoons water.

Turn heat down to a simmer; slowly stir in the slurry until the liquid begins to thicken. Add the mint leaves, salt and pepper. Remove from heat and taste. The taste will be fruity and spicy.

Set aside in a warm place.

Pork loin steak

SAFFRON CREAM SAUCE

10 threads	saffron
½ cup	white wine
1	lime juiced
1 teaspoon	XXX sugar
2 cups	heavy cream
½ teaspoon	salt and pepper (white pepper)

Boil saffron threads in wine down to one tablespoon of liquid. Strain liquid into cup. In the same pan add heavy cream and turn to high heat and reduce to one cup liquid. Add lime, sugar, salt and pepper, and saffron liquid. Set aside in warm place.

PASTA AND VEGETABLES

4 oz	dry weight angel hair pasta
2 tablespoons	zucchini
1 tablespoon	yellow squash
4	artichoke hearts, quartered\tab
2 oz	virgin olive oil
1 teaspoon	salt and pepper mix.

Cook the pasta in three quarts salted and oiled rapidly boiling water. The salt (one tablespoon) seasons the pasta, the olive oil (two

Chapter Four • FLOWERING of AMERICA

tablespoons) keeps the water from overflowing, the rapid boil and oil keeps the pasta from sticking together. Cook ten minutes until the pasta is the way you like it, be it with a slight crunch (al dente) or soft.

Grate the vegetables so that they are in long, thin strands. Add to pasta water for the last minute of cooking.

Strain, rinse, and toss the pasta and vegetables with your favorite virgin olive oil. Salt and pepper.

THE LAMB

1	1 pound lamb loin, trimmed of fat and silver skin
2 tablespoons	all purpose flour
3 tablespoons	blend oil (10% olive, 90% corn)

Heat the skillet and add the oil. It must be very hot. The oil will be clear. Dust the lamb with the flour. Add the lamb as soon as the oil turns clear.

With a pair of tongs add the lamb from one end to the other, not all at once. If you add all at once it cools the skillet and the meat will stick. Shake the pan as you add the lamb. Brown both sides one to one and half minutes, and then turn heat down to medium. The rest is up to your choice of temperature. A common medium will take about four minutes per side. Rare to medium rare is 118°. Remove from heat and set aside to let the meat rest. This allows the fibers of the muscle to close back together; hence you don't lose all the good flavors when you slice it.

After the meat has rested, slice the lamb in twelve thin slices.

THE PLATE

Spread each sauce on opposite sides of the plate. Place the pasta down the middle. Lay the lamb along the pasta. A good garnish would be a sprig of mint and three slices of apple.

ALTERNATE ENTREE

Now, as a final way of showing how sauces are able to interact with totally different foods we will prepare the above sauces and pasta with a fish dish. You can use turbot, flounder, sand dabs, halibut, and even tilapia for this dish. The most interesting thing about this dish is the use of a Japanese snack called Wasabi Fried Green Peas. They are slightly hot, sweet and crunchy.

The Seventh Menu

WASABI GREEN PEA TURBOT

2, 6 ounce	boned turbot fillets
1 cup	rice flour
2	eggs
4 ounces	cold water
5 ounces	wasabi fried green peas
4 ounces	peanut oil

Divide flour in half. Place half in one pan and the other half with the peas. Prepare the egg wash by whipping the egg and water together. Set aside in pan. In food processor crush the peas and flour together into a coarse mixture. Place in pan.

Dust the turbot in the flour, and then coat with egg wash. With your left hand lift the turbot out of the egg and set in the crushed peas. With your right hand press the fish down into the peas and turn it over until all of the fish is crusted with the peas. Set on plate.

Heat sauté skillet with the peanut oil to a medium heat. Add the turbot and cook four minutes, turn heat down to medium low. Turn the fish over and cook another four minutes. Turn again and cook two minutes. Turn and cook one more minute. The fish will be crispy with a light tan and green color.

Follow the same procedure for plating as with the lamb dish. This preparation is also good with a fruit salsa or fruit chutney.

DESSERT

EACH... OTHER. This is the end of the book and you need to spend a little time just doing nothing other than sipping your favorite beverage, being close and enjoying your life together.

OK, enjoy each other if you will, but there really is a last dessert.

CHOCOLATE DECADENCE

This is an old war horse of the California cuisine movement. I was first introduced to this cake at St. Orres in Gualala, California in 1980. It has since shown up in cookbooks from the California cuisine to Caribbean cuisine. The original cake is attributed to Narsai David of the late restaurant, Narsai's in Kensington, California. I always thought we were the first, but I guess firsts in food is really just a frame of regionalism and of mind. So, from my ancient notes here is the recipe as I first made it.

Chapter Four • FLOWERING of AMERICA

THE CAKE ITSELF

1 pound	semisweet chocolate
10 tablespoons	unsalted butter
1 tablespoon	sugar
1 tablespoon	all purpose flour
4	whole eggs, large

You will need one 8 or 9 inch round cake pan, parchment paper, two large mixing bowls, a large soup pot, a flexible wire whisk, a firm wire whisk, a rubber spatula, a food processor, and fine strainer.

Set your oven on 425°. Cut the parchment paper to fit the cake pan. Rub butter or spray can baking oil, spray over all the insides of the pan. Pour in a cup of flour. Shake it around to cover all the surfaces. Pour out the excess flour. Set the pan aside.

Fill the soup pot halfway with water and bring to a boil. Put the chocolate and butter into one of the mixing bowls. Set the bowl on top of the boiling water. This is called a double boiler. As the chocolate melts stir it with the firm whisk so that it melts smooth and uniform. Set aside in a warm place.

In the next large mixing bowl put in your eggs and sugar. Set inside of the double boiler, and with the flexible whisk beat until the eggs are at least 165°, this is lukewarm. Remove from heat and continue to whisk until they are thick and yellow like a custard.

This stage is a switching back and forth kind of thing: Fold the flour into the eggs. Now each of you holds one of the pans: stir a fourth of the eggs into the chocolate. Then, with the rubber spatula fold the chocolate mixture into the rest of the whipped eggs. Make sure it is folded, not stirred or whipped, and the mixtures are incorporated into one another to create a chocolaty liquid whole. To tell you the truth I prefer to use my hands for the folding in stage. As long as they are clean and you don't mind, what the hell, get into the food.

Chocolate Decadence

Pour the batter into the cake pan and bake for fifteen minutes. Don't worry, the center is supposed to be liquid. Take it out of the oven and let it come to room temperature. Freeze it. Do not remove from freezer until it has had a chance to actually freeze, at least overnight.

Time to eat. Remove cake from freezer and set aside. The cake will be firm throughout.

Here we whip more cream and puree more fruit.

THE WHIP CREAM, TOPPING AND RASPBERRY SAUCE
| 1½ cups | heavy cream |
| 1 tablespoon | sugar |

TOPPING
| 1 cup | shaved semi sweet chocolate (use grater) |

SAUCE
| 1 pint | fresh raspberries, or frozen if you must |
| ¼ cup | sugar |

In a small mixing bowl combine the cream and sugar and beat with a flexible wire whisk to stiff peaks. Chill.

Puree the raspberries and sugar. Strain through a fine sieve to remove all the seeds and all that remains is a smooth puree. Chill.

Using either the edge of a sharp knife, or the slicer part of a four sided cheese grater shave a cup of semi sweet chocolate onto a cold plate…Cold so that the chocolate doesn't melt.

To shave with a knife: lay the chocolate down flat on a damp cloth, hold the knife with both hands, one at the point and the other on the hilt, pull the blade across the chocolate so that thin curls of chocolate follow the blade as you pull. This seems more difficult than it is, just have a firm grip and don't try to cut, you are shaving.

If you have a pastry bag here's a place to use it by using a star tip and making little whip cream crowns all over the top of the cake, if not then just scoop the whipped cream in tablespoons around the top edge of the cake, then spread a thin layer over the center part of the cake.

Shake the chocolate shavings over the cake. Pour two tablespoons of the puree on each dessert plate. Cut the slices you need. Set in center of raspberry puree. Have at it, this really is a decadent dessert.

Set on dessert plate. Garnish with a sprig of mint. A strong espresso, cognac, or grappa will fit right in with this dessert.

I could wave flags,
I could pretend a million things,
I could search to see and taste
all the herbs and foods
the world has to offer,
and yet there is no one flag,
and there is no Oz Wizard
to show the heart and mind within,
but there is this,
this you that I open to
like morning glories to the sun.
And I will always be there
at the end of the day
and throughout the night,
there if not beside you
then within you as thought as spirit.

GLOSSARY

EDIBLE FLOWERS

The listed flowers are easy to grow; don't use chemical insecticides on them and you will have a long and happy life.

BORAGE: Light blue to purple and pink petals. Cucumber taste that suits fish, salads and even adds a nice flourish to cold drinks.

CHAMOMILE: You know, the tea flower. White to yellowish petals. Good for tea as a nightcap, or salads and garnishes.

CHIVE FLOWERS: Light purple. Grow on the tips of chives and have that light chive taste. Good for fish and salads.

CHRYSANTHEMUMS: I don't use these often only because I've never grown them. If you do have access you will be surprised at the range of tastes that accompany this legendary blossom. Blanch before using to soften them up. Taste is from pepper to something like cauliflower. As with all flowers you can cure them in vinegar by pushing the petals into a bottle and pouring rice or cider vinegar in, capping it and storing in a dark, cool cabinet for at least two weeks for the flavor to become infused. It, like all vinegar, keeps quite a while, up to two or three months. Use the vinegar for salad dressings. Or, after blanching the flower (dipping in boiling water) you can garnish salads with the petals.

DAISIES: Yellow and white petals. Don't use the center, it's tough. Mint and clover taste. Interesting with salads and lamb.

DANDELION: The ones in your yard. Bitter like endives. Good for salad.

DAY LILIES: On the roadside, in your garden, they grow wild all over America, and are just great. They have orange and yellow petals that work either whole or as petals for salads, stews, soups, lasagna, and desserts. When they're not available use dried tiger lily flowers, which we will see a lot of in the recipes in this book. Lilies are my favorite for cooking as they add a slightly sweet flowery scent that always reminds me of windy, clean weather. Dried tiger lily flowers will also lightly thicken a sauce.

GERANIUMS, SCENTED: A long time ago on the Northern California Coast I was lucky enough to live close to a family of herbalists who grew at least 40 different varieties of geranium. It was by this farm that my appreciation of all the possible edible flowers and herbs fully developed. The era of the geranium has fallen back in these times, but if you have the chance to grow any of the scented varieties, do it. Pick a couple of flavors that you like (they are frequently named

Glossary

by taste) and use them for salads and cakes. The most popular flavors are lemon, mint, and rose. Use the leaves on the bottom of a cake pan for scenting cakes. Use the petals for salads, and as final seasoning for fish and chicken dishes.

HONEYSUCKLE: Yep, honeysuckle, you know it from the fences and bramble. Who hasn't had the moment of standing by wild honeysuckle vines and pulled the stamen out to have that tiny drop of liquid, so sweet and honey-like? Of course it's good for cooking and garnishing. Use on ice creams, fresh fruits, cheese plates, salads and cold as well as hot chicken dishes.

LAVENDER: Purple petals and mint. Strong taste, so use sparingly. Lavender grows easily, and is a wonderful ingredient for oils and vinegars.

MARIGOLDS: Almost all vegetable gardens have marigolds growing around them as a natural guardian against insect and animal invaders. Use the yellow and orange petals. They have a peppery taste. I highly recommended them. Use the petals all over the place, salads, sauces, soups, fish, stews and roasts. When using for cooking, add near the end of the cooking time.

NASTURTIUM: A lot of colors: yellow, orange, red, rusty and dark brown. You can use the flowers and leaves, the flowers are mild to strong pepper-radish, and the leaves are simply strong radish. They grow wild all over the northwestern coast, and can be cultivated elsewhere. They should be grown with care, they are as prolific as mint and will take over a garden if you let them. Very popular for salads.

PANSIES: All colors. Easy to grow. Grape and clover taste.

ROSE PETALS: Use for anything and everything, and use often. Grow them, cook with them, make salads of only rose petals, make vinegars and oils, give them to people, smell them, use for tea, dip whole buds in simple syrup and candy them, dry them, there is no end to the use of roses. They are more than metaphor; they are one of the essences of the sensual life.

SQUASH BLOSSOMS: Great as an addition to sautéed vegetables, or they can be fried and stuffed. And of course they have the taste of the particular squash you have removed them from.

VIOLETS: Light blue and purple petals. Sweet. They are good in the regular places, salads and garnish; delicious when crystallized and used on desserts.

Glossary

MUSHROOMS

BUTTON: Your basic Pennsylvania cave grown mushroom. Firm, white and not much flavor, but they are good. They are at their best when eaten raw, and that is their main purpose, as a raw ingredient.

CRIMINI: Similar to the button, but darker and more intense flavor. Lately I've found them for the same price in the grocery store, and I do suggest buying them instead of the more common button when you need an inexpensive mushroom for cooking. Better taste and holds up to heat.

CEPES: Thick, pale yellow with an intense flavor that smells of oak. They are the classic Italian mushroom. Great grilled. Sliced thin and added to tomato sauces they broaden the flavor of the dish to include an earthy balance to the acidity of the tomato.

CHANTRELLE: Trumpet like with lots of extensions. Pale yellow to white. Trim the chewy root off before cooking. Good marinated. Okay in sauces, but are best sautéed with the dish you are cooking. The flavor is mild

ENOKI: Small white to yellow arrow shaped mushrooms with a watery texture and taste. Used mostly as a garnish.

HARISIUM: A true unheralded prince of mushrooms. White and bearing the look of urchins. They have a mild chalky flavor all their own. They take on the characteristics of marinades and sauté ingredients rather well. I've stuffed them with shrimp and baked them. I've grilled them plain. I've stuffed them with crab, wrapped in bacon and grilled on skewers. They sauté well with tofu and vegetables. They can be a little chewy and juicy, which is a good thing.

MAITAKE: King of the woods. White, succulent, filled with nutritious aspects from being delicious to curing specific cancers. It is also under study as one of the kind of mushrooms that purify the ground around dumps both toxic and "normal".

Ginger, Lily & Sweet Fire

Glossary

HEN OF THE WOODS: Same as Maitake.
OYSTER: Pale white, fan shaped, mild taste that when cooked has a hint of chicken to it. For some reason vegetarians always dispute the origin of the taste when I've used it in soups, they seem to think it's a meat. Sorry, it's not; it's a fungus, a mushroom. Great for soups and cream sauces.
PORTOBELLA: Brown, meaty, deep taste that is wonderful when grilled. Can be stuffed and served like a pizza. Good for sauces and simply sautéed in olive oil. One of my favorites. They are 3 to six inches across when mature.
SHIITAKE: The shiitake is rich, meaty and smoky flavored, cooks well with anything that needs a mushroom, and is my most used mushroom besides the crimini. Shiitake stems are not much good except for in stocks or as part of a paste. Along with Maitake they shiitake has healing properties.
WOOD EAR: Dark Chinese mushroom with a deep flavor. Good in soy based stir-fries and clear soups.

There are many more mushrooms in the world than I can enumerate at this time. As always, all I can say is to read and to explore the world around you.

PASTAS WEST AND EAST

If you ever want to cause a bar fight between Chefs just stand up and say you have the best method for cooking pasta and will take down any who disagree. A good way to start a WAR is to stand in a room of Mainland Chinese and Italians and state that one of them not only created pasta but has the best techniques for making the pasta itself.

Shape is another thing altogether though; and this holds from group to group: The coarser and larger the pasta the coarser and larger the sauce ingredients. So linguini needs a thin, buttery sauce with fine ingredients, and penne needs larger cut ingredients from chunky tomato to whole cashews and chopped chicken.

For me, pastas originated in the East and I am more inclined towards their varieties and ingredients for lighter sauces, fully flavored, but more refined with pastas like shiritaki, udon, soba, and for heavier Asian I like wu ma, Canton and rice cakes. When cooking aggressive tomato or meat sauce it is going to be penne, shells, fusilli, pappardelle and fettuccine; for lighter we go with farfalle, linguini and capellini.

Glossary

Boiling the pasta: when cooking pasta the salt is for seasoning and the oil is to keep the pasta from sticking together as it cooks. Any other detail is myth. Salt is for flavor only. Period. Nothing more. Rinse pasta after cooking only if it is going to be used in a cold dish or if it is not going to be used immediately. Best to cook and use in the same hour or few minutes.

Always save some of the pasta water to thin and season pasta sauces.

Cooking pastas: 1 pound of pasta per 4 quarts of water. Dry pasta will absorb one quart of water. When boiling the pasta absorbs the water and expands, if you were to observe this action under a microscope it would appear that the noodle explodes or bursts but holds together. Stir infrequently as it cooks. If the box says cook three minutes then cook two minutes. It cooks after removed from water. So basically you cook $1/3^{rd}$ less than the instructions on the box tell you to cook it.

By way of America's Test Kitchen we find that the best dry pastas are American made. The best of that group is Ronzoni.

To myth and legend. Pasta was being made in Asia in 3000 B.C. Etruscan tomb paintings show pasta being extruded in 4th century Italy. Thomas Jefferson introduced the Macaroni machine to America after his return from France. The first mass marketing of pasta in the New World was in 1848 Brooklyn by a Frenchman. The kind of wheat, or even potato, rice or citrus starch is what determines the dough. Millet was used in ancient China, Durum is American and soft red is what the Marco Polo Italians used.

The thing about pasta is that it is as simple as mixing flour and water, as with bread. It is what we do to it that brings about the differences. Fresh is not better or worse than dried; and dried is no better or worse than fresh. It is a difference in texture, and fresh will usually have egg involved.

There are over 350 advertised shapes. That's a lot of pasta. We call most Asian pastas noodles, but it is still the same thing just a way to divide the kind of pasta, and that is by East and West. Durum semolina, whole wheat, egg noodle, alternative grains including gluten free are the kinds of "flour or starch" used in making pastas. Spelt and quinoa are gluten free.

This list is by no means exhaustive, in fact it is exclusionary in that these are the ones I like to use, hence they are what I would recommend. Know what I mean?

Glossary

    Pastas are also divided by shapes, tubular, strand, ribbon, stuffed and micro.

CONCHIGLIE: shell shape, fine dice ingredients, medium to heavy sauces

FARFALLE: bow tie shape, light to mid range sauces

GEMELLI: two strands twisted together, heavy sauces

ORECCHIETTE: little ears, smooth tomato, meat sauces

LINGUINI: oval, long, thin, very good for light cream or olive oil/butter sauces

FETTUCCINE: wide, flat, most common other than spaghetti.

PENNE: quills/pen, hollow, angle, heavy tomato sauces or cream

RIGATONI: tube shape, a little bigger than penne or ziti, straight cut

ROTELLE: wagon wheel shape good for cold dishes as well as soups

MANICOTTI: large, ridges, used for stuffed pasta more than as in a sauce

PAPPARDELLE: wide, heavy sauces

ROTINI: two edges, spiral but not twisted like gemelli or wide like fusilli

SPAGHETTI: round, medium to heavy sauces

CAPELLINI: angel hair, very thin, light sauces, and aromatic sauces

BUCATINI: straw, like a straw, good with any style

FUSILLI: spiral shape, good for cold dishes as well as medium range sauces

LASAGNE: flat sheets or smaller, baked pasta, heavy sauces

MACARONI: hollow, short tubes, heavy cream sauces

EGG NOODLES: various shapes with the most common being 1 inch long, thin

SHIRITAKI (LINGUINI SHAPE): Japanese sweet potato and lime starch and water,

Very healthy and light, gluten free. Every application has worked well.

SHIRITAKI (FETTUCCINE SHAPE): has tofu in addition to yam and lime.

WU MU: wheat flour and water, flat not as wide as fettuccine, soft, buttery flavor

LO MEIN: a kind of spaghetti style egg noodle, very good with clear sauces

RICE CAKE: rice flour and water, thick, round to oblong, heavier sauces

CELLOPHANE: same as mung bean, alternate name, when fried

puffs up and is crunchy snack or garnish for chicken and fish dishes.
VERMICELLI: mung bean starch and water, used in Viet dishes
RICE STICKS: rice flour and water, usually thin
SOBA: buckwheat flour is the most common, soba is Japanese for noodle
UDON: wheat flour, soft, elastic, soaks up clear sauces quite easily and is most commonly used in soup style preparations.
RICE PAPER: rice and wheat flour, water, thin, used for spring rolls

MELONS

Other melons that you should buy at some time in your life:
CASABA: Rippled yellow skin, elongated, with little smell. The flesh is white to yellow green. The taste has hints of pineapple and pear. When vine ripened the flesh is softer and juicier than cantaloupe or muskmelon (the American cantaloupe).
CRENSHAW: Smooth yellow gold skin, large and oval shaped. The flesh is golden, crisp and has a taste reminiscent of banana and cantaloupe. I've had some that actually reminded me of mango.
CHRISTMAS: A December purchase, but also available late summer into autumn. Elongated, green veined yellow skin. Flesh is greenish to yellowish. It's an odd melon whose taste is not as deep as the others, but is unique to me because it always tastes different. Sort of a banana-honeydew-cantaloupe taste.
HONEYDEW: Round, firm green skin. Common ones are green to white fleshed while there are varieties that are pink. Frankly, it's hard to find the perfect honeydew anymore because of the mass production. The good ones are like their name, sweet and a little sticky. The grocery stores like to stock the crisp flavorless ones. Shop wisely. Shelf ripen in a dark place and it should come around to it's reputation as one of the better melons.
WATERMELON: How many kinds of watermelon are there? I don't know. Round green. elongated yellow veined green, smooth skin, rough skin, five pound to fifty pound, red fleshed to yellow fleshed, Basketball, Crimson, Sugar Babies, Cannonball, and there may be more varieties. There are seedless ones, but we don't want to talk about that. My favorite method of checking watermelons is the classic thumping that is taught to all Southerners by the age of seven. Put your ear to the melon and thump it with your middle finger, it should ring deep and basso. If you buy it at a roadside stand the vendor will usually let you plug it to check for the perfect melon. There is nothing

Glossary

worse than cutting open a melon and finding a dry, pink-white mass of cotton imitating melon.

TUBERS

I'll skip descriptions of the more familiar and shoot right to the point:

BONIATO: the true sweet potato not to be confused with the yam. The flesh is pale white to a deep red-orange. Yams are scruffy and hairy and are rounder than sweet potatoes/boniato. It's become trendy to make the distinction and I'm OK with that as long as boniato that are Island are properly identified as boniato, and that the Alabama sweet potato is just that, an Alabama sweet potato. The Alabama and Mississippi varieties are sweeter than the Island kind. Remember the difference in soil produces a difference in vegetable or fruit. Think wine. We should be just as big on the truth and history of what we eat as we are about what we drink. Also, potatoes are always referred to in terms of nutty and citrus.

YUCCA: also known as cassava (not the melon). We are more familiar with it as the base for *tapioca*. The flour is often used for baking breads, same way we use potato for potato breads. They are long with a bark like skin. The flesh is hard and white and as versatile as the potato. Great for chips, or mashed and baked with butter. I find it has a bit of a citrus flavor. Use tapioca flour in place of cornstarch and you will taste the difference between the two starches.

TARO: the more familiar to me is the one that is lilac-gray and has a slight nutty flavor. The skin is kind of hairy. Good for chips, mashed, pureed as a thickener, or roasted.

MALANGA: my favorite. Almost sweet, and a bit nutty. They fry wonderfully, and are good when diced and added to soups and sauces. They have a bit of a lavender vein to the flesh, it's pretty. Some cookbooks will tell you that malanga is an acquired taste, well isn't everything?

ABOUT COFFEE

Coffee legend: Coffee is native to Ethiopia. It was discovered by an East African goat herder who observed his goats becoming somewhat hyperactive after eating the red berries of a low growing tree. He thought it must be good so he tried it out, and yes, the caffeine did make him energetic. Time and trial led to the brewing and eventual styles of roasting. Turkish, Cowboy or Sheep herder coffee is when you just put the grounds in a pot with water and boil it till it's dark and thick. For some, as found with the use of the French Press we've sort of gone back to the beginning.

This is just a partial list of the hundreds of coffees on the market now, and the list is particular to my own tastes, so note the absence of any flavored coffees.

COLOMBIAN: rich and deep flavor, high caffeine
KENYA AA (my favorite)**:** full flavored, medium caffeine, holds well
ZIMBABWE: a bit like Kenya AA but a little lighter
JAMAICAN BLUE MOUNTAIN: a light, slightly winery bean that is regarded by some to be the best there is with a low caffeine count.
HAWAIIAN KONA: also a light, winey coffee with low caffeine
JAVA ESTATE: From the Island of Java. Bold, rich, full bodies with low acidity, the taste has smoky undertones.
MOCHA JAVA: a blend of Yemen Mocha and Indonesian Java. Deep almost chocolate, medium caffeine

The list is huge, and these are just a few representatives of the vast population of coffee. There is even now a rise in what are called estate coffees, and organic coffee beans, not unlike estate wines. Just study the coffee section of the grocery store, you'll see. Also check out your local heath food stores, they often carry a nice variety. If there is a local roaster, go and see how it's done. As a coffee drinker I love every bit of it.

ABOUT ROASTS
AMERICAN: a medium light brown roast
FRENCH: dark and strong, a brown to red brown color
EUROPEAN: a blend of one part French and two parts American
VIENNESE: one part American and two parts French
ITALIAN: the darkest, black red bean, this is the espresso bean.

The reason for the different roasts is to match desired intensity of flavors for the coffee drinker. Some people don't really like the Italian and French roasts because the taste is sort of burnt and too heavy for them. The American roast is good for lighter, fruitier coffees.

COFFEE REGIONS
As far as global regions go it is difficult to stereotype beyond the effect of volcanic ash, rain, sun, soil, etc. and this is where the pleasure of buying estate coffee comes in. But I will give you a little guide:
HAWAIIAN: light and fruity

Glossary

INDONESIAN: spicy and bold
EAST AFRICAN: brisk with less caffeine
CENTRAL AFRICAN: rich and medium caffeine
CENTRAL AMERICAN: medium caffeine and light
SOUTH AMERICAN: full bodied and lightly acidic, caffeine medium to high octane.

Best way to brew coffee? The big question that depends on what you like. The argument is never settled. A few examples: we all know the drip kind, an acceptable coffee that is only as strong as the basket will let you make it. The percolator: a good brew really, that can be made as strong as you like by allowing it to perk longer. The French Press which is good for estate and gourmet coffees because you make it per cup with as much coffee as you like. It's a favorite.

And of course, the espresso machine. The force fed hot water into the coffee basket creates a dark, thick foamy cup that is in actuality of a lesser caffeine content that drip style. It just tastes bolder.

The grind also dictates the flavor. Powder for espresso and Turkish (more than thick), fine for French Press, fine to medium for drip, coarse for percolator method. Friends from New Orleans and my parents swear by the percolator. I prefer French Press, and the Espresso machine. I like my coffee thick, rich and full bodied. In the afternoons I sometimes enjoy a light drip blend. It just all depends, and coffee, like tea, wine, scotches, cognacs, house beers and grappa all rest on your level of curiosity and experimentation. Explore. Go to your local **INDEPENDENT** coffee shop and taste the different brews, and then decide for yourself what most satisfies you. It's a great moment when a couple agrees on a coffee or tea. Agreeing on wine is easy, coffee and tea is not.

EASY SEAFOOD LIST

The seafood, meats and produce that we have used for the recipes in this book all abide by what is known as sustainable. Sustainable means that we do not harvest at a rate greater than reproduction and that there is little to no impact on surrounding ecosystem.
AMBERJACK: a firm thick fleshed fish with a hearty flavor.
BARRACUDA: rich flavorful meat, high oil content, grayish colored meat cooks up snowy white (k'aku). Use only Hawaiian.
BARRAMUNDI: Australian farm fish, medium flavor, salty, warm water to brackish water, firm, white flesh.
BLACK BASS: Atlantic bass, rich, firm, grassy to salty flavor. White

Glossary

meat, flakey.
CAVIAR: Do not use imported, **ONLY** American farm.
COBIA: mild. White. Very, very firm.
CORVINA: mild, firm, white flesh, mild to sweet.
DORADE: Mediterranean fish, firm, white, salty.
ESCOLAR: white mackerel, pacific, buttery, firm, steak-like, medium (wa'loo).
FLOUNDER: mild, sweet, thin flaked.
GROUPER – mild to sweet flavor with semi-firm flesh, usually use red or black grouper.
HALIBUT: very mild. Firm white flesh with a delicate flavor. Dense with firm flakes.
HAMACHI: (or yellow tail) sushi quality, medium flavor with light oil.
HAPU'UPU'U: Hawaiian sea bass/grouper; white meat, large flakes, crunchy to soft texture.
HEBI: Hawaiian spearfish; small, steaky, salty firm, great medium flavor. We offer this one quite a bit.
KAJIKI: firm white meat, moderate to high oil content, cooks up like steak, striped marlin.
MAHI MAHI: lean, white and tender. Firm with large, moist flakes
MONCHONG: sweeter than Opah, deep water, firm. Grey to white, the best
NAIRAGI: firm orange to white meat, steak, salty, high oil content, blue/coral marlin, from Hawaii.
ONO: smooth and firm, textured meat, mild to rich taste, cooks up white, also called Wahoo.
OPAH: moonfish; firm, sweet. Pink to orange, the second best.
OPAKA PAKA: white flaky fish, great sashimi, clear translucent meat, buttery flavor, a snapper, so it is firm.
POMPANO: one of the greatest coastal Florida fish. White, good salty flavor.
RAINBOW RUNNER: firm rich meat, cooks up white, high oil content, buttery flavor.
RAINBOW TROUT: thin with a mild, nutty flavor and tender, soft flakes.
RED SNAPPER: lean and moist flesh, semi-firm with mild sweet flavor. Hawaiian is Opaka Paka.
REDFISH: oily and strong flavored with a soft, flaky texture there is

Glossary

a reason it is blackened and strong is why. Also known as agria. It is a drum.
SALMON: pink flesh, full flavor with sufficient firmness, fatty, Chinook, Coho, Silverbrite, Pink and Sockeye.
STRIPED BASS: medium, moist and slightly salty; lean, flaky firm flesh this is both a farmed and wild fish.
STURGEON: fresh water American farmed; very steak like. Rich flavor.
TAUTOG: mild, sweet, with a moderately firm texture, deep Atlantic waters.
TILAPIA: mild, salty, tender flakes, farm raised red perch, also called Nile or Green Perch. Fresh water fish, eco friendly, farmed.
TORO-TORO: is the belly of Big Eye and Yellowfin tuna, some of the very best fattiest, richest, melt in your mouth goodness there is in the tuna world.
TREVALLY: Hawaiian jack that is smaller, more round and of a slightly saltier flavor than amberjack.
TUNA— BIG EYE: a very rich red tuna, a favorite as it almost melts when you eat it rare to medium rare, it is that rich. Hawaiian, so it's very, very fresh. This is what we use for the Ahi Tataki plate.
TUNA— SKIP JACK: smaller tuna, great healthy stock, very good grilled, the reddest of the tunas.
TUNA— TOMBO: white tuna, also known as 'Albacore' salty, lean and firm.
TUNA— YELLOWFIN: firm, sushi- quality tuna. Usually seared rare to med rare. Ruby red in color, white when cooked.
TURBOT: a mild, sweet, north Atlantic, thin flake.
WAHOO: med flavor. It is bluish in color, white when cooked, great for people with a fear of full flavored fish. When it's used in Hawaiian sushi grade call it Ono.
WOLF FISH: Atlantic is white, sweet and the taste between lobster and scallops as this is their primary diet. The Mediterranean is saltier and smaller.

Index of Terms for "Ginger, Lily and Sweet Fire: A Romance With Food"

Bread
   French, 59, 85, 189, 209, 213
   Italian, 85, 115, 123, 198
   Ladyfingers, 106-107
   White
   Yellow Corn Tortilla, 229

Dairy
   Butter
      Unsalted, 117, 144, 167, 182, 197, 204, 205, 227, 234
   Cheese
      Alabama, 119
      Cream Cheese, 82-83, 91, 106, 156, 165, 168
      Feta, 14, 18, 27, 85-86, 96, 196
      Gouda, 13, 18, 67, 70, 81, 208-210
      Jack, 81, 208
      Montrachet Goat Cheese, 119
      Mozzarella, 8, 15, 115, 117, 119, 172
      Parmesan, 14, 15, 76, 78, 80, 85-90, 108, 110, 112, 172
      Port Wine Cheese, 18, 201, 206
      Ricotta, 14, 75, 76, 82-83
      Smoked, 18, 208-210
      Vermont, 91, 119, 209
      White Cheddar, 15, 93, 95, 96
   Cream
      40% Whipping Cream, 176
      Half and Half, 93-94, 113, 219
      Heavy Cream, 8, 24, 30, 53, 58, 88, 90, 96, 98, 121, 144, 154, 157, 200, 208, 228, 231, 235, 242
      White Cream
   Eggs
      Yolks, 53, 83, 106-107, 113, 150, 157, 165, 166, 199
   Yogurt
      Lemon Yogurt, 50
      Plain Yogurt, 60
      Vanilla Yogurt, 98

Fish
   1½ inch thick Sashimi Grade Tuna Loin, 159
   Amberjack, 14, 61, 93, 95-96, 161, 246
   Carrabolla from
   Catfish
   Pompano, 13, 61, 63, 65, 247
   Salmon, 18, 22, 23, 55, 61, 86, 89, 130, 133, 173, 190-193, 248
   Striped Bass, 8, 61, 131, 203, 248
   Tilapia, 12, 13, 24, 27-29, 203, 232, 248
   Trout, 13, 61, 67, 69-70, 173, 248
   Turbot, 232, 233, 248
   Wahoo, 18. 95, 201-204, 223. 225. 247. 248
   Wreck Fish, 17, 61, 95, 137, 170, 172, 203

Fruits
   Apples
      Golden Delicious, 18, 160, 201, 206
      Granny Smith, 14, 42, 76, 78, 103, 178, 230
      Juice, *see Pantry Items*
   Apricots, 17, 33, 37-39, 44, 69, 137, 178, 182-183, 219
   Bananas, 12, 13, 17, 33, 39-40, 55, 56, 60, 61, 63-65, 70, 76, 138, 141, 165, 167, 168, 243
   Blackberries, 12, 48, 49-50, 84, 91, 97
   Blueberries, 84, 91, 97, 125, 144, 194, 195
   Cantaloupe, 14, 31, 85, 90, 243
   Currants
      Black, 8
      Juice, 204
   Dates
      Medjool, 164
   Figs, 18, 77, 201, 206
   Grapes
      Black, 205-206
      White Grape Juice, 46
   Honeydew, 243
   Kiwi, 18, 65, 121, 190, 194
   Lemons, 14, 28, 30, 34, 50, 56, 70, 82-83, 85-86, 88-90, 115, 120, 121, 142, 144, 164, 167, 175, 178, 184, 192, 196, 197, 225
   Limes, 8, 17, 24, 30, 34, 43, 50, 56-57, 62-64, 69, 70, 92, 103, 110, 112, 117, 121, 140, 144, 147, 154, 162, 165, 174-176, 231, 242
   Mandarin Oranges, 18, 106
   Mango, 8, 12, 13, 16, 18, 24, 30-31, 62, 65, 71, 87, 98, 112, 121, 138, 140-141, 152, 155-156, 160, 163, 179, 185, 196, 228, 243
   Nectarines, 65
   Oranges
      Juice, *see Pantry Items*

Index

Zest, 124-125, 199
Papaya
    Ripe, 17, 31, 47, 61, 62, 98, 112, 121, 141, 145, 155, 160, 165, 168, 179, 227
Passion Fruit, 16, 112, 137, 138, 144-145, 164
Peaches, 46, 65, 91, 112, 170, 194, 195
Pears
    Anjou, 30, 66, 70
    Asian, 18, 30, 31, 146, 191-193, 226
    Bartlett, 30, 146
Pineapple, 8, 16, 60, 159, 161, 163, 167, 243
Plums, 15, 65, 122, 125-127, 153, 172
Pomegranate Seeds, 145, 203, 204
Preserves, 83, 127, 128-9
    Apricot, 38, 69, 182, 219
    Blackberry, 50
Raisins
    White, 191
Raspberries, 12, 18, 56, 84, 91, 97, 113, 125, 194
    Whole Frozen, 60, 120-121, 235
Star Fruits (only buy yellow), 121, 137, 145, 167
Strawberries, 18, 65, 84, 97, 121, 125, 160, 175, 194, 208, 213-214, 227-228
Tangerines, 12, 36, 42, 46, 47, 151, 155, 160
Watermelon, 243

Herbs/Spices

Allspice, 16, 85, 102, 108, 149, 159, 161, 179, 182, 193
Annatto Seed
Basil
    Holy, 63, 177
    Opal, 230
    Purple, 63
Bay Leaf, 93, 122, 181, 218
Black Pepper
    Ground, 27, 88, 140
Caraway Seed
    Ground, 102
Cardamom, 18, 27, 35, 70, 103, 149, 162, 178-179, 190, 191, 213
Caribbean Jerk Seasoning Mix, 179
Cayenne, 17, 161, 163, 178-180
Chinese 5 Spice Powder, 152
Cilantro, 17, 18, 25, 27, 34, 38, 56-58, 68, 103, 112, 160, 167, 170-171, 193, 196, 209, 217, 230
Cinnamon
    Stick, 157
Cumin, 22, 139, 141

Dried Chili Flakes
Fenugreek, 22, 226-227
Garlic
    Roasted, 8, 14, 15, 86, 93, 95, 97, 115, 117, 119, 172
Ginger, 8, 11, 13, 20, 22-26, 30-31, 34, 38, 41, 50-52, 56, 64, 67, 69, 70, 105, 141, 144, 146, 147, 154, 160, 162, 165, 168, 174, 180, 181, 182, 185, 205, 206, 209, 213, 216-217, 224, 220
Horseradish
    Prepared, 38, 50, 69
Karachai (Baby Ginger) = Fingeroot, 23, 25, 147
Lemongrass, 8, 12, 13, 22, 23, 24, 27, 33-36, 56-57, 60, 63, 67-70
Marjoram, 111, 114, 122
Mint
    Spearmint, 139
Oregano
    Dried, 88
Paprika, 22, 44, 101, 141, 161
Parsley, 27, 79-80, 96, 100-102, 147, 215
    Italian Flat Leaf
Rosemary, 18, 19, 23, 72, 108-109, 111, 136, 196-197, 215, 220
Saffron, 19, 72, 149, 229, 230, 231
Sage, 8, 15, 115, 117, 118
Sesame Powder
    Black
    White
Sichuan Peppercorns, 23, 56, 63, 159, 191, 217
Thyme, 18, 35, 88, 93, 101, 115, 161, 190, 191
Turmeric, 22, 63

Methods

Bake, 85, 119, 123, 198
Cook on Big Green Egg, 162
Grill, 140, 162, 165, 188, 218
Pan Frying
Sautéing, 97, 165
Slow Cook > various methods < , 22
Steaming, 63, 127, 148, 181
Stir Frying
Wok, 8, 37-38, 42, 52, 97, 139

Noodles

Bean thread, 68
Buckwheat soba. 219
Chinese Wide
Rice Sticks, 44, 155, 243

Index

Oils
- Corn Oil, 23, 29, 37, 74, 95, 159, 160, 163, 166, 171, 208, 216
- Olive Oil
  - Extra Virgin, 75, 88, 101, 109, 130, 196, 226
  - Virgin, 37, 74, 78, 96, 102, 111, 166, 178, 230-232
- Peanut Oil, 23, 24-25, 27, 37, 44, 49, 51, 58-59, 62, 64, 68, 70, 74, 146-147, 168, 193, 233
- Sesame Oil, 23, 29, 38-39, 171, 219, 224
- Special Oils
  - Prickly Ash Oil, 23
- Walnut Oil, 8, 107, 191, 229-230
- Wasabi Oil, 23

Pantry Items
- Active Dry Yeast, 117
- Almonds
  - Crushed, Toasted, 156
  - Sliced, 103, 191
- Apple Cider, 230-231
- Apple Juice, 38, 94, 103, 110, 140, 174, 178
- Beans, 15, 16, 22, 51, 56, 62, 70, 105, 107, 108, 110-111, 122-124, 126, 129, 147
- Cannelloni, 122
- Capers, 14, 93, 95-97
- Cashews, 12, 16, 18, 24, 27-29, 45, 58, 127, 138, 144-145, 179-180, 201, 240
  - Whole Halves, 27, 204-205
- Chinese Sweet Bean Chili Paste, 224
- Chipotle Chili Sauce (the thick kind), 230
- Chocolate
  - Milk Chocolate, 107
  - Semisweet, 234
  - Unsweetened Cocoa, 214
  - White Chocolate, 16, 46, 60, 121, 146, 150-151, 176, 190, 194
- Coconut Cream, 12, 16, 33, 39, 60, 63, 138, 139, 188, 220
- Coconut Milk (canned), 22, 24, 39, 58, 59, 60, 65, 139, 146-147, 174
- Corn Syrup, 227
- Cornmeal, 33, 68, 119, 216
- Cornstarch, 43, 121, 126, 157, 174, 205-206, 223, 231, 244
- Cranberry Juice, 204
- Cream of Tartar, 150, 175
- Crème de Cassis, 18, 190, 194

- Curry Products
  - Curry Paste, 22, 56-59
  - Curry Powder (madras), 23, 166
- Dark rum, 152
- Egg Roll Wrappers, 168
- Espresso, 15, 19, 99, 106, 108, 112-113, 198-199, 200, 223, 227, 228, 235, 245, 246
- Fermented Black Beans, 56
- Fish Sauce
  - Golden Fish Sauce, 226
- Flour
  - APF = All Purpose, 38, 82, 126, 139, 156, 182, 193, 199, 204, 227, 232, 234
  - Unbleached Bread, 117
- Ginger Beer, 16, 17, 138-140, 178, 179-180
- Graham Cracker Crumbs, 156
- Graham Crackers, 18, 176, 201, 206
- Great Northern, 122
- Harissa, 14, 100, 102-103, 105
- Honey, 38, 39, 50, 60, 65, 85, 91, 106, 109-110, 144, 158, 164, 174, 175, 182-183, 202, 205-206, 217, 225, 226
- Mango Puree, 121, 141
- Maple Syrup, 151, 220
- Mesquite Seasoning (buy it), 17, 165, 167
- Mirin, 26, 215, 216-217, 224
- Mustard
  - Brown, 38
  - Dijon, 109
  - Raspberry, 212
  - Seeded Dijon, 212
- Olives
  - Amfissa, 17, 170, 171
  - Black, 27, 118
  - Conservolea Olives
  - Kalamata, 118
  - Spanish, 118
- Orange Juice, 60, 150-151, 202, 205
- Orange Liquor, 106, 112
- Papaya Juice, 140
- Peach Juice, 34, 140
- Peanuts, 45, 58
- Pear Juice, 34, 204
- Pecan, 15, 122, 144, 162, 227
  - Halves, 124-125
- Phyllo Dough, 152, 155-156
- Pine Nuts, 15, 92, 108-109, 125, 212
- Pink Guava nectar, 176

Ginger, Lily & Sweet Fire • 251

Index

Pistachio Nuts, 14, 18, 93, 95, 96, 159, 164, 196, 198, 199
   Raw/Green, 199
Powdered Nori (toasted seaweed), 8, 159, 229
Raspberry Puree, 212, 235
Red Miso, 19, 215-217, 224
Red Pepper (ground), 139
Rice, *see Rice*
Rice Paper (sheets round), 19, 223-224, 243
Rum Extract, 157
Salt
   Kosher, 35, 118, 129, 132, 149, 161, 166, 171
   Rock, 37, 132, 139, 140 141
Sambal Oelek, 8, 16, 22, 24, 25, 44, 57, 102, 137, 141, 152, 154, 204-205
Sesame Seeds, 23, 38, 68, 159, 170, 171
   Black,163, 170, 202
   White, 163, 202, 224
Soy Sauce
   Dark, 43, 181, 213
   Indonesian Sweet, 42, 179
   Mushroom, 23, 68, 70, 152, 197, 215
   Sweet, 8, 22, 69, 160, 224
   Thin Soy Sauce, 147
Sugar
   Brown, 14, 38, 42, 43, 78, 82, 93, 97, 126, 140, 141, 152-153, 168, 183, 198-199, 205-206
   Confectioners (XXX Sugar), 106, 113, 114, 228, 231
   Granulated, 22, 53, 69, 117, 126, 150, 156, 175, 176, 194, 214
   Light Brown, 22, 98, 161, 164, 182, 213, 227
   Molasses, 16, 17, 22, 43, 140, 141, 151, 152-153, 182-183, 230
   Powdered, 157
   Unsulfured, 182
Sunflower Seeds, 14, 43, 76, 78
Sweet vermouth, 126
Tamarind Juice, 60, 152
   Use 4oz. of Tamarind
Tamarind Paste, 152, 164
Tea
   Jasmine, 179
   Oolong, 179
Tomato Juice, 103, 123
Tomato Paste, 58, 59, 103
Tomato Sauce, 15, 34, 79, 108, 110, 112, 138, 239, 242
V-8 Juice, 87, 123

Vanilla Extract, 53, 112, 113, 194, 199, 219
Vinegar
   Apple cider, 103, 163, 202
   Balsamic, 51, 77, 78, 79, 93, 95, 96, 109, 211
   Chinese Black, 181
   Red wine, 77, 140, 181, 196, 211
   Rice, 12, 18, 24, 26, 42, 43, 56, 62, 68, 69, 70, 190, 191, 209, 216, 224, 226
Walnuts, 82, 144
Wasabi Fried Green Peas, 8, 232, 233
Wine
   Red Table Wine, 124
   Sherry, 44, 215
   Marsala, 106-107
   White wine, 43, 103, 191, 209, 212, 218, 231
      Chinese Cooking Wine, 44
   Zinfandel, 19, 215, 217, 218
Worcestershire Sauce, 22, 218

Pasta
Angel hair, 97, 230, 231, 242
Capellini, 240, 242
Fettuccine, 38, 240, 242
Orzo, 15, 122, 124-125
Penne, 14, 58, 76, 78, 79, 240, 242

People/Mentors/Associates
St. Orres, 3, 189, 233
Louis Osteen, 3, 9
Jacque Pepin, 3, 9
Norman Van Aiken, 3
Alice Waters, 3, 77, 189

Places/Cuisines
Caribbean, 136-183, 178, 233
China, 4, 7, 8-9, 56, 133, 182, 240, 241
Hong Kong, 8, 23, 67, 189
Italy/Italian, 8, 27, 62, 72-127, 148, 172, 190, 198, 239, 240-241, 245
Mediterranean, 8, 14-15, 71, 72-127, 130, 131, 178, 247, 248
New World Cuisine, 7, 8, 186-236, 241
Southern, 24, 122, 140, 148, 155, 243
Thailand, 8-9, 12, 20-71, 132, 147

Proteins
Beef, 8, 14, 18, 100, 102, 104, 105, 122, 208, 209-212
   Tenderloin Filets, 209

Index

Chicken, 8, 12, 13, 15, 16, 23, 24-25, 33, 37, 38, 42, 44, 56-59, 67, 68, 88, 102, 103, 115, 117, 118, 119, 122, 129, 140, 146, 148, 149, 152-153, 155, 159, 161-163, 178, 208, 218, 224, 238, 240, 243
    Sautéed, 37, 38
    Sesame, 12, 33, 38
    Steamed
Duck, 17, 19, 131, 137, 178, 179-182, 223-224
Lamb, 73, 102, 109, 125, 130-131, 152, 233, 237
    Leg Steaks, Bone In, 15, 122, 124
    Loin, 19, 124, 229, 230, 232
Pork, 8, 16, 22, 122, 129, 130, 138, 140, 141, 209, 211, 213, 231
    Bacon, 80, 108, 130, 135, 239
    Loin with Chop Bones, 213
    Pancetta, 15, 80, 108, 109
    Prosciutto, 17, 80, 86, 108, 178-179
    Smoked Italian Sausage, 210
Turkey, 19, 129, 215, 219
    Breast Steaks, 217

Rice
    Arborio, 88
    Basmati, 18, 48, 51, 196, 197
    Glutinous White Rice, 218
    Jasmine, 12, 24, 29, 48, 51, 140, 147
    Nishiki
    Sushi, 65, 202, 218
    Uncle Ben's Long & Wild, 48, 111

Shellfish, 73, 132
    Calamari, 16, 22, 72, 136, 137, 138, 139-140
    Clams
    Crabmeat
        Blue fin, 209
        Lump (fresh), 165
    Lobster, 16, 95, 152-154. 248
        Tail Meat, 154
    Mussels, 12, 36, 132
        Black, 33-34
    Oysters, 8, 22, 116, 240
    Scallops, 16, 140, 154, 248
        Large Sea, 146-147
    Shrimp, 8, 12, 14, 16, 22, 25-26, 42, 44-45, 47, 48, 49-50, 65, 85, 86-87, 89-90, 100, 116, 136, 138, 139-140, 230, 239

Stock
    Chicken, 24, 88, 103, 208

Clam, 209
Marinade, 23, 43, 140-141, 162, 167, 179, 190, 226, 229, 239

Tofu, 12, 19, 48, 51-53, 229-230, 239, 242
    Eggroll skins, 67
    Extra firm, 51, 219, 229-230
    Firm, 140, 224

Vegetables
    Artichoke, 14, 15, 74, 115-116
        Fresh, tight, no brown leaves, 115-116
        Heart (canned), 14, 76, 79-80, 125, 154, 231
    Asparagus, 17, 38-39, 51, 58-59, 147, 178-179, 223
    Avocado, 15, 58-59, 122, 124, 125, 165
    Banana Leaf, 13, 61, 63-65, 70
    Bean Sprouts, 8
        Kidney, 215
        Lima, 215
        Mung Bean, 64
    Bok Choy, 57, 64, 181, 197
        Baby Bok Choy, 181, 197
    Broccoli, 12, 24, 29-30, 42, 44, 51, 57, 147, 155
    Cabbage, 42, 44, 57, 226
        Green, 12, 24, 26-27, 44, 163
        Napa, 64, 226
        Red
    Carrot, 25, 38, 42, 44, 58-59, 70, 88, 112, 122-123, 149, 205-206, 223
    Celery, 51, 57, 64, 79, 88, 105, 112, 122-123, 149, 165, 179-180, 197, 223, 230
    Coconut, 8, 12, 16, 17, 22, 23, 48, 49-50, 61, 65, 162, 170, 172, 185
    Corn, 8, 18, 57, 142, 181, 190, 191, 192-193, 203, 208-209
        On the Cob, 213
        White, 208
        Yellow, 192, 208
    Cucumber, 12, 16, 24, 26-27, 159, 161, 237
        Seedless, 163
    Eggplant, 13, 15, 57, 108-109, 110-112, 140, 149, 197, 224
    Ginger, 8, 11, 13, 20, 22, 23, 24-25, 26, 34, 40-41, 50, 51-52, 56, 64, 67-70, 105, 138, 141, 144, 146-147, 154, 160, 162, 165, 168, 174, 181, 182, 185, 189, 205-206, 209, 213, 216-217, 224, 229
        Crystallized, 30-31
    Green beans, 15, 51, 61, 62, 70, 105, 122, 129
    Hericium

Index

Horseradish, 12, 38-39, 48, 49-50, 69, 160, 226
Leek, 57, 88, 197
Mushrooms, 8, 14, 23, 24-25, 51, 57, 68, 70, 76, 79, 86, 123, 134, 152, 155, 197, 209, 215-216, 239-240
    Crimini, 15, 51, 57, 79, 122, 147, 215, 239, 240
    Portabella, 18, 51, 79, 122, 196, 240
    Shiitake, 8, 19, 51, 57, 79, 215, 240
    Snow crab, 51
Onion, 14, 18, 25, 33-34, 57, 58-59, 69, 70, 80, 87, 88-89, 95, 100-101, 105, 112, 122-123, 160, 161, 165, 167, 179-180, 205-206, 209-212, 215, 223
    Pearl Onion, 51
    Red, 12, 18, 24, 26, 163, 201-202, 229
    Scallion, 14, 25, 44, 52-53, 68, 70, 76, 78, 161, 162, 163, 171, 181, 210, 224
    Shallot, 12, 48, 51-53, 62, 63, 108, 109-110, 202, 211-212
    Yellow, 38, 64, 79, 89, 97, 149, 154, 162, 208, 218, 226
Peppers
    Ancho, 102
    Green Bell, 208, 223
    Golden, 19, 223, 225, 226
    Jalapeno, 16, 18, 23, 70, 76, 110, 138, 146-147, 181, 196, 230
    Poblano, 14, 18, 19, 23, 76, 85, 86, 87, 89, 108, 109-110, 160, 165, 190, 191, 192, 208, 226
    Red Bell, 14, 27, 51, 68, 89, 93, 94, 102, 105, 109, 154, 167, 179, 196, 219, 223
    Serrano, 14, 23, 62, 76, 78, 110
    Thai Bird Chili, 22
Plantains, 16, 137, 138-139, 159, 161, 163
    Yellow, 163
Potato, 8, 14, 57, 100-101, 105, 129, 138, 142, 154, 174, 190, 191, 192, 193, 205, 241, 244
    Boniato, 174, 179-180, 244
    Malanga, 174, 175, 230, 244
    Red, 100, 174, 192
    Sweet, 138, 193, 226, 242, 244
    Taro, 174, 175, 179, 192, 230, 244
Pumpkin, 12, 48, 53-54, 193
    Puree, 53
Roses (flower), 18, 46, 70, 177, 190, 191, 207, 238
    Hips, 19, 215, 217-218
Salad Greens, 62
    Arugula, 8, 226
    Head (Iceberg)
    Mixed Field Greens, 109

Romaine, 14, 65, 76, 78, 109, 152, 212
Snow peas, 51, 58-59, 64, 105, 122, 174-175
    Sugar Snap Peas, 51, 105, 122, 197, 219
Spinach, 8, 12, 14, 18, 42-44, 57, 63-64, 93-94, 122, 124, 125, 147, 190, 191, 208, 209-210, 219
Squash, 24, 87, 122, 238
    Patty Pan, 197
    Yellow, 8, 25, 38, 51, 57, 67, 231
    Zucchini, 8, 14, 25, 64, 67, 87, 93, 95, 97, 149, 223, 231
Sunflower seeds, *see Pantry Items*
Tiger Lily (flower), 8, 23, 178, 237
Tomato (s), 12-17, 27, 33-34, 36, 39, 73, 75, 84, 86-90, 110, 114, 115, 117-118, 138, 146, 148, 149, 170, 171-172, 230, 239, 240, 242
    Cherry, 62
    Paste, *see Pantry Items*
    Roma, 43, 79, 85-86, 112, 119, 212, 229
    Sundried, 13, 67-68, 74
    Tomatillo, 19, 229
    Yellow Pear Tomato, 196
Wasabi Powder (your choice) real or not?, 160, 202

ABOUT THE LUMMOX PRESS

Lummox Press was created in 1994 by RD Armstrong. It began as a self-publishing/DIY imprint for poetry by RD. Several chapbooks were published and in late 1995 RD began publishing the *Lummox Journal*, a monthly small/underground press lit-arts mag. Available primarily by subscription, the *LJ* continued its exploration of the "creative process" until its demise as a print mag in 2006. It was hailed as one of the best monthlies in the small press.

In 1998, Lummox began publishing the Little Red Book series, and continues to do so today. To date there are some 59 titles in the series (as of 2010) and a collection of poems from the first decade of the series has been published under the title The Long Way Home (2009); it's a great way to explore the series.

Together with Chris Yeseta (Layout and Art Direction since 1997), RD continues to publish books that are both striking in their looks as well as their content…you'd think he was aping Black Sparrow, but he is merely trying to produce the best books he can for his clients, the poets, and their customers, you, the readers.

The following books are available directly from the Lummox Press via its website: **www.lummoxpress.com** or from Lummox c/o PO Box 5301, San Pedro, CA 90733. There are also E-Book (PDF) versions of most titles available. Most of these titles are available through other book sellers online, as well.

The Wren Notebook by Rick Smith (2000)
Last Call: The Legacy of Charles Bukowski edited by RD Armstrong (2004)
On/Off the Beaten Path by RD Armstrong (2008)
Fire and Rain—Selected Poems 1993-2007 Volumes 1 & 2 by RD Armstrong (2008)
El Pagano and Other Twisted Tales by RD Armstrong (short stories—2008)
New and Selected Poems by John Yamrus (2009)
The Riddle of the Wooden Gun by Todd Moore (2009)
Sea Trails by Pris Campbell (2009)
Down This Crooked Road—Modern Poetry from the Road Less Traveled
  edited by RD Armstrong and William Taylor, Jr. (2009)
Drive By by John Bennett (2010)
Modest Aspirations by Gerald Locklin & Beth Wilson (2010)
Steel Valley by Michael Adams (2010)
Hard Landing by Rick Smith (2010)
A Love Letter to Darwin by Jane Crown (2010)
E/OR—Living Amongst the Mangled by RD Armstrong (2010)